MW00824410

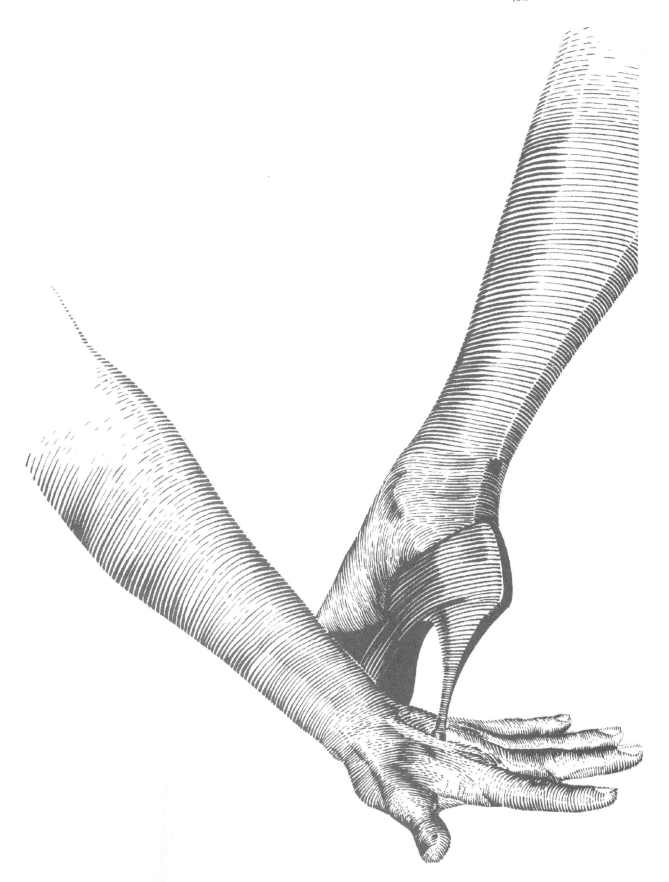

GRINDHOUSE

THE FORBIDDEN WORLD OF "ADULTS ONLY" CINEMA

EDDIE MULLER
and
DANIEL FARIS

ST. MARTIN'S GRIFFIN ≋ NEW YORK

Writer and designer: Eddie Muller
Materials and research: Daniel Faris
Photography: Andrew Taylor
Copy Editor: Erik S. McMahon

Entire contents designed and packaged at
St. Francis Studio, Alameda, California.

All photos and art in this book, including cover images,
are courtesy of the authors' collections with the exceptions of
the bottom photo on page 112 (courtesy of James Singer)
and on page 134 (courtesy of David F. Friedman).

Library of Congress Cataloging-in-Publication Data

Muller, Eddie.
Grindhouse : the forbidden world of adults only cinema/
by Eddie Muller and Daniel Faris.
p. cm.
ISBN 0-312-14609-4
1. Erotic films–United States–History and criticism.
I. Faris, Daniel. II. Title.
PN1995.9.S45M85   1996
791.43´6538–dc20   96-26667
CIP

First St. Martin's Griffin Edition: November 1996
10 9 8 7 6 5 4 3 2 1

ST. FRANCIS
STUDIO

Coming Attractions

Acknowledgments

Tribute must first be paid to Fred Klein, whose nocturnal expeditions long ago set this project in motion. Without his archeological skills, this volume would not exist. Thanks and praise are also due Gordon Van Gelder, editor at St. Martin's Press, who jumped in where others feared to tread, and assistant editor Corin See. David Friedman, who pops up in these pages like a ribald master of ceremonies, generously provided brilliant background and perspicacious perspective to the research. Dave is a gentleman of rare order and a raconteur of first rank. Erik S. McMahon provided invaluable input on the manuscript, and remains the keenest copy editor on the planet. James Elliot Singer and Lisa Petrucci also provided valuable assists. The Cinema Shop in San Francisco deserves special recognition for providing many of the posters in this book.

Dan issues a big thank you to The Cinema Shop's Steve Imura, and also to Sandy Sandifer, who showed him the humor in all this. Special appreciation goes to his wife, Melinda, for her patience and support over the years.

Eddie would like to extend depthless gratitude to the person who makes it all possible, and worthwhile, his wife Kathleen.

Foreword

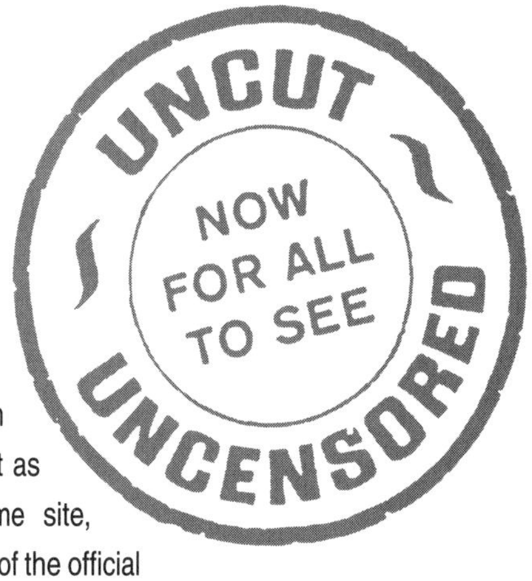

As in a corner of Rome where rows of modern coffee shops and hair salons are abruptly intruded upon by newly excavated fragments of gods and monsters, the words and images in this book force on us their already archaic brand of noise and neon. Here, in fact, is a portion of the groundwork for a cultural archaeology of modern America. The digging is necessary because so much was buried; and just as Schliemann found a succession of different Troys occupying the same site, *Grindhouse* uncovers an alternate country co-existing within the boundaries of the official America.

And what a country it was: a place where whatever was despised or concealed on Main Street displayed itself just around the corner in forms grotesque and ravaged, in that mournful theater where desire and revulsion circled around each other in a mordant and perpetual dance.

While not a full-scale history, this book performs the invaluable service of rapidly sketching out the phases and turning points of the process by which "adults only" cinema emerged from the shadows — a process crucial to any understanding of how American culture got the way it is. The amazing thing is that until very recently hardly anyone thought such a project worth undertaking. The films discussed here — from primeval exploitation fare like *Mad Youth* and *Slaves in Bondage*, to such choice '60s titles as *Sin in the Suburbs* and *The Orgy at Lil's Place* — are not discussed in standard film histories; until recently their very existence was scarcely acknowledged.

The authors take us from a time when Caesarean operations and venereal sores were exhibited as forms of erotic entertainment, through all the curious hybrid genres of the '50s and '60s grind circuit (nudie-cutie, roughie, mondo), to that era of porno chic (more recent but already surprisingly remote) when ads for sex movies ran daily in *The New York Times*. To look at the advertisements for desire which fill their pages is to glimpse a paradise of panderers, in which anything at all can be sold to an audience so desperate as scarcely to care whether the product delivers.

Yet if anything remains alive out of this world of filmmaking, it is not so much the films themselves — of which, for the most part, the less said the better — than the energy of their promoters. As necessary, the exploitation experts could mimic the rolling sanctimony of the professional guardian of morality or the leering, cajoling spiel of the sideshow barker, and their ear for the come-on was infallible. It's hard, for instance, not to react with numbed awe to the ad copy for *Olga's House of Shame:* "This picture shows what Freud only hinted at!"

Grindhouse also makes clear that when the concealed culture of exploitation went mainstream in the 1970s — when the movies that had been barely tolerated at the margins of public exhibition became at once widely acceptable and infinitely more explicit — the result was a major cultural shift whose aftereffects we are still living with. To go half a century from a cinematic condition in which almost nothing was permissible to one in which virtually everything is: this was culture shock indeed. What better time than the aftermath of such a cataclysm to review the path that led to it? If that path seems to lead through an endless succession of half-lit back alleys, we can nonetheless be certain of ending up back in the glittery, open-all-night multiscreen complex we now call home.

— Geoffrey O'Brien
New York, 1996

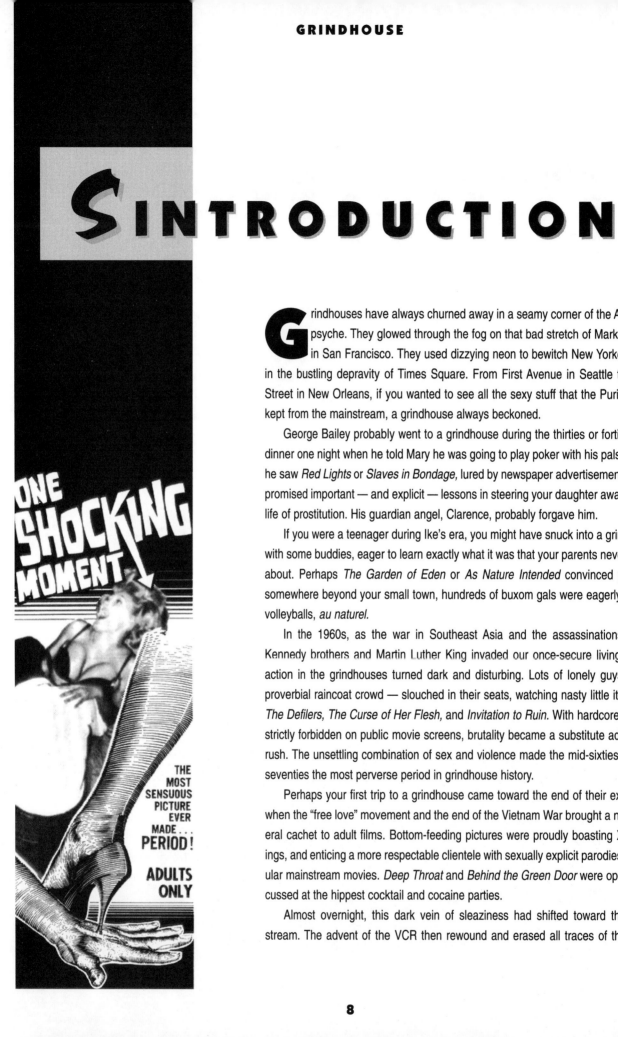

ONE
SHOCKING
MOMENT

THE
MOST
SENSUOUS
PICTURE
EVER
MADE . . .
PERIOD!

ADULTS
ONLY

SINTRODUCTION

Grindhouses have always churned away in a seamy corner of the American psyche. They glowed through the fog on that bad stretch of Market Street in San Francisco. They used dizzying neon to bewitch New Yorkers even in the bustling depravity of Times Square. From First Avenue in Seattle to Canal Street in New Orleans, if you wanted to see all the sexy stuff that the Purity Patrol kept from the mainstream, a grindhouse always beckoned.

George Bailey probably went to a grindhouse during the thirties or forties, after dinner one night when he told Mary he was going to play poker with his pals. Maybe he saw *Red Lights* or *Slaves in Bondage,* lured by newspaper advertisements which promised important — and explicit — lessons in steering your daughter away from a life of prostitution. His guardian angel, Clarence, probably forgave him.

If you were a teenager during Ike's era, you might have snuck into a grindhouse with some buddies, eager to learn exactly what it was that your parents never talked about. Perhaps *The Garden of Eden* or *As Nature Intended* convinced you that somewhere beyond your small town, hundreds of buxom gals were eagerly spiking volleyballs, *au naturel.*

In the 1960s, as the war in Southeast Asia and the assassinations of the Kennedy brothers and Martin Luther King invaded our once-secure living rooms, action in the grindhouses turned dark and disturbing. Lots of lonely guys — the proverbial raincoat crowd — slouched in their seats, watching nasty little items like *The Defilers, The Curse of Her Flesh,* and *Invitation to Ruin.* With hardcore sex still strictly forbidden on public movie screens, brutality became a substitute adrenaline rush. The unsettling combination of sex and violence made the mid-sixties to early seventies the most perverse period in grindhouse history.

Perhaps your first trip to a grindhouse came toward the end of their existence, when the "free love" movement and the end of the Vietnam War brought a newly liberal cachet to adult films. Bottom-feeding pictures were proudly boasting XXX ratings, and enticing a more respectable clientele with sexually explicit parodies of popular mainstream movies. *Deep Throat* and *Behind the Green Door* were openly discussed at the hippest cocktail and cocaine parties.

Almost overnight, this dark vein of sleaziness had shifted toward the mainstream. The advent of the VCR then rewound and erased all traces of the grindhouse. You no longer had to leave your house to see what, or who, was going down in the wrong part of town.

You've never been to a grindhouse? Then consider this volume a guided tour of back alley Americana. We promise you a trip that is safe, sordid, amusing, enticing, and highly informative.

The makers of Adults Only movies, with rare exceptions, are part of a long thriving tradition of American hucksterism. From carny barker to holy-rolling evangelist, to grindhouse sleazemeister, the goal has always been the same: promise something extraordinary, get the cash up front, then get the hell out of town.

The modern era of exploitation began in the 1920s. It was created through the efforts of several do-gooders who, in their quest to ensure America's moral purity, forged two lasting accomplishments: they taught all future exploitation producers how it was done, and they pioneered a thriving and lucrative fringe enterprise that made millions off the public's fearful desire for "forbidden" subjects.

Louis Sonney was an Italian immigrant who, in 1919, as the sheriff of Centralia, Washington, captured notorious railroad bandit Roy Gardner. Sonney used the reward money to start his own company, Sonney Amusement Enterprises. Its first production was *The Smiling Mail Bandit* — based on the exploits of Roy Gardner.

As an independent, Sonney had little hope of cracking the monopoly the major Hollywood Studios held on the nation's theater chains; instead, he "roadshowed" his film, traveling around the country, setting up screenings in independent theaters, saloons, Elk's lodges, tents — wherever he could gather a crowd.

Sonney was part of the show, lecturing on "The Dangers of Crime" to rapt audiences. When his crime schtick wore thin, he segued into "The Dangers of Sex." Louis and his sons would eventually move to Southern California, and produce more than 400 exploitation pictures.

The other original exploitation pioneer was Florence Reid (known to movie fans as actress Dorothy Davenport). The nation was stunned in March, 1922 when her husband, matinée idol Wallace Reid, the original Boy Next Door, was revealed to be a morphine addict. "The King of Paramount" was committed to a sanitarium to take "the cure." He died in a padded cell on January 18, 1923.

Immediately, a new calling blossomed for Florence. She hit the road, Sonney-style, with a film entitled *Human Wreckage*. It depicted the tortures of drug addiction, and was promoted as "The Greatest Production in the History of Motion Pictures."

If you want to understand the psychology and economics of Adults Only movies, you have to start with traveling carnivals. The tent show at the farthest end of the midway, off-limits to youngsters, was the precursor of the grindhouse. Film offered an easier way to distribute forbidden thrills. As producer/carny David Friedman has noted, "After Mr. Edison made these tintypes gallop, it wasn't but two days later that some enterprising guy had his girlfriend take off her clothes and that's how exploitation began."

Reid rode the rails, lamenting her dear dead husband, screening the film, and selling pamphlets warning about the evils of a wayward life. She turned a steady profit. After grinding *Human Wreckage* for more than a year she did the circuit again, with another cheapie, *Broken Laws.*

Even as silent pictures gave way to sound, and Wallace Reid faded from public consciousness, Florence Reid still trouped along, screening cautionary tales such as *The Road to Ruin* — a film that dutifully depicted all the sex and vice she railed against.

Louis Sonney and Florence Reid showed how road-showing could profitably skirt the stranglehold of the Hollywood studios. In so doing, they laid the groundwork for the theatrical exhibition of Adults Only movies.

Thanks to the efforts of film archeologists, many of these old grindhouse spectacles are now available on videotape. The contemporary viewer will be surprised by the timidity of tawdry concoctions from the thirties through the fifties. Like most temptations, expectation and anticipation far exceeded the delivered goods. In the early days, grindhouse patrons would have to endure the full 60 minutes of some indescribably absurd howler like *Maniac* for the briefest glimpse of the bizarre and sanguinary: the reanimation of a negligée-wearing corpse; the ripping off of said negligée by a drug-crazed rapist and a hair-pulling, clothes-tearing catfight between two women in a dirty cellar (the picture's loony climax). Gradually, with each passing decade, the ratio of passagework to payoff (story to sex) shifted.

We've now come full circle. Today, there's rarely a storyline to engage a viewer's interest, or any of the amusing moral rationalizations producers used to justify the prurient content of their films. Now, it's just modern hardbodies pistoning away like steroid-infused sex machines. Call us old-fashioned, but we find the weirdly entertaining strategies of yesterday's low-rent hucksters infinitely preferable to the siliconed, moussed — and boring — big-business porno of today.

We offer several caveats before we begin our whirlwind tour. If you're looking for an in-depth study of forbidden films, filled with biographical information on performers and directors, you'll find this book merely scratches the surface. Our goal is to tell a colorful story, and to that end we believe it's better to be accessible than definitive.

Sticklers may also take exception to some of the chronological groupings used within, for example, considering "nudie-cutie" movies as a phenomenon of the fifties when in actuality most such films were released in the early sixties. Containing films within certain decades is a convenience; our groupings have more to do with the sociology of different eras than with the significance of exact release dates.

Similarly, this isn't a detailed academic study of American sexuality; you're better advised to augment this tome with further research. This is not even a book about sexuality, *per se:* rather, it's a story about how sex was sold in a culture with very conflicting beliefs and emotions about the concept of sex — let alone the concept of sex as entertainment.

This volume does not consider the immense avalanche of X-rated video that has appeared since 1975. One of the things that inspired our account was the revelation that the video generation has little notion of the grindhouse experience; they would be stupefied to learn that people once congregated in small public venues to view the type of movies that are now confined to the back room of the local video rental parlor.

A final note: this book is more about money than sex. It presents, and ponders, a major tenet of America's cultural experience: exploiting people's fears and desires for fun and profit. To accomplish this, the sex huckster worked with limited tools. Their wares couldn't be advertised on radio, or later, television. Print was the primary advertising medium, and producers and distributors were brilliant at milking every last drop of titillating temptation out of their promotional material, while keeping it just this side of unprintable. The paper legacy we present in these pages is exciting, unnerving, and ridiculous: a perfect reflection of our culture.

We don't condemn, nor do we celebrate, the gaminess of our nation's back alleys. We do, however, believe that there's plenty to learn in the grindhouses there, particularly if you walk softly and carry a healthy sense of humor.

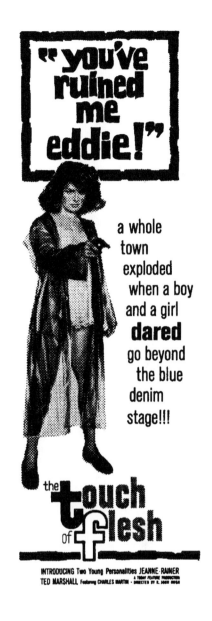

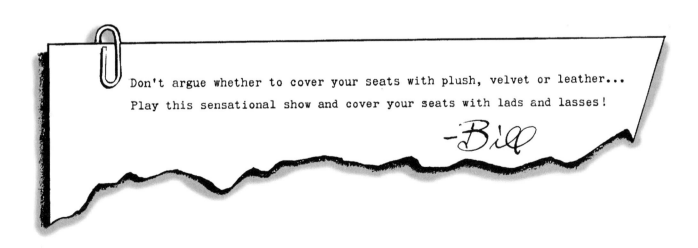

Don't argue whether to cover your seats with plush, velvet or leather...
Play this sensational show and cover your seats with lads and lasses!

—Bill

THE 30s
THE ROAD TO RUIN

The modern era of exploitation burst on the American scene after the Big Crash and before the New Deal. It was Hollywood itself that tilled the soil on which grindhouses would grow, through the creation of the Production Code Administration, commonly known as the Hays Office. Will Hays was a former Postmaster General and professional lapdog bureaucrat chosen by the studios to serve, at $100,000 per year, as the industry's censor.

Prior to the creation of the Hays Office, movies eagerly depicted all sorts of sex, vice, and general moral corruption, from "exposés" of white slavery like *Traffic in Souls* (Universal, 1913) to grandiose epics that featured nubile Christians lashed naked to the stake (Cecil B. De Mille's *Sign of the Cross*) and all-out orgies (Erich von Stroheim's *The Merry Widow* and *The Wedding March*).

Hollywood's excesses didn't go over well with the puritan movement that was exerting itself in American culture. Many high-minded community leaders believed that America, having beaten back the Kaiser in World War I, was destined to be a moral utopia. The Volstead Act, prohibiting the distribution of liquor, was soon enacted. Obviously, if reality could be regulated, so could the movies.

The media circuses of today didn't begin with television. In the early 1930s, American newspapers were crammed with stories of crime and vice. Sensational tales of white slavery rackets were screened in upscale theaters until Hollywood's self-imposed Hays Code pushed such sordid subjects into the "adults only" venues.

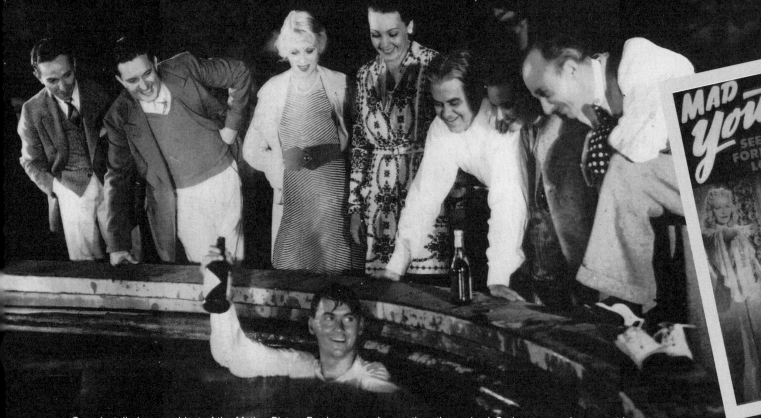

Once installed as president of the Motion Picture Producers and Distributors Association of America, Will Hays created a list of "Don'ts and Be Carefuls" in response to growing pressure by politicians and churches over Hollywood's salacious image.

Talking pictures were still a rumor when Hays became Hollywood's morality czar. With the advent of sound, his job became tougher. Subtlety and innuendo crept into the movies, and Hays was overwhelmed. Then the stock market crashed, scaring the hell out of the East Coast financiers whose money fueled Hollywood. The movie business, even with the advent of sound, was in a precarious state. Hollywood couldn't afford to offend anyone, lest the studios lose their vital Wall Street backers.

Into the breach stepped a Catholic layman named Martin Quigley, moneybag publisher of *Motion Picture Herald,* who was well-connected to the church's hierarchy. Quigley deemed Hays' "Don't List" inadequate: Hollywood needed a guiding light, Quigley believed, to ensure that films strengthened moral character. He nominated himself for the job. Investors convinced themselves that Quigley's holier-than-thou approach would sanitize their Hollywood product for public consumption.

In practice, the revised Code was much more stringent about sex than it was about violence. Quigley and Joe Breen, who would later run the Production Code office, were both Irish-Catholics. As MPPDA staffer Jack Vizzard noted in his 1970 memoir *See No Evil: Life Inside a Hollywood Censor*, the Irish culture "dreaded sex as being identified with darker forces," but didn't mind brutality as much, since it wasn't deemed to be "catching."

From 1930 to 1968, Joe Breen's Production Code office previewed 98 percent of the movies released in the United States. Because major studios controlled most film distribution in the country, Breen had almost complete control over the subject matter viewed on America's movie screens. A movie couldn't be screened in a first-run house without the PCA seal. Studios wouldn't allow their films to be shown on a double bill with a film that wasn't PCA-approved.

It could be argued that the day Hollywood accepted the revitalized Production Code — February 17, 1930 — was the day that the "Golden Age" of exploitation began.

For out of this moral lock-down emerged The Forty Thieves: A loosely affiliated cadre of independent producers not only from Los Angeles, but Texas, Florida, New York,

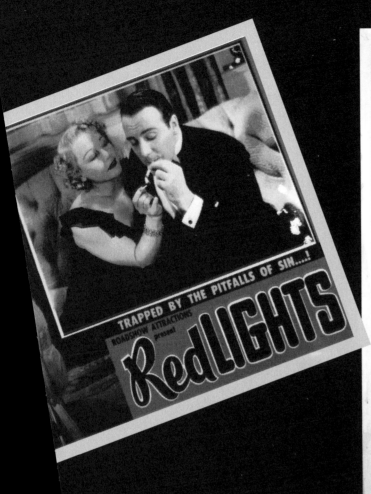

The "Hays Code," Hollywood's answer to its morally high-minded critics, succeeded in creating a fertile market for exploitation producers. Grindhouse fare displayed all the skin, sin, and moral turpitude that Hollywood was afraid to show. Producers avoided state and local obscenity laws by disguising their films as cautionary moral tales.

Fools of Desire (above) may have been a thirties-style re-release of an old film called Wild Oats, made in 1919. At least they shared identical poster art. The sexy graphics don't tell the whole story: it's about venereal disease.

Opposite page and left: Girls of the Underworld (1932). Classic Prohibition-era vice: drunken carousing leads straight to a game of strip-dice. Guess what? The boys always won.

Chicago, and other predominantly rural territories on what they called "the Sucker Belt." Former carnival operators, con men, roadshow hucksters, the self-annointed "Thieves" saw Hollywood's new code as the opportunity of a lifetime. Will Hays' list of dreaded DON'TS — white slavery, vice, nakedness, prolonged love scenes, gambling, drunkenness, and depictions of the underworld — provided the essential ingredients for dozens of low-budget melodramas sold as the Shocking Truth for ADULTS ONLY.

The Forty Thieves were jacks of all trades. Some were primarily distributors, some producers, others mainly exhibitors. In operation, everybody in the dodge had a hand in everything. Exhibitors might finance their own product, then sell it outright to distributors in other territories. Producers didn't just make films, they often acted as distributors as well. Some Thieves, like Dwain Esper, did everything from loading the film in the camera to threading it through the projector in some scratch-house on the roadshow circuit. What united them was their willingness to handle the types of films that Hollywood shunned.

The Thieves who worked roadshows were a cross between cowboy and carny: cruising the overheated Plymouth across the American outback, Omaha one night, Cedar Rapids the next, showing in tiny grindhouses, staying in

Too Hot for Hollywood

A staple attraction on the early grindhouse circuit was *High School Girl* (1935), produced by Bryan Foy, who as a child was one of the "Seven Little Foys" of vaudeville fame. Foy opted for an independent career in exploitation after he had the distinction of directing Warner Bros.' first all-talking picture, *Lights of New York*, in 1928. *High School Girl* dared to depict the trials of teenage pregnancy, a definite Hollywood taboo. The Forty Thieves ground it on the roadshow circuit for more than a decade. After WWII, *High School Girl* had some fresh clinical birth footage inserted and was reborn as *Dust to Dust*. It continued to play small towns in America's "Sucker Belt" into the early 1950s.

flops to keep overhead low. Schmoozing exhibitors to stay on their good side, hoping to hit a "red one" (carny lingo for a big payday) in the next town. Traveling salesmen of cinematic sin.

And, of course, they were characters. S. S. Millard, nicknamed "Steamship," was a Thief in good standing. He made a couple of early exploitation films in the late twenties, *Pitfalls of Passion* and *Is Your Daughter Safe?*, but spent most of his life as an itinerant showman, buying, selling, and in some cases, stealing films. A favorite story about Millard holds that, being of Romanian extraction, he conned his way into a three-day wining and dining binge in San Francisco with the visiting ex-queen of Romania, passing himself off as a stateside old country diplomat. By day, he was probably grinding *Jungle Virgins* at a dingy sleaze-pit on Market Street.

Howard "Pappy" Golden was another of the Forty Thieves who lived up to the larcenous nickname. He had a reputation for swiping films from exchanges, and hitting the road with purloined promotional material.

J. D. Kendis operated two production companies, Jay Dee Kay and Continental. He was a jeweler from Sedalia, Missouri, who moved to Hollywood and started out as a tour guide at MGM. Rumor had it that he had a cousin at the studio who ended up bankrolling his exploitation exploits.

Compared with contemporaries like John Dillinger and Pretty Boy Floyd, the

Thieves were harmless fun. They were, after all, just giving the public what it wanted. In the depression era, when the major theater chains resorted to Bank Nights and dish giveaways to lure customers, putting some sex in a picture to boost receipts was a temptation

even Paramount found hard to resist. While the Hays Office kept the big boys in line, the Forty Thieves ran amok. Between 1931 and 1934 more than thirty Adults Only films played around the country.

In a typical grindhouse potboiler, there might be five minutes of "forbidden" action. This usually took place in the roadhouse, a location central to exploitation films of the period. All manner of sordid deeds transpired in a smoky juke joint across the county line, where the innocent heroine got her first taste of that tempting stew of liquor, smoke, and music. Often, it made her surrender to a cad in the backseat of a steamy Packard. Many roadhouses were situated near the lake, to accommodate spontaneous late night skinny dips.

The films were an extension of carnival tease. As David F. Friedman, a carny publicist turned film producer, explained, "The whole secret to the scheme was that the sucker never really saw it all, but, 'Boy didja see that preview for next week's show? We're really gonna see it then.' Of course, they never did. But hope springs eternal in the human breast."

As for exhibition, the Forty Thieves had no use for classy theaters. They took pride in being able to travel with a single print of a film, secure a few nights in a dilapidated downtown theater, and rake in cash before the local authorities rousted them.

If they couldn't book a theater, they'd use a tavern. Failing that, they'd pitch a tent on a dry lot across the city line and grind away. It was utter failure to leave town without

Ingredients for Adults Only Potboiler Stew

J. D. Kendis, one of the original Forty Thieves, helped create the basic recipe for exploitation chefs in his 1931 production *Guilty Parents*. Patrons left thirsty by the Volstead Act were shown lots of drinking, either in swanky urban social clubs or in grungy rural roadhouses. Fallen women presided over gambling dens, wearing filmy negligées. The heroine, typically a corn-fed blonde, had her hands full fending off the heavy-petting wolf who lived to corrupt her.

the rubes' money, so they had to be resourceful.

Selling sin and sex to the suckers was a rolling shell game. Circumventing state and local obscenity laws was a big part of the fun. Many of the states in which the Forty Thieves thrived had their own censorship boards: New York, Pennsylvania, Virginia, Maryland, Massachusetts, Ohio, and Kansas. Other states applied laws capriciously and arbitrarily, depending on the pressure from church campaigns or politicians trying to garner newspaper write-ups.

This led to many different versions of a film like *Lash of the Penitentes*. Some states had no tolerance for the scenes of an "added" featured actress being stripped naked and tortured. When these scenes were cut, *Lash* returned to its original state — a documentary about a sect of Christians in New Mexico who ritualistically torture and crucify each other every Easter.

The Thieves specialized in outsmarting the censors. On a circuit, the roadshower would travel with the films in his car, and a trunk full of posters and handbills promising an unflinching look at the most forbidden secrets of

Grable's Grindhouse Origins

Even fledgling Columbia Pictures, a Poverty Row studio climbing to the top rank, edged into the Forty Thieves' territory with *What Price Innocence?*, a film about the dire consequences of pre-marital sex that was branded in many regions with an Adults Only label. Years before she'd become the favorite pin-up of WWII GI's, a teenage ingenue named Betty Grable "went too far" in the film, and ended up in a home for unwed mothers. An even younger Betty appeared, at age 16, in the 1932 grinder *Probation*, as a girl who "likes to fool around."

our society. He'd cut a deal with a local exhibitor, plaster the town with advertising — and watch the money pour in. Typically, he'd split the take fifty-fifty with the exhibitor.

All that action, of course, often brought the cops calling. As soon as word of a raid came down, the agent would zip straight to the projection booth. All the "hot" spots were flagged on the reels, and with a few quick snips, he'd cleanse the purportedly "filthy" movie. (Scripts for exploitation films were always written so that the nasty bits could be excised quickly.)

After a while the cops, no doubt bored and disgruntled, would drift back to their beat. In order to avoid a riot among the disappointed paying customers, the agent would then pull out the "square up" reel, a hot little item he never let out of his hands.

The square-up contained just the juicy parts. Never outright pornography — and only used as a desperate last resort to soothe a riled-up audience — the square-up might feature prolonged takes of nude actresses and maybe even flashes of pubic hair.

An alternative to roadshowing was the outright sale of Adults Only films through the States Rights network. This was an organization of 32 film exchanges around the country in which regional distributors bought films for their geographically defined territories. Producers could get a fast return on their films by selling prints outright to, say, the Central States or Southeast territory. A distributor who bought a film for his territory assumed responsibility for its success: he could rename it, recut it, whatever he wanted.

The States Rights system made it even tougher for the Hays Office to keep the nation's screens free of sin and salaciousness. Regional distributors could splice anything into, or out of, any picture they bought. Producers routinely offered hot and cold versions of their films, giving exhibitors lots of leeway in determining just how "adult" an Adults Only attraction would be.

Haven't I Seen You Somewhere Before?

Selling films outright to various territories under States Rights agreements meant that patrons of the film *Red Lights* might years later have the strange feeling that they'd seen this strip poker game somewhere before. Films popped up over and over again, each time with a new name and fresh publicity campaign, promising *The Shocking, Naked Truth Behind Today's Headlines! Nothing Like It Ever Seen Before! Revealed Here for the First Time on Any Screen!*

DWAIN ESPER
KING OF THE ROADSHOWS

Here's Hollywood's boss censor, Joe Breen, assessing the merits of a low-budget motion picture entitled *The Seventh Commandment:* "The whole play is the most thoroughly vile and disgusting motion picture which the three members of this staff, who saw the picture last night, have ever seen. It is thoroughly reprehensible in all its details. In addition, it is poorly produced and poorly photographed. The portion of the film given over to the Caesarian operation suggests a foreign picture, possibly a foreign medical picture. The whole thing is very offensive and disgusting."

Few people have ever understood the work of Dwain Esper so well.

What's odd about Breen's tirade is that it was directed at a production which had absolutely no use for the Hays Office's Seal of Approval. Breen must have simply been furious that a man such as Dwain Esper existed at all, a man whose movies were designed to stir up controversy — and dollars. Esper's only failing was that he was a genuine triple-threat: he couldn't produce, write, or direct with any detectable coherence. Esper made Ed Wood look like Orson Welles.

But what Esper lacked in filmmaking talent, he made up for with roadshowing savvy. He was a legend among the Forty Thieves, earning the nickname "King of the Celluloid Gypsies."

Esper's biography is sketchy, as befits a man who lived most of his life on the road, one step ahead of the law. He was born in the early 1890s, served in World War I, and worked as a building contractor in Los Angeles in the 1920s, when the arid basin was burgeoning. But Esper shunned a life of real estate development in favor of the movie business — even though his films were of sub-Poverty Row standard.

Esper and his wife, Hildegard, understood that Hollywood's new censorship meant there was a nasty niche to be carved in the movie business. They leapt right into the breach, creating some of the most infamous Adults Only exploitation films of the decade.

Narcotic (1933) depicted, on-screen, the ravages of opium and heroin addiction; the aforementioned *The Seventh Commandment* (1933) was a film about venereal disease which featured the Caesarian delivery of a dead baby; *Maniac* (1934) purported to be a clinical study of psychosexual madness; *Modern Motherhood* (1934) deals with a young, fast lane couple considering an abortion, and Esper's

In 1937 Dwain Esper somehow talked John Barrymore's wife, Elaine, into appearing in a film he was making. The end result was a scratch-house short called *How To Undress in Front of Your Husband.* It's hard to imagine debutantes lining up for that one. Never one to waste a good idea, Esper also roadshowed the rare little oddity seen here. The man obviously was not shy about tackling the crucial issues of the day.

most famous film, *Marihuana* (1936), warned against the evils of the Devil's weed. In 1936 he bought the rights to *Tell Your Children*, an anti-dope film financed by a Los Angeles church group. Esper topped off the turgid production with some skin shots and retitled it *Reefer Madness.* (We'll discuss that film's history later on.)

Several characteristics unified the Esper *oëuvre:* the insistence on controversial subjects, a bargain-basement approach to production, a disdain for coherent storytelling, and a guarantee that at some point —

amidst the numbing sermons on morality and the hammy acting — there would be flashes of nudity.

Esper created dingy, prurient imagery framed within scripts of fervid moral righteousness. The result was a head-spinning, hellfire-and-brimstone huckster's stew, just like they served at a carnival geek show.

Esper formed companies the way most people change clothes: Hollywood Producers and Distributors, Roadshow Attractions Company, and Dwain Esper Productions were a few of them. He operated on a shoe-string, often taking pictures on the road himself. He'd barnstorm regions with a trailerhouse in tow, stuffed with all his lurid promotional material. A preferred strategy was to rent an entire theater for a week or so, and take over the whole operation (known in the trade as "four-walling"). In true roadshow fashion, Esper put more energy into the enticing theater fronts than he did into the films. Showings of *Narcotic* featured glass-encased displays of phony drug paraphernalia and the mummified corpse of outlaw Elmer McCurdy, propped up to display the ultimate fate of the drug addict. Esper had purchased McCurdy from Louis Sonney for a six-month "tour."

After World War II, Esper stopped making pictures, but he continued to roadshow, even as the practice started dying out. In a deal that to this day is considered suspect, Esper secured the "rights" to the 1930 Tod Browning classic *Freaks*. He toured the country with it, running it under the title *Forbidden Love*. As David Friedman recounts in his riotously funny book *Youth in Babylon*, Esper learned the hard way that the new title was no good. A crowd in North Carolina, primed for skin, threatened a riot when the reti-

Who Needs the Hays Code?

As these rare stills show, *Narcotic* (1933), Esper's first film as an independent producer-director, contained heroin use, prostitution, and some drug-infused sex (suggested, not shown). The story concerns a doctor turned hop-head. Although he tries to clean up, a car accident lands him in the hospital, where he becomes addicted to heroin. The doctor ends up on the carny circuit, selling the brilliant medicinal cure-all he'd hoped to patent as a sleazy snake-oil remedy. He finally shoots himself. Among its other delights, *Narcotic* depicts a Caesarian operation performed on a dead mother to save her unborn child.

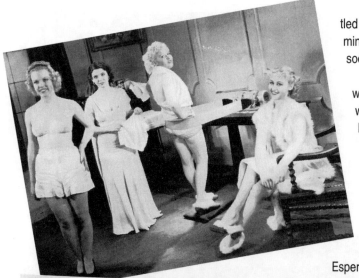

tled *Freaks* didn't deliver. Unfazed, Esper handed the projectionist a ten-minute reel of "pickles and beaver" (frontal male and female nudity) and soothed the savage crowd.

Switching the title to *Nature's Mistakes*, Esper roadshowed *Freaks* with an assortment of actual human oddities, including Sam "The Man with No Face" Alexander. He let his crew run their own gaffs in theater lobbies, selling potions, bibles, whatever.

It was no mean feat to be considered a pariah within a band of renegades like the Forty Thieves. But Esper managed to do it by adhering to none of the "gentlemen's" rules that kept the Thieves in line. He was notorious for selling states rights to his films, but secretly keeping one or two prints for himself. On many occasions, distributors would find Esper in their territory four-walling a film to which they'd just bought the exclusive rights.

Esper's antics were infuriating enough that Pappy Golden, one of the Forty Thieves, had bogus FBI Wanted posters of Esper printed up and distributed in territories corresponding to Esper's travel itinerary. But Esper turned the prank to his advantage. Whenever one of the Thieves threatened to sue him over some transgression, Esper, who claimed to be an attorney in addition to everything else, would threaten a countersuit alleging defamation of character, libel, the whole nine yards — based on the anonymous FBI poster. And Esper was enough of a wild man to scare rivals into dropping their lawsuits.

Toward the end of his roadshow career, when he was four-walling at a dilapidated burlesque house in Chicago, Esper brazenly operated, without any union involvement, a combined film-striptease show. According to Friedman, the young union agent sent to roust Esper was slipped a Mickey Finn by a dancer, separated from his streetclothes, and left dangling in the dust from Esper's trailerhouse.

The King of the Roadshows finally cashed in, at the age of 89, in 1982.

Esper's Bizarro "Masterpiece"

Maniac is one of the craziest films ever made. Under the guise of a serious study of various mental disorders, Esper ladles on all kinds of naughty weirdness: rape, fleeting nudity, catfighting women, wild hallucinations (lifted from another film) — all within the loose confines of a barely coherent plot. The film's most memorable moment occurs when the frenzied vaudeville actor who is impersonating a crazy German doctor (don't ask...) chases a cat around the lab, gouges out its eyeball, and eats it. When Esper initially inflicted *Maniac* on the public, it died. Later he sold the film to Sonney Amusements, which re-released it with a new title: *Sex Maniac*. Business picked up considerably.

SEX HYGIENE MOVIES

Dwain Esper's *The Seventh Commandment* was by no means the first film about venereal disease. During the 1930s, enough such pictures were produced to constitute an entire genre: the sex hygiene movie.

The first artistic broaching of the once unspeakable subject of venereal disease was the 1913 New York stage production of Eugene Brieux's *Damaged Goods*. Despite much concern over whether the scourge of syphilis was appropriate subject matter for the public boards (the *New York Times* feared that it would "appeal to the merely curious and morbid minds"), the play enjoyed a successful, if controversial, run. It became a *cause celebre* for Manhattan's upper crust, and a special performance was even staged for President Woodrow Wilson. In 1914, it was made into a film, leading to a barrage of sex hygiene films such as *Wild Oats*, produced by Samuel Cummins' Social Hygiene Films of America.

The real reason these films were tolerated by the ruling patriarchy was the subtext — that the freshly minted "aristocracy" (upper middle class whites with delusions of grandeur) needed to protect itself from the disease carrying lower classes streaming into the country and tearing at its social fabric. The moral of the story, as it would be in every sex hygiene film to come, was that dalliance with women of lower standing would lead not just to tainted blood and oozing sores, but soul corruption and social chaos.

By whatever name, the 1937 sex hygiene melodrama *Damaged Goods* was a durable roadshow attraction of the thirties and forties. Some distributors later played it as *Forbidden Desires*, sexing up the promotion by highlighting the curvaceous extras...

...while on yet another spin through the roadshow circuit it was called *Marriage Forbidden*. This version used the morality play approach, promising that the dark mysteries of sex would be revealed in shocking detail.

One Moment of Bliss – A Thousand Nights of Hell.

The only thing missing here is the main attraction: clinical footage of the ravages of venereal disease. Other than that, these lobby cards pretty much summarize the entire plot of every sex hygiene movie. An upstanding young man is betrothed to a fine young woman. Their future seems bright and secure. Then temptation weasels its way into the picture...

"What If You Are Getting Married! Tonight is Tonight. Tomorrow's another Day!"

Frivolity and Folly Climax George Dupont's "Bachelor Dinner"

Henrietta's father, Ignorant of George's Physical Condition, Refuses to Delay the Ceremony!

George's Family is Informed of His Ailment!

"I Forbid Your Marriage!"

George's Mother Takes Full Blame For Not Telling Her Son of Life's Greatest Pitfall and Begs Henrietta to Forgive Him!

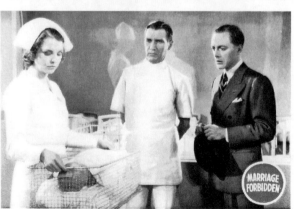

George's Child is Born — a weakling — It's Blood Tainted with the Result of George's Final Bachelor Night of Love!

Once the Hays Code banned any explicit sexual subject, America's sex education was pretty much left in the hands of the Forty Thieves. They resurrected the sex hygiene film with a vengeance in the 1930s, under the guise of educational imperative.

VD movies were always presented in the thickest of moral cloaks, because the makers were courageously showing the TRUTH that no one else dared to expose. In 1933, Weldon Pictures produced *Damaged Lives* (not to be confused with *Damaged Goods*, although the stories are almost identical), a better-than-average VD film directed by Edgar G. Ulmer. The original *Damaged Goods* was remade again in 1937 by Criterion. More than thirty other sex hygiene films appeared between those two, both melodramas and documentaries, encompassing subjects such as straight sex education, venereal disease, abortion (rare) and childbirth. It was

more than the Catholic Legion of Decency could stand.

The Legion, declaring that these scandalous films were the work of "foreign producers" trying to undermine the wholesomeness of Hollywood movies, pressured the Hays Office to exert more control over the nation's film exhibitors. But times had changed. President Roosevelt's surgeon general initiated a VD awareness campaign in 1936, and opinion polls showed the public favoring government distribution of sex hygiene material. Soon, regular movie houses, in defiance of the Production Code, were screening what the films' producers called "clap operas."

The come-on, in true carny fashion, was the promise of seeing something sensational. Often it would be the actual birth of a baby. Or producers would ferret out medical

footage depicting the horrors of advanced VD. Some of it was gleaned from medical school libraries, some came from the military. A tidy morality play was wrapped around the hot stuff. As Eric Schaefer has analyzed it in his doctoral dissertation, *Bold, Daring, Shocking, True! A History of Exploitation Films, 1919-1959*, there were five functional characters in every clap opera: the Innocent, in dire need of sexual awareness; the Corrupter, a lower-class man or woman who leads the Innocent into sexual temptation; the Parents, typically ignorant sorts who fail to impart the facts of life to their offspring; the Crusader, a pragmatic teacher or reporter campaigning for sexual responsibility, and the Charlatan, usually a quack who takes advantage of the innocent, selling them useless cures for their embarrassing ailment.

And, of course, the consequences of fooling around were often tragic. In *Damaged Lives* the disgraced fiancée of a syphilis victim commits suicide!

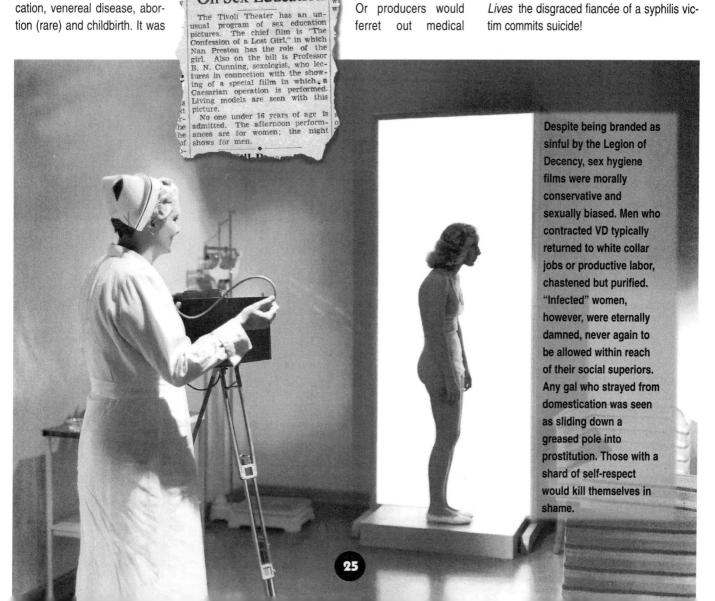

Tivoli Has Films On Sex Education

The Tivoli Theater has an unusual program of sex education pictures. The chief film is "The Confession of a Lost Girl," in which Nan Preston has the role of the girl. Also on the bill is Professor B. N. Cunning, sexologist, who lectures in connection with the showing of a special film in which a Caesarian operation is performed. Living models are seen with this picture.

No one under 16 years of age is admitted. The afternoon performances are for women; the night shows for men.

Despite being branded as sinful by the Legion of Decency, sex hygiene films were morally conservative and sexually biased. Men who contracted VD typically returned to white collar jobs or productive labor, chastened but purified. "Infected" women, however, were eternally damned, never again to be allowed within reach of their social superiors. Any gal who strayed from domestication was seen as sliding down a greased pole into prostitution. Those with a shard of self-respect would kill themselves in shame.

POVERTY ROW

Major motion picture studios such as Metro Goldwyn Mayer, 20th Century-Fox, Warner Bros., and Paramount controlled the vast majority of America's cinematic product. The cadre of former East Coast tailors and junkmen that ruled Hollywood liked to bill themselves as Dream Makers. Men like Martin Quigley and Joe Breen were hired to ensure that the dreams stayed clean and wholesome.

But there was another level of studios, existing in a low-budget independent world between the majors and the Forty Thieves. Companies like Monogram, Chesterfield, Reliable, Progressive, Mascot, Majestic, and PRC — nicknamed Poverty Row — cranked out a steady stream of films, specifically designed to fill out the bottom half of double bills.

The most important ingredient in a Poverty Row production was an enticing title that would pop off the lower half of the billboard. *Dance Hall Hostess*, *Sister of Judas*, *The Slums of New York*, *Her Re-Sale Value*... they were exploitive in nature, but not quite the type of exploitation films that were the Forty Thieves' stock in trade. Some were even tight little examples of pre-WWII *film noir*, made more than two decades before the term *film noir* was coined.

For Poverty Row producers, it was essential to wring every last penny out of a shoestring production. That often meant selling prints outright in states rights fashion. If a film had a provocative title, its chances of a second life on the grindhouse circuit increased. Taking a page from the Forty Thieves' operating manual, Poverty Row producers often squeezed a nightclub scene into a script, providing an opportunity for a sexy dance number. The scene might be shot in a hot and cold version, allowing a print to be modified later according to regional and local laws.

If a second-tier "star," someone like Jack LaRue or Otto Kruger, was in the film, grindhouse distributors might cut them from the advertising: patrons knew that such stalwart veterans would never appear in a truly "dirty" movie.

Poverty Row was the tabloid television of the time. It sold exposés of sensational subjects such as the "Yellow Peril," in films like *Captured in Chinatown* (Superior, 1935), *Yellow Cargo* (Pacific Grand National, 1936), and *Law of the Tong* (Syndicate, 1931). Grinders always loved the word "Tong" in the title. Forget that it actually meant any type of family group. On American screens, Tong conjured up images of hatchet wielding maniacs dragging nubile innocents into the back of a steamy laundry for a fate worse than death.

This lobby card from *The Sin of Nora Moran* (1933) is a classic example of how Poverty Row producers marketed films. You'd never know from the sexy Vargas-style painting and suggestive title that the movie was actually about a woman taking the rap for a crime her lover committed. Star Zita Johann had slipped off a hot career track when she made this picture — the previous year she'd been the female lead in *The Mummy*, and starred opposite Edward G. Robinson in Howard Hawks' *Tiger Shark*.

PRIMING THE PROFIT PUMP

Promotion was the name of the game, whether an Adults Only picture was sold via states rights or roadshowed. Often, the cost of marketing films far exceeded the cost of making them. *Secrets of a Model*, produced in 1939 by J. D. Kendis, was a prime example of a more-than-modest little film that had "legs" in the nation's grindhouses. Kendis knew that the advertising was more important than the film, so his company, Continental Pictures, would provide "a complete exploitation campaign and special lobby, gratis, with every Continental roadshow unit."

This was Kendis' way of helping out the states righters who purchased his films. Unlike the major studios, which could conduct national advertising blitzes, states righters were often solely responsible for marketing a film in their territory. A good, spicy promotion might mean the difference between the purchase of one or ten prints within a region.

Each film exchange had a set percentage deal for the territory it covered. Charlotte, for example, was a three percent territory; Chicago a six percenter. So if it cost Kendis $10,000 to make *Secrets of a Model*, and he wanted to make $100,000 on his investment, he knew what to ask for in each states rights market. To make his "expectancy" in Charlotte, Kendis would ask for a $3,000 advance for the picture. In Chicago, he'd ask for $6,000.

Producers might sell their films to an exchange for several years, or in perpetuity. The exchanges would keep a cut of the gross rentals, and remit the rest to the producer. Needless to say, none of this was cut and dried, particularly where the Forty Thieves were concerned.

Pressbooks, like the one shown here, were provided to the various film exchanges by the production company. They were catalogues of all available "paper" the exchanges could provide exhibitors to attract customers. The contrast between the come-on — "Laying Bare the Private Lives of Glamorous Girls in Glittering Hollywood" — and the actual film was pretty typical. *Secrets of a Model* was about a struggling car-hop who becomes an artist's model to pay for the life-saving operation her mother desperately needs. The art class was a staple of grindhouse fare. Artsy and immoral bohemians would later become an entire sub-genre of Adults Only cinema.

EXPOSING THE
VICE RACKETS

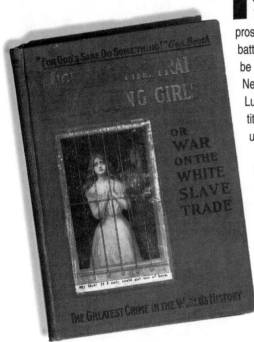

It always helped if an Adults Only picture could trumpet that it was *RIPPED FROM TODAY'S HEADLINES!* New York's crusading prosecutor Thomas Dewey's highly publicized battle against gangland racketeers proved to be perfect grist for the grindhouse mill. Newspapers followed every lurid detail of Lucky Luciano's 1936 prosecution for prostitution, whetting the public's appetite for unflinching exposés of sex for sale.

Although vice racket movies flourished in the thirties, they actually originated in 1913, when Universal scored a box office bonanza with *Traffic in Souls*. Like its descendents, the film claimed a basis in government-sanctioned fact — in this case the John D. Rockefeller Report on white slavery. Although the industrialist and banker denied any connection between the two, the publicity — and

all-important cloak of moral concern — led to huge business.

Its success spawned *Inside the White Slave Traffic*, a documentary look into New York's red light districts. The actual depiction of prostitutes plying their trade was too much for American screens, and the film's producer, Samuel H. London, was tried and convicted of "presenting an indecent exhibition and corrupting the public morals."

Florence Reid even got into the vice act later, when she presented *Red Kimono* (1925). Filmed in her solemnly draped Hollywood office, Mrs. Reid warned America's young women of the dangers that faced "hometown girls" when they wandered into the urban jungle.

One white slavery film that strayed from the typical farm girl sucked into the urban nightmare scenario was a nasty number called *Trapped by Mormons*, in which the followers of Brigham

Tomes such as *Fighting the Traffic in Young Girls* (1910), published by the Illinois Vigilance Association, purported to detail the inner workings of the white slave trade. "Ice cream parlors of the city and fruit stores combined, largely run by foreigners, are the places where scores of girls have taken their first step downward," the book warned.

When prostitution rackets became a hot subject in the late thirties, *The Pace That Kills*, a 1935 film about the evils of cocaine addiction was retitled *Girls of the Street* and recirculated with an appropriately salacious Adults Only campaign.

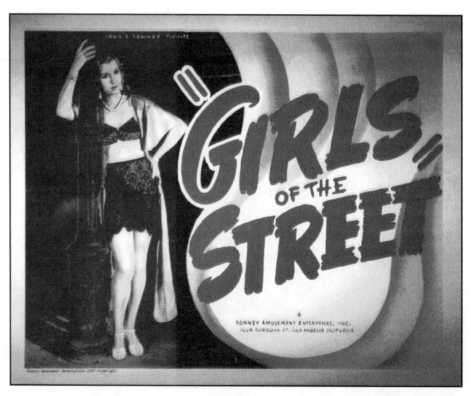

Young are shown using Svengali-like powers to lure unsuspecting women into lives of polygamy.

The backbone of most vice films, however, was the tale of an innocent girl led into a life of prostitution by a cosmopolitan cad. This premise played strongly on the roadshow circuit: Most Americans of this era lived closer to farmland than to skyscrapers, and vice pictures played on their fear and awe of teeming cities. Small-town parents who worried that their daughters would leave them for the bright lights found no solace here: the villains were often theatrical agents who promised stardom, but delivered fat, slumming businessmen primed for "servicing." This was nicely ironic, as the exploiteers were happy to sell the public an image of film and theater people as being one step above sewer scum.

Intense coverage of the Luciano case also allowed people's worst fears about immigrants to be exploited. With the drums of war beating across the Atlantic, "pure" Americans looked suspiciously on any organization of foreigners. Three pimps in a pool hall suddenly became a "vice trust." The new face of crime was swarthy and southern European, and was more likely than not portrayed by Willy Castello, a "specialist" in thuggy brutes with awkward accents.

In *Smashing the Vice Trust*, produced by Willis Kent in 1937, Castello played Lucky Lombardo, and the picture hewed closely, if clumsily, to the facts of the Luciano case. In its courtroom climax, a fiery Dewey-like prosecutor calls for Lucky's conviction, declaring "The truth must be self-evident! You've seen how they've debauched American womanhood!"

Kendis Plays a Pair

Two of the most durable vice racket pictures were *Slaves in Bondage* (1937, a. k. a. *Crusade Against the Rackets*) and *Gambling with Souls* (1936, a. k. a. *The Vice Racket)*, both produced by J. D. Kendis. In *Slaves*, Lona Andre, once a promising Paramount feature actress, played a manicurist at a beauty parlor that's a front for a prostitution ring. In *Souls*, Martha Chapin is a doctor's wife whose gambling debts make her an easy mark for vice lord Lucky Wilder, portrayed by the ubiquitous Wheeler Oakman (see page 31). The "Adults Only" visuals consisted mostly of prostitutes paraded around in bras and half-slips.

The producers, of course, rarely missed a chance to show American womanhood in lacy brassieres and diaphanous slips and panties. And it was always made clear that these women were at least partially responsible for their own degradation, since it was their quest for fame, fortune, romance — or, God forbid — "a good time," that got them in trouble in the first place. The moral was simple: stay in your place and let Dad run the show. Women's desires, whether material or sexual, could only lead to disaster.

Willis Kent was one of the most prolific producers of Adults Only fare, having made *The Pace That Kills* (1935), *Race Suicide* (1938, about an abortion racket), *Mad Youth* (1939, escort bureaus), and *Souls in Pawn* (1940, a stripper adopts a baby on the black market), among many others.

Kent devised one of the more outlandish exploitation gimmicks of the time, with yet another Willy Castello grinder, *Wages of Sin* (1938). The storyline is archetypical: hard-working Marjorie Benton toils in a laundry to support a miserable family that doesn't deserve her. She decides to go out with a girl-friend to blow off some steam. At a club called the Hideaway, vice boss Tony Kilonis (our man Willy) takes a shine to her. He fixes it so Marjorie will be fired and have to turn to him for help. He promises marriage, but in no time has her working as a prostitute in his stable. (Marjorie has had many chances to escape but — *guilty, guilty* — she can't quite shake her desire for Tony's fast life and all the baubles it might bring.) She's ensconced in Fat Pearl's whorehouse up the coast, but escapes. When she finds Tony back in his city apartment with a new girl, she shoots him to death. The story ends with Marjorie on trial, awaiting the verdict of an all-male jury.

Here's Kent's twist: there is no resolution.

Willy Castello, as the swarthy immigrant, menaces the pure Constance Worth.

Audiences were invited to write short essays arguing whether Marjorie's crime was justi-fied, with Kent promising $1,000 for the best answer submitted to his Los Angeles Office of Real Life Dramas.

Kent's ultimate racket film, however, must be *Confessions of a Vice Baron*, in which Willy Castello resurrected the character of Lucky Lombardo. Not that the public demand-ed it. Rather, the resourceful Kent made a "new" film by simply hacking five other films of his apart and gluing the juiciest parts back together, bookended by Lucky's death-row spiel warning about the pitfalls of a life of crime.

Confessions of a Vice Baron was fifty-nine minutes, total: only eight new minutes of Castello. *That's* exploitation!

The Lord of Vice

While mainstream movies made gun-toting icons out of Jimmy Cagney, George Raft, Paul Muni, and Edward G. Robinson — "Adults Only" budgets dictated stars like Wheeler Oakman. Here he's seen in a deceptively tender moment in the 1941 film *Escort Girl,* yet another vice racket exposé produced by J. D. Kendis. The actresses who filled out the brothel scenes in vice pictures no doubt came to Southern California with grand ideas of trading their small-town beauty queen status for a movie career. They dreamed of kissing Clark Gable but ended up in a Poverty Row studio fending off Wheeler Oakman. "Go ahead and yell your head off!" Wheeler would sneer when an ensnared lovely realized her fate. Troublesome dames who didn't "play along" were usually dropped in a lake by Wheeler's fellow heavy, John Merton. Whether he was menacing Tim McCoy in a cheap Western or Flash Gordon in a space age serial, Oakman was the most utilitarian of Grade-C villains.

Like tabloid television shows of the 1990s, early exploitation producers kept an eye out for "social problems" that could be profitably exploited. History shows little genuine concern, circa 1934, regarding the "issue" of forced sterilization. Yet a big grindhouse earner that year was *Tomorrow's Children*, starring Sterling Holloway and Crash Corrigan as wacked-out hospital workers who cruise around in an ambulance picking up morally unfit people for unscheduled spaying and neutering.

The southern circuit being particularly lucrative, producers created a subgenre of "hillbilly" pictures. Sturdiest — and dirtiest — of these films was a controversial backwoods saga called *Child Bride* (1939), which billed itself as an exposé of under-age marriages.

A young, progressive-thinking schoolmarm ventures into the sticks to bring enlightenment to the peckerwoods. She's quickly abducted by a redneck vigilante who doesn't appreciate her educatin'. She's stripped to the waist, tied to a tree and flogged. That scene wouldn't raise an eyebrow today. But the shots of 13-year-old Shirley Miles splashing naked at the swimming hole — well, Humbert Humbert would blush. The leering treatment of the little girl makes *Child Bride* one of the few old grinders that might still be taboo today.

Here is a page from the book of life. The characters are real people who live deep in the heart of Thunderhead Mountain. In dramatizing life among these "back yonder" folks — we aim neither to ridicule nor defend their way of living. And if our story will have helped to abolish Child Marriage — it will have served its purpose.

—Opening "Square Up" from *Child Bride*

Once upon a time there was a young Austrian woman named Hedwig Eva Maria Kiesler, who dreamed of becoming a famous movie actress. She met a man named Gustav Machaty, who said that if she followed him into the forest near Prague, he could make her dreams come true. He was making a beautiful art film, one that would earn them renown the world over. *All you have to do, Hedwig, is take off your dress and go for a swim.*

Sounds like the tried and true recipe for a sleazy little stag film, doesn't it?

Well, yes and no. *Extase*, made in Czechoslovakia in 1932, takes a now-familiar plot — the dissatisfied young wife seeking to release her pent-up sexual urges — and turns it into a stylized frenzy of romantic erotica. The film was a minor scandal when it was originally released in Europe, due mainly to its brief and shimmering nudity and the purple symbolism used to evoke young Hedwig's orgasmic release. Rearing stallions, howling winds, surging flames — it was all there.

Of course, it wasn't until Hedwig Kiesler came to Hollywood in 1937 — at the behest of MGM boss Louis B. Mayer — that *Ecstasy* became the most notorious sex film ever made. The story goes that when Mayer learned of the film's existence, he sought out every copy, to ensure that the studio and his newfound star, renamed Hedy Lamarr, would suffer no further embarrassment. More believably, Mayer was milking every last drop of sensational publicity.

(Hedy's first husband, millionaire Fritz Mandl, had already bought up most of the circulating prints. She left him for Hollywood; he left her for Hitler, for whom he made munitions.)

Whatever the real story, Hedy had nothing to worry about. While this 64-minute import achieved legendary status as the ultimate smut film, it actually helped, rather than hurt, her career.

Ecstasy has historical significance beyond the presence of a future movie star appearing unabashedly nude. It's the first example of the sexy art film from Europe: although choppy and technically erratic, *Ecstasy* is full of dynamic visuals and genuinely exciting bits of business. It's the *Battleship Potemkin* of sex pictures.

The approach to sexuality is at least an ocean away from what was passing for sex on American movie screens. Lamarr portrays a woman who abandons the affluence of her cold, older groom in a search for "ecstasy." And although her fulfillment has tragic consequences — her estranged husband shoots himself — she is not punished for her desires.

The most whispered about picture in the world—

Hedy LAMARR *in* **A BOLD STORY OF A DELICATE SUBJECT!**

DARING! REVEALING! SHOCKING!

ECSTASY

THE STARK NAKED TRUTH OF A WOMAN'S DESIRE FOR LOVE

In an American film of the same era, the "fallen" woman, consumed with guilt, would have thrown herself in front of a train. Here, she merely boards the train and heads off into an uncertain future.

These intensely erotic close-ups were scandalous for their time. Stories vary on how Hedy, a notoriously stiff actress, conveyed such believeable rapture. One version has it that she was administered a Teutonic "tongue-lashing" off-camera. The less spicy account (and Hedy's own) has it that the director jabbed a pin in Hedy's derriere to get the required response.

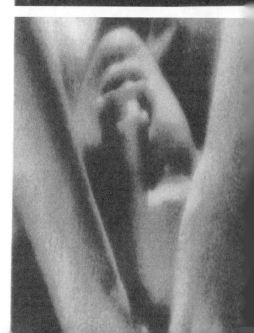

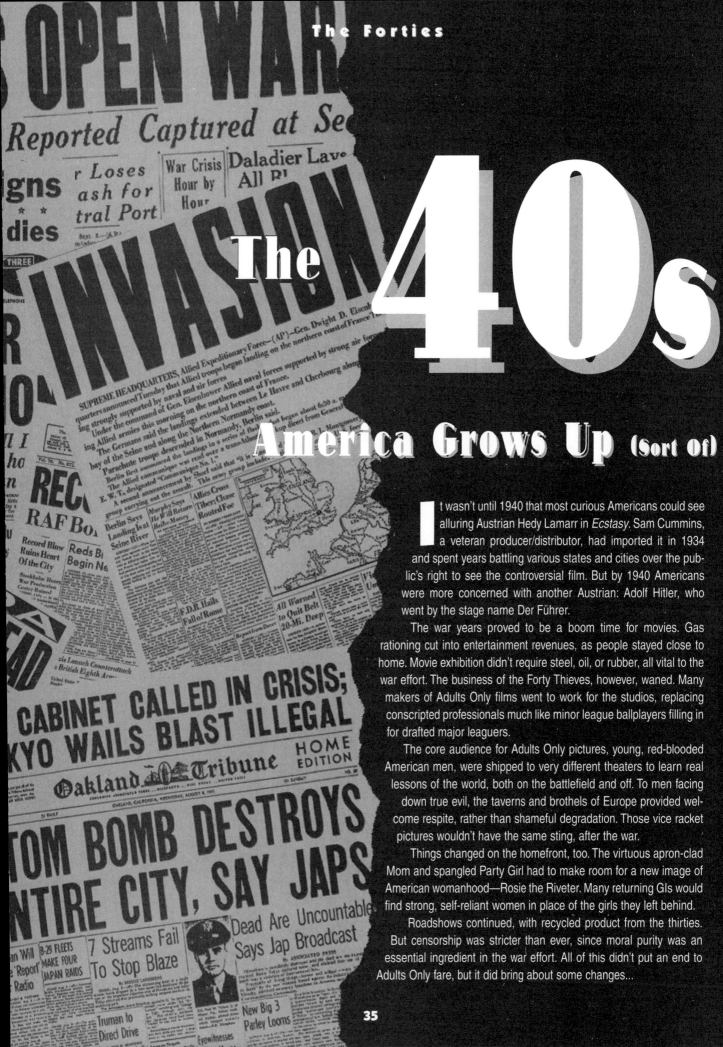

The 40s

America Grows Up (Sort of)

It wasn't until 1940 that most curious Americans could see alluring Austrian Hedy Lamarr in *Ecstasy*. Sam Cummins, a veteran producer/distributor, had imported it in 1934 and spent years battling various states and cities over the public's right to see the controversial film. But by 1940 Americans were more concerned with another Austrian: Adolf Hitler, who went by the stage name Der Führer.

The war years proved to be a boom time for movies. Gas rationing cut into entertainment revenues, as people stayed close to home. Movie exhibition didn't require steel, oil, or rubber, all vital to the war effort. The business of the Forty Thieves, however, waned. Many makers of Adults Only films went to work for the studios, replacing conscripted professionals much like minor league ballplayers filling in for drafted major leaguers.

The core audience for Adults Only pictures, young, red-blooded American men, were shipped to very different theaters to learn real lessons of the world, both on the battlefield and off. To men facing down true evil, the taverns and brothels of Europe provided welcome respite, rather than shameful degradation. Those vice racket pictures wouldn't have the same sting, after the war.

Things changed on the homefront, too. The virtuous apron-clad Mom and spangled Party Girl had to make room for a new image of American womanhood—Rosie the Riveter. Many returning GIs would find strong, self-reliant women in place of the girls they left behind.

Roadshows continued, with recycled product from the thirties. But censorship was stricter than ever, since moral purity was an essential ingredient in the war effort. All of this didn't put an end to Adults Only fare, but it did bring about some changes...

BURLESQUE

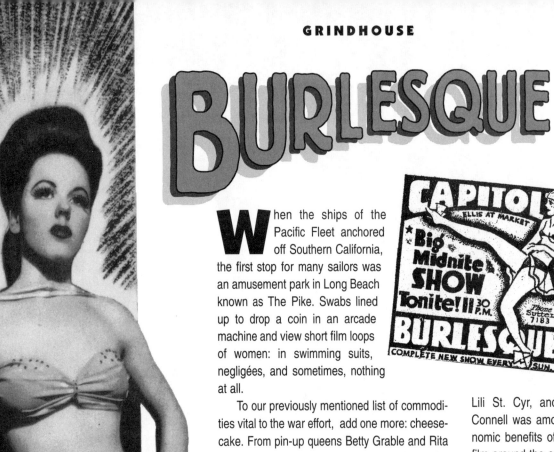

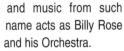

When the ships of the Pacific Fleet anchored off Southern California, the first stop for many sailors was an amusement park in Long Beach known as The Pike. Swabs lined up to drop a coin in an arcade machine and view short film loops of women: in swimming suits, negligées, and sometimes, nothing at all.

To our previously mentioned list of commodities vital to the war effort, add one more: cheesecake. From pin-up queens Betty Grable and Rita Hayworth, to the glamor girls painted on the noses of fighter planes, to nude photos passed around the barracks, female pulchritude was considered downright patriotic. Keep the boys' morale high, give 'em something to fight for and protect.

A direct outgrowth of WWII cheesecake imagery was the burlesque film. Producers in Los Angeles who'd seen the huge business for arcade "peep shows" during the war decided to go the theatrical route. Quality Studios, founded by Merle Connell — a jack of all cinema trades from rural Yakima, Washington — started producing burlesque shorts in 1947, using dancers from L.A. houses,

and music from such name acts as Billy Rose and his Orchestra.

When the old Red Cars were running in Los Angeles, you could grab one headed Downtown and take it to 5th and Main, where the "Bur-Le-Qs" thrived, and bump-and-grind queens like Aleene, Lotus Wing, Evelyn West, Lili St. Cyr, and Tempest Storm held sway. Connell was among the first to realize the economic benefits of filming these shows: shipping film around the country was far easier and more lucrative than doing the shows live.

For a relatively small fee up front, the

Hollywood Revels (1946) was one of the first burlesque features. Shot at the Follies Theater in downtown Los Angeles, it presented a complete burlesque show on film, including not just striptease artists, but singers, production numbers, and comedy sketches.

gals would do an extra performance, just for the camera.

In the period just after the war, the filming of burlesque routines was seen as something of a novelty—far from the grand vaudeville tradition that produced striptease.

The "golden age" of burlesque was the mid-twenties to mid-thirties, when ecdysiastical luminaries such as Gypsy Rose Lee, Georgia Sothern, and Ann Corio strutted their stuff in the popular vaudeville venues of Manhattan's Times Square. The Minsky Brothers were the reigning kings of sexy live shows, interspersed with comedy acts such as the young Abbott and Costello. But NY mayor Fiorello LaGuardia chased burlesque out of Times Square in 1937. He alleged that it was inspiring a rash of sex crimes. Others contend that LaGuardia had made a sweetheart deal with midtown theater chains who wanted the real estate.

In any case, burlesque languished until the immediate post-war period, when it returned with renewed vigor. Action heated up in theaters around the country. The ranks of dancers swelled into the thousands on the two "wheels"—Mutual and Columbia—that composed the striptease circuit. These were, by and large, professional, unionized operations. If you performed on the Mutual Wheel, you didn't work the Columbia circuit, and vice-versa.

The $50,000 Treasure Chest

Evelyn West was a headline performer, billed as "The Original Hubba-Hubba Girl." Her promotion included the first example of a now-familiar exploitation ploy: having her breasts insured by Lloyds' of London. According to the Paul M. Nippert Company, which handled Ms. West's management, her bosom carried a value of fifty thousand dollars. Nippert's posting of the insurance certificate outside the theater may not have been such a good idea: "...indemnity for loss of either one or both breasts by reason of removal on account of accident or disease—subject to the seven day survival clause..." just doesn't add much to Evelyn's otherwise obvious allure.

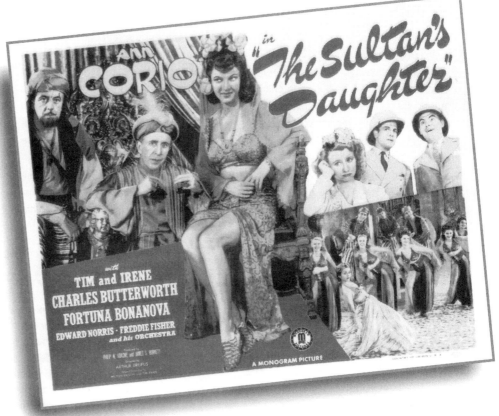

Undressed for Success

Ann Corio was one of the very few "ecdysiasts" of the Golden Age of Burlesque to make it in the movies. Granted, she never achieved stardom beyond the Poverty Row level of films, but she enjoyed a steady run of success in B-pictures such as *Sarong Girl* (1943), *The Sultan's Daughter* (1943), and *Call of the Jungle* (1944).

While the wheels rolled through the big cities, burlesque films often played small towns that didn't have a grind emporium. And the movies allowed new producers to crack the entrenched burlesque establishment. Veteran impresarios like the Minskys missed the boat entirely, figuring film could never duplicate the thrill of a live show.

One who did make the transition was San Francisco's Harry Farros, who owned a chain of burlesque houses on the West Coast. Candy was his ticket to the show; his family was one of the first indoor concessionaires in the movie business. Farros formed Broadway Roadshow Productions, and cranked out a

slew of revealing reels in the late forties and early fifties.

Some charter members of the Forty Thieves, such as the Sonney family and Willis Kent, produced numerous feature length films: *Midnight Frolics*, *Hollywood Revels*, *A Night at the Follies*, and *Striptease Girl* were but a few of the titles.

The big attraction for the Sonneys, notorious penny-pinchers, was that it didn't cost much to make a burlesque film. One camera set-up, third-row center, some old painted vaudeville flats as a backdrop, a record player instead of a live band

— ten minutes later you had a short film. These films were extremely versatile, had a long life, and were a surefire investment. A print could circulate for years, and since it was typically constructed of separate segments it could be cut up and reedited with newer footage in endless combinations. Individual acts could be cut out and turned into "loops," from which prints were struck for the arcade machines in the Adults Only sections of amusement parks. Later still, the clips

The Classiest Act in Town

Lili St. Cyr, born Marie Van Shaak, in Minneapolis, in 1918, represented the royalty of burlesque. The most classically beautiful of all striptease artists, she was a model and chorus girl in Los Angeles during her teens, where she performed at the posh Florentine Gardens, earning $27.50 a week. When she learned that nude dancers made $500, Lili lost her inhibitions.

Although she suffered from notorious stage fright, she became the most renowned striptease star of the forties, due to her penchant for enacting storylines in her exhibitions (such as "In a Persian Harem"). Women enjoyed her act, because Lili wore only the most opulent wardrobes, and would sometimes perform her act backwards — making the act of dressing up sexy and exciting. For the short film *Love Moods* (1952), producer Dan Sonney paid Lili $5,000 for one day's work. At her peak, Lili was pulling down more than $200,000 a year.

On trial in L.A. in 1951 for "lewd and lascivious" performances, she volunteered to take a bath in the courtroom to prove her tastefulness. The judge demurred, and the jury declared her work to be "art." Today, Lili maintains an interest in a lingerie shop on Melrose Avenue.

could be distilled down into 8mm mail-order films, of the type popular with Elks, Mooses, and Rotarians the world over.

Two things were different about burlesque films, from the perspective of Adults Only entertainment. The first rank of headliners, like Tempest Storm and Lili St. Cyr, were the very first "stars" of unabashed sexuality. These weren't actresses hinting at sensuality. They were sex performers, wildly popular because there was no shred of pretense about what they were selling.

In addition, these films broke the unwritten rules of voyeurism. In previous Adults Only films, the audience was pure voyeur, watching the travails of innocent maidens corrupted and disrobed. But the women of burlesque looked back! They knew they were being watched, they smiled, they encouraged the viewer's arousal. Critics can argue about how these productions objectified women, but there's little doubt that burlesque films were the first to allow women the conscious choice of being sexually expressive, without the assumption of dire consequences.

So what did a burlesque viewer see? That depended on the territory. Because of state and local censor rules, films were always made in as many as three versions. In the coolest, the dancer would perform in an exotic costume, revealing little more than long legs, a sly smile and some suggestive moves. She'd exit to much applause on the soundtrack. Often, that was the whole show. In the warmer version, she'd come back for an encore, and strip down to a g-string and pasties or a sheer brassiere. Only the most daring dancer took it to stage three, baring her nipples and wearing only a "merkin" to cover her genitalia.

Strange as it sounds today, one of the most marketable aspects of these films was that they showed American men all different types of women. In the days before television was commonplace, men wondered about "other" women. Southerners wanted to get a look at "Yankee" girls. And Yankees wanted to know if all that sun really gave California girls an all-over glow.

For all their repetition and low-brow humor, burlesque films seem innocent and even quaint today. By 1990s' standards, none of these women revealed enough to make it into any video by Aerosmith or Whitesnake.

J. D. Kendis surfaced again in 1953 with a compilation burlesque film called *Vegas Nights*. Although most of the film was made up of shorts previously shot by veteran Klayton Kirby, Kendis spliced in new footage of the sultry Elvira Pagan and issued the film, in true Forty Thieves fashion, as a new feature.

"Oh, yeah? How fat is she?"

One of the holdovers from burlesque's vaudeville origins was the inclusion of comedy sketches as interludes between the dancers. The comedy was strictly low-brow Borscht Belt schtick, delivered by comics such as Jackie Mann and Dave Carr. This combination of sexiness and silliness continued right through the fifties, when Hugh Hefner placed "Playboy's Party Jokes" on the back side of his magazine's centerfolds, mirroring the burlesque experience.

To my El Rey Fans
Tempest Storm

No burlesque performer had the longevity of Tempest Storm, nor a life story that lived up to her adopted name. Born Annie Blanche Banks in 1928, to a sharecropping family in Eastman, Georgia, she left home at 14 after being gang raped by local boys and abused by her father. She found her way to Los Angeles, worked as a cocktail waitress, and landed at the Follies Theater, in the chorus line. She told talent coordinator Lillian Hunt that she was embarrassed by her prodigious breasts, to which Hunt replied "They don't make breasts too big for my business."

Tempest became the last of the classic burlesque stars, appearing as a headliner in 1950 at the El Rey Theater in Oakland, California. The photos of Tempest on this page, from *French Peep Show*, were shot at the El Rey by a young cameraman named Russ Meyer (his obsession with cavernous cleavage already apparent), who would himself become a legendary part of Adults Only cinema.

Tempest worked steadily for an astounding forty years, during which her ability to shatter social taboos didn't stop at stripping. She had affairs with Sammy Davis Jr., Nat King Cole, Elvis Presley, and (reputedly) John F. Kennedy. She continued to disrobe in public until the age of 65, when she hung up her g-string for the last time.

Who knew when *Teaserama* was released in 1955 that it would, decades later, represent a one-shot meet-

ing of two future American sex legends. The picture was made by a portly little purveyor of mail-order dirty pictures named Irving Klaw, who owes his sliver of fame to the everlasting charms of model Bettie Page. An aspiring showgirl who posed provocatively to pay the rent, Bettie was a real life version of the "good girl gone bad" story typical of grindhouse fare — except that she giggled her way through the whole thing and eventually disappeared to lead a normal, happy life.

When Klaw decided to upgrade his product from mail-order to theatrical distribution, he enlisted the services of Tempest Storm as headliner, and included a scene in which Bettie played the subservient maid to Tempest's domineering sexpot.

It was all so coy and innocent it's hard to believe films like *Teaserama* were ever considered racy. Klaw took low-budget production the next level down: everything was shot by a single static camera in a single room, with lurid, mismatched drapes and threadbare furniture changed from one scene to the next. Who knows, maybe *Teaserama* provided an early influence on David Lynch.

NEW and NAUGHTY
TEMPEST Storm
Beautiful Productions Inc. presents
'TEASERAMA'
featuring BETTY PAGE

IN Beautiful EASTMAN COLOR

SEE THE STRIPTEASE QUEENS IN ACTION

BETTIE's PAGE

AMERICA'S FEARLESS KROGER BABB YOUNG SHOWMAN

No figure looms larger in the history of exploitation films than one Howard W. "Kroger" Babb. An all-American huckster, Babb celebrated the Allies' victory in the great world war by creating, in the words of his protegé David Friedman, "the biggest and best-organized bunko game in American show business history."

The heart of Babb's glorious gambit was a presentation called *Mom and Dad*, a truly dull retread of the 1935 film *High School Girl*. It didn't matter a whit that *Mom and Dad* — like most all of Babb's "creations" — was leaden and preachy. It was Babb's showmanship that was breathtaking. This guy could sell a beggar a bottle of rain.

Babb was born in Lees Creek, Ohio, in 1907, and grew up as an energetic and enthusiastic hard-charger with a gift of gab. After picking up his nickname as a clerk at a Kroger's grocery store, Babb worked as a newspaper reporter and advertising manager before landing a job as publicity manager of the Chakeres-Warners theater chain in the mid-thirties. There had to be carny in his blood somewhere, for Babb immediately showed a talent for staging Derby Nights and other promotional gimmicks to lure customers into his theaters. He once had a man buried alive before the entrance of a theater as a publicity stunt.

Babb parted company from Chakeres – Warners to work for an established roadshowing outfit, Cox and Underwood. He took their aging birth-of-a-baby grinder *Dust to Dust* (actually the retitled *High School Girl),* out on the route. In no time, Babb was itching to run his own "gaff," having convinced himself that he could make a sex hygiene picture and ballyhoo it to undreamed-of fortune.

In 1944 he charmed twenty investors into putting up $62,000 in production money and enlisted the services of William Beaudine, a Hollywood director long on output, short on ability. Beaudine had

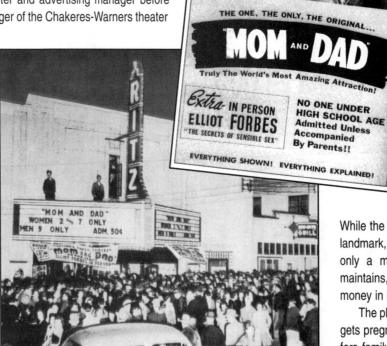

hacked out literally hundreds of Poverty Row quickies in every genre.

Having pilfered the script of *High School Girl* almost verbatim, Babb had his product without delay. Then his real work began: convincing legitimate neighborhood theaters — not grindhouses — to run a sex hygiene film that culminated with the actual on-screen birth of a baby.

Playing "legit houses" became a crusade, and his timing couldn't have been better. Four years of fear and uncertainty were over. Soldiers were free and eager again, ready to resume pursuit of the opposite sex. Women who'd labored on the home-front were feeling a new sense of personal independence. And theater exhibitors were looking for something new, a hook, that would pull these restless folks in off the street.

So, despite a dreaded "C" (condemned) rating from the Catholic Legion of Decency, selected theaters across America started screening *Mom and Dad* — A Hygienic Production. While the leap to legitimate houses was a landmark, Dave Friedman notes that it was only a matter of time: "Exhibitors," he maintains, "will eat their own kids if there's money in it."

The plot was simple: young Lois Austin gets pregnant, is dumped by the cad, suffers family trauma, and gives birth to her love child. A crusading high school teacher excoriates parents, school, and church for not providing the type of sex education that could have prevented Lois's plight. That's it. But what a circus Babb wrapped around it!

In a calculated effort to attract more women viewers, Babb contractually mandated that audiences be segregated: there was a 2 p.m. matinée for Women and Teenage Girls, another Female Only show at 7 in the evening, and a final Men and Teenage Boys show at 9 o'clock.

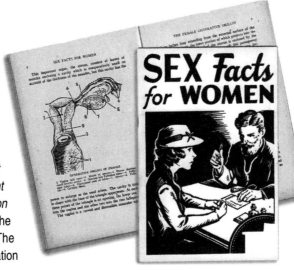

Like all successful hucksters, Babb was a psychologist. As women viewed the film, hour after hour, hormonal pandemonium swelled outside the theater. *What were the girls seeing? Is it different than what we'll see? I'll bet our version will be hotter!* Riled-up crowds for the Men's show were nicknamed "The Thundering Herd." It was sex education straight from the carnival midway.

In the middle of the film, as the promise of never-before-seen sexual mysteries loomed, the projector stopped. Out walked eminent sex hygiene commentator Elliot Forbes, who delivered a stirring talk about the need for openness and education in sexual matters. At the conclusion of his lecture, Forbes directed the young nurses on duty (just in case anyone passed out from the startling frankness) to distribute some essential — and affordable — hygiene pamphlets to those who valued sexual knowledge over shameful ignorance. The books, *Man and Boy* and *Woman and Girl*, cost one dollar.

Under the guise of eradicating ignorance, Babb had found the huckster's Holy Grail: the big score. Ticket sales boomed, and Babb kept every cent of the book sales. As many as twenty-five units of *Mom and Dad* were on the road simultaneously, playing one- and two-night stands, split weeks, Mondays-Saturdays, all across America. Before *Mom and Dad* finally ran out of gas (it still played in some backwaters into the 1970s!), it earned total revenues in excess of $100 million.

Babb began billing himself as "America's Fearless Young Showman."

Elliot Forbes, of course, was a phony. There were dozens of Elliot Forbeses all along the route. Most were old vaudeville comics who'd mastered the art of stand-up no matter how drunk they were. Enraptured by the undiluted facts of life, audiences apparently had no idea that "sexologist" Elliot Forbes was actually Moe Schwartz, a baggy

trousered retread straight from the Catskills.

The Legion of Decency was outraged by the whole thing, and Hollywood's purity czars, Martin Quigley and Joe Breen, detested Babb's wild success in skirting their rules. Once, when Quigley made particularly loud noises in his *Motion Picture Herald* about the scurrilous *Mom and Dad*, Babb took out a full-page ad in the rival trade paper *Boxoffice*, to trumpet his pending (and bogus) production: *Father Bingo! — An Exposé of Gambling in Parish Halls*. Babb really loved to stir it up.

Underneath all the boozy bluster, Babb was actually a diehard campaigner for the separation of church and state, who never missed an opportunity to go head-to-head with the Catholic Legion over the right to exhibit his films, and the public's right to attend them. He relished having picketers from the Knights of Columbus or any quasi-religious organization lining up outside his theater. To him, it was just more attention, more publicity, more tickets.

The success of *Mom and Dad* did not go unnoticed in Hollywood. In 1948, Universal produced *The Story of Bob and Sally*, a saga of two young couples' battles with all sorts of problems: venereal disease, alcoholism, abortion. It was directed by Earle Kenton, a Hollywood veteran, and is a fairly dramatic and frank consideration of these serious issues. The Hays Office stomped all over it, assuring Universal that there was no way, ever, that the film would carry the PCA Seal of Approval.

Elliot Forbes Speaks...

"These books are offered exclusively to the patrons of this presentation at a slight charge over the actual cost of printing and distribution. That price — a single dollar. One dollar a copy, two dollars for the set. Think of it — for less than the cost of a carton of cigarettes, you can have a set of these vitally important books to read in the privacy of your own home, and I believe with all my heart that a set of these fine books belongs on every bedside table in every home in this great land. Attendants will pass among you. Simply raise your hand, and please, if possible, give the attendant the exact amount of your purchase. Thank you for your kind attention. In closing, I'd like to wish each of you a very long life, a very happy life, but above all — a very healthy life. Thank you, good night, and God Bless You." Says David Friedman of Wally Nash, perhaps the finest "Elliot Forbes" of them all: "He was the crudest human being who ever lived, but God, could he sell books!" Women paid a dollar for books like the ones above to get the ovulation chart within, so they could calculate when they could — and couldn't — get pregnant. "Vatican Roulette," as Friedman calls this propagation of the rhythm method.

Rather than burn the negative, Universal sold it to Gidney Talley, who owned a string of theaters in Texas. He presented *Bob and Sally* under his Social Guidance Enterprises banner. According to Friedman, Talley had a long-standing grudge against the Catholic church. Apparently he had an aunt who was loaded, but instead of leaving a hefty inheritance to her family, she willed it all to the church. Talley was eager to have *Bob and Sally* piss off the pious. Using Babb's formula, Talley roadshowed *Bob and Sally* with a challenging promotional campaign: "Just How Much Truth Can You Stand?" blared the advertisements. This time, "Roger T. Miles" essayed the role of the guest lecturer.

Street Corner, made in 1948 by Wiltshire Pictures Corp., is less ambitious in its range of woe, focusing on a single out-of-wedlock pregnancy. The father is killed in a car wreck. The young mother suffers through a botched abortion. A good doctor rails against the ignorance of the girl's parents. Floyd Lewis, a Chicago-based distributor, bought the rights to the film, and gave it the Babb treatment: "Lifts the Iron Curtain of Ignorance" and "Sweeps Away Superstition, Illusions and Hypocrisy!" Some illusions remained, of course: lectures were conducted by Curtis Hayes, Alexander Leeds, Carlton Cox — take your pick.

At the end of the decade, the distributors of all these competing films decided to consolidate their carnival under one tent, forming Modern Film Distributors. It's interesting to note that during the height of the baby boom, while the Hays Office was paring "objectionable" dialogue from *A Place in the Sun*, and worrying whether Judy Holliday's walk was too suggestive in *Born Yesterday* — Modern Film Distributors ran its own sex education clinics in theaters coast-to-coast.

Because of Eve was the most notorious of the MFD quartet. It had the flimsiest of plots, but it was a true carny freak show:

"That picture had something nobody'd ever seen before," says Friedman. "A guy's joint and a gal's ussypay, eighty feet tall."

That's right, *Because of Eve* contained the first full frontal nudity ever seen in domestic movie theaters. Unfortunately, in the section of the film called "The Story of VD," those penises and "ussypays" were oozing pus and crackling with all kinds of nauseating sores.

The standard information on menstrual and reproductive cycles was rounded out by up-close clinical footage of a natural birth, and a complete depiction of a Caesarian operation. Even today, not too many camcorders would record *that* for posterity.

In 1949, Dave Friedman, one of the Modern Film mavens, took *Because of Eve* through New England — the most staunchly Catholic territory in the nation. "I cleared over one hundred and fifty thousand dollars," he recalls. "It was my biggest run ever."

It's All Eve's Fault

Because of Eve (pictured here) features characters called Bob and Sally, but it's a different film from *The Story of Bob and Sally*. Got it? Poor sleepy Bob gets VD when his good buddy buys him a prostitute before he goes off to war. Sally, his girlfriend back home, is ashamed to enter the clinic when she realizes she's pregnant — *by Bob's buddy!* The film contains one hilarious scene: the engaged couple visit their doctor for the results of their pre-marital check-ups. "Sally, you'll be happy to know that first baby didn't hurt you a bit," the doctor blithely tells her, in front of slack-jawed Bob. "And Bob, don't worry — there's not a trace left of that VD." *Whoops — the marriage is off!* Not to worry. The good doctor's soothing words, and a forced viewing of hideous examples of venereal disease, childbirth, and a bloody Caesarian section, bring Bob and Sally together again.

NAKED NATIVES

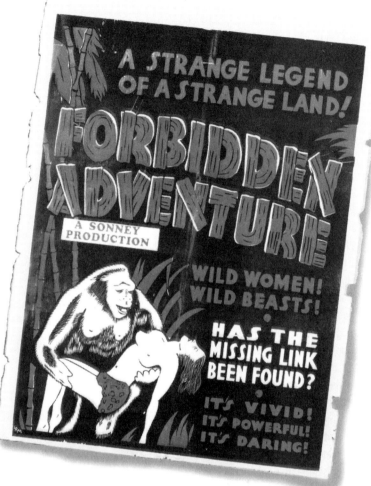

Jungle pictures, or "goona-goonas" in industry argot, were a staple of the Adults Only circuit for decades. Most of them were cobbled together from bits and pieces of travelogues, either purchased or purloined. That's why during a time of wartime rationing, goona-goona films could still be easily made and released.

Goona Goona (1932) was the name of a French film made in Bali by André Roosevelt (Theodore's nephew) and Armand Denis. The eponymous substance was a plant tribespeople smoked, which acted as an aphrodisiac. Uninhibited natives had no idea that the resulting sexual escapades, captured on film, would be watched in dark theaters by civilized voyeurs in a place called the United States.

The goona-goona formula was simple: exotic locations, some "barbaric" shocks (allowing slumming viewers to feel superior to the savages), and, most vitally, nudity. Censors passed goona-goona movies for a disturbing reason: to be concerned about the nakedness of Africans or Balinese was to admit that they were, on the evolutionary scale, closer to white people than animals. From the 1930s through the 1960s, state censor boards went into shock whenever a white woman threatened to slip out of her brassiere. "Colored" women, however, displayed breasts and buttocks with impunity. Only pubic hair was entirely forbidden, lest the moral infrastructure of the nation collapse. This double standard was the entire *raison d'être* of goona-goona movies.

The nudity in these films was either documentary footage, or newly shot inserts used to enliven antiquated stock. Much of the old material came from the 1920s, when dozens of adventurous cameramen combed the world, capturing unusual spectacles to display theatrically. Most followed in the footsteps of Robert Flaherty, whose *Nanook of the North* (1922) was a landmark in anthropological filmmaking. To others, like Martin and Osa Johnson, makers of *Headhunters of the South Seas* (1922), *Congorilla* (1932), and *Baboona* (1935), natives were straight men for far-flung vaudeville schtick: big laughs when pygmies encountered their first firecrackers, monkeys were fed beer, etc. The festivities ceased when Martin Johnson's plane went down in 1937.

Ingagi (1930) stands as a prototype for most "gorilla and the maid-

It's Angkor Again!

By the time the Sonney family bought *Forbidden Adventure* from Dwain Esper, it had been recut and retitled many times over. Despite borrowing huge chunks of footage from other goona-goona films, this version was a strong earner throughout the forties.

en" films to follow. A pair of great white hunters journey to darkest Africa in search of a tribe that worships ingagis (bogus "African" word for apes). They learn that nubile maidens mate with the vile but virile gorilla-gods, and after observing all the wild dances and rituals the hunters set the world right by killing everything in sight. *Ingagi* was a complete hoax. Many of the clips were leftovers from films such as *Heart of Africa* (1914) and *Chang* (1928), a hugely ambitious project undertaken by Merian C. Cooper and Ernest Schoedsack that turned out to be the *Heaven's Gate* of its time. Before they made *King Kong* and saved their hides, Cooper and Schoedsack sold off *Chang* footage to pay their bills.

When *Ingagi* producer Nathan Spitzer tried to play it in legitimate theaters, passing the film off as authentic, his grip slipped off the vine. The Hays Office took an affidavit from the actor who played the ape, and it was revealed that the pygmies were black children from East L.A. and the "dusky queens" cocktail waitresses.

But *Ingagi* would rise again, with pieces of it reappearing in another fraudulent gorilla picture, *Angkor*, produced in 1937 by Harry Warner and Roy Purdon. Dwain Esper got his hands on *Angkor* in the early forties, retitling it *Forbidden Adventure* (a. k. a. *Gorilla Woman*) and cutting in new nubile maiden footage. Samuel Cummins also bought *Angkor* footage, from whom it's anybody's guess, and released his own *Love Life of A Gorilla*. It played for years under various titles, including *Kidnapping Gorilla*, *Jungle Gorillas*, *Gorilla Kidnappers*, and *The Private Life of Ingagi*.

When Esper acquired, in 1942, a goona-goona called *Rama*, he tacked on a square-up that managed to tie the whole goofy mess into the war effort: "The persistent pursuit of pleasure and ambition to obtain wealth without working as the sole aims of modern existence are stripping the vitality of our national life. The decay of democracy could well be laid at its feet... The simplest life well lived according to God's standards of common goodness holds more true happiness than is available to the greatest dictator on earth. With this thought in mind we present *Rama* as a simple tale of every man when shorn of superficial aspiration of present day civilization."

Even Kroger Babb tried his hand at a goona-goona, albeit relatively late, with *Karamoja* (1954). The film was shot by William Treuttle, a dentist who learned he had only six months to live and winged off to Africa with a 16mm camera to live with a remote tribe. He documented naked dances, body scarification, and cattle slaughtering. Just the stuff for a Kroger Babb promotion, whose ad campaign featured ritualistically disfigured natives and carried the tag line: "In the age of jet travel, Africa is only hours away — *Meet Your New Neighbors!*"

Accuracy?
Try National Geographic

Goona-goona movies featured topsy-turvy world geography. The lovely L.A.-based jungle maiden seen here in *Gorilla Woman* (circa 1942) wears a Polynesian costume for her confrontation with an actor garbed as an African gorilla. Hunters on the veldt were often surprised by Bengal tigers suddenly leaping through tall grasses. Borneo, the Congo, it made no difference as long as the breasts were authentic.

A Genuine Flak-Catcher

In 1954 vagabond cameraman Elwood Price (whose day job was selling Ramblers in San Bernardino) went to Kenya, where he documented the Mau-Mau revolt for independence led by future Kenyan president Jomo Kenyatta. All U.S. television networks passed on the footage. Price and his partner, Joe Rock, ended up selling their film to Dan Sonney, son of exploitation pioneer Louis Sonney. The product wasn't quite hot enough for Sonney's taste, so he hired some local African-Americans to flesh out the storyline: a bit more butchering, several rapes, and so forth. Veteran television newsman Chet Huntley pocketed a few bucks for providing the narration.

A not-too-distant relative of the goona-goona is the atrocity movie. Jungle films, although indiscriminately prejudiced and insensitive, were benign spectacles aimed at titillating the audience. Atrocity pictures, on the other hand, dealt in outright revulsion. Again, the specter of the carnival midway loomed: *We want only the bravest souls among you to step behind this curtain, where you will see the most shocking sights your eyes will ever behold!*

Most atrocity pictures were made in a similar fashion to their jungle brethren: existing documentary film spliced in with newly shot action. Some were imported from overseas, such as *Nightmare in Red China*, shot in India and brought to the States in the early fifties by Lloyd Friedgen. *Nightmare* tells the tale of a young Hindu physician helping guerillas battle the Communist Chinese. When the doctor's relatives tell him of various horrors committed by the Communists, jarring scenes are cut in depicting the acts. Not surprisingly, these atrocities frequently involve topless Chinese women.

Of course, no exploitation genre is complete without a film from Dwain Esper, and in 1948 he distributed *Love Life of Adolf Hitler*. Esper was a fanatical collector of World War II film footage, and apparently he gleaned much of his material from U.S. government sources. The only thing approaching sex in this brutal hodgepodge was some film of Eva Braun in a bathing suit.

Perhaps the most disturbing example of exploitation was Kroger Babb's 1953 release (on the bill with *Karamoja*) of *Halfway to Hell*, a film that billed itself as a warning about the evils of fascism while presenting graphic documentary evidence of the horrors of the Nazi death camps.

In his exhaustive and insightful *History of Exploitation Films, 1919-1959*, Dr. Eric Schaefer suggests that these films drew on post-war anxiety by "focusing on ghastly acts brought on by modern warfare, technology, and crumbling political systems." He makes a reasoned and forceful case, but in the end another, simpler, explanation seems more apt: people will always — *always* — pay money for the "privilege" of being shocked.

Funny How They All Look Alike

Atrocity films, like goona-goona movies, had no use for accuracy. The 1949 film *Atrocities of Manila* was made in the Philippines, and depicted the trials of Filipino guerillas trying to fight off the Japanese invasion. The rebels obviously chose their leader based on breast size. Producer Lloyd Friedgen picked the film up for U.S. grindhouse distribution, cutting in fresh nudity and torture shots, and released it as *Outrages of the Orient*. It contains a documentary "insert" shot from the Japanese invasion of Manchuria in the early thirties, in which a baby is thrown in the air and caught on a Japanese soldier's bayonet. That image was used, *ad nauseum*, in numerous atrocity films. This same movie was later released as *Beast of the East*, to exploit another round of fear and hatred brought on by the Korean War.

Sex-Crazed Dope Fiends

Narcotics and sex go together like Astaire and Rogers, at least on America's movie screens. For exploitation filmmakers, drugs were the perfect hook on which to hang a woman's discarded clothes. First, producers could claim the high moral ground, as protectors of youth. Secondly, it allowed the innocent heroine of the story (bad girls were never the protagonists) to act wild and uninhibited because she was, sadly, out of her mind. Two hits on a reefer and the good girl next door needed to jitterbug out of her dress in the worst way. At least until square-jawed Joe arrived to put her back on the right track.

As loopy and inaccurate as grind-house films were about narcotic use, they at least addressed the subject. Hollywood studios shied away from drug use as a subject until the 1950s, when the controversial *Man with the Golden Arm* (1956) stirred up considerable debate. Without any open discussion of the realities of narcotic use, the public was left to imagine. By and large, it imagined the same sort of ominous lower-class threat that inspired vice and VD films.

In fact, until narcotics use came to be identified with lower classes, the subject was treated less sensationally by the government and the media. In the 1870s, when rail barons were using Chinese "cooley" labor to build the nation's railroad network, many states passed anti-opium ordinances, inspired by tall tales of how the demonized foreigners smoked opium to fuel their manual labor. Apparently, the bosses were afraid opium might not mix with the massive amounts of alcohol and tobacco that "real" workers consumed.

Narcotics that would later become anathema to Americans were routinely included in medicines and consumer products in the early 1900s, from toothache powders to Coca-Cola. Narcotic-imbued remedies could be purchased over-the-counter for every-

Toked-Up Youths Craving Snacks!

It's certainly true that the Nazis had the most sophisticated intelligence operation in the world, but whether they used it to peddle dope to America's teenagers — the plot of J. D. Kendis's *Devil's Harvest* (1941) — is highly speculative. In reefer movies, kids always went on violent rampages; it was more cinematic than the more accurate alternative: sitting quietly, staring out the window, wondering what's to eat.

MARIJUANA
....THE SMOKE OF HELL!

"DEVIL'S HARVEST"

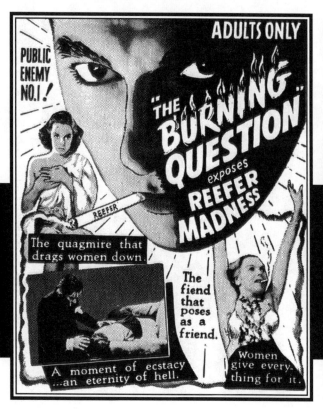

thing from earaches to menstrual cramps. The Pure Food and Drug Act of 1906 wasn't a ban on such practices, but a labelling act, informing consumers of which narcotic they might be ingesting. Cocaine was so common as a remedy that its use inspired the colloquial expression "In a pinch."

When the nation realized that these substances could be dangerously habit-forming, The Harrison Narcotics Act of 1914 was enacted, regulating the sale, importation, and distribution of opiates, cocaine, and other potentially addictive substances. Embarrassed and chastened by this development, the middle class was ripe for exploitation. *The Drug Terror* (Eclair), *The Derelict* (Kalem), and *The Cocaine Traffic* (Lubin) were all released in 1914, playing on the public's newfound fear of drugs. As WWI bolstered the nation's determination to be both morally and physically fit; the focus on drugs subsided.

But 1923 brought the Jazz Age, and with such hedonism came more drug use. When movie star Wallace Reid died in 1922, strung out on morphine, his wife, actress Dorothy Davenport, hit the roadshow circuit with the anti-drug tale *Human Wreckage*, making a small fortune lecturing and selling pamphlets,

in a fashion Kroger Babb later emulated with *Mom and Dad*. Her success spawned other films such as *The Drug Monster*, *The Greatest Menace*, and *The Drug Traffic*. In 1928, exploitation producer Willis Kent, one of the charter members of the Forty Thieves, released *The Pace That Kills*, about cocaine addiction. It formed the mold for almost all 1930s grindhouse plots: country girl goes to the city, mixes with the wrong crowd, does drugs, gets pregnant, commits suicide.

Some drug references even snuck by Hollywood censors. In *Little Giant* (1933), Russell Hopton, cracking wise while perusing Edward G. Robinson's modern art collection, says "I ain't seen nothing like that since I been off cocaine."

Up through the mid-thirties, most drug films depicted the use of "hard" drugs such as cocaine, heroin, and opium. But then in 1935 a church group in Los Angeles produced a film about the dangers of marijuana called *Tell Your Children*. The atrociously bad film, in which dope smokers blast away at each other with guns and leap out windows in fits of insanity, would have sunk without a trace but for one man. That's right... Dwain Esper. Esper bought the film, retitled it *The Burning*

Question, and exploited it like mad. It earned enough on the circuit that he produced another doper, *Marihuana* (the spelling perhaps intended to assist audiences in identifying the evil herb).

Soon, marijuana was a national menace.

In fact, hemp, as it was commonly known in English, had long been one of the country's premier cash crops, dating back to Colonial days. Used to make everything from rope to varnishes to workclothes, hemp was a utility. Tobacco, by contrast, had only one luxurious use. Migrant mexican workers, however, had long smoked the hemp plant *(marijuana* in Spanish) as a folk remedy, in the same way cocaine and opium were considered medicinal in the U.S. middle class. Cowboys and ranch hands had always been familiar with the extra high a hemp smoke provided. Even early Bronco Bill westerns contained references to loco-weed (by which they meant either hemp or jimson weed).

When public attention focused on marijuana in the thirties, its use was revealed to be most prevalent among Mexicans and blacks, especially jazz musicians. Few whites had cared when Cab Calloway sang "Reefer Man" in *International House* (1933) or

Gertrude Michael performed "Sweet Marijuana Brown" in *Murder at the Vanities* (1935). But after 1936 — and the fear that the lower classes might spread this scourge — weed became Public Enemy Number One.

In *The Burning Question*, Dr. Alfred Carroll (no doubt related to Elliot Forbes) lectured the PTA on the case of a young lad, high on reefer, "who killed his entire family with an axe." Few stoners have ever showed such vitality.

The floodgates were open, and marijuana films played on the grindhouse circuit well into the 1940s. *Assassin of Youth* (1937), *The Green Monster* (1936), and *The Devil's Harvest* (1941) were only a few of them. The strategy behind the marketing of these films was insidiously clever: the hot versions played the Adults Only houses, while cold versions (with all the sex snipped out) were retitled and sold to schools. Some played in classrooms into the 1960s.

In 1948 Hollywood star Robert Mitchum and his buddy Robin Ford got pinched for marijuana possession. Partying with them was a sexy bit player named Lila Leeds, who was also arrested. Mitchum refused to cop a plea, did thirty days, and let the papparazzi shoot him swabbing down the jailhouse. It did wonders for his tough guy image. His next film, *Rachel and the Stranger*, was RKO's top grosser of 1949.

It's the Real Thing

Adults Only films may have traded in gross caricature and distortion, but they didn't just make this stuff up. They often drew inspiration from the crime beat, as evidenced by this wire service story:

NEW YORK, Nov. 8, 1947—HELD ON DRUG CHARGE—Joyce Mintz (left), 18, a model, and Marguerite Pierce, 19, a chorus girl whose stage name is Christine Johnson, stand in the anteroom of Felony Court here after they were arrested today and charged with possessing narcotics. The girls were rounded up by police in a raid on a West 52nd St. apartment along with a dozen youths and teenage girls and quantities of marijuana, cocaine, and hypodermic needles.

Things were a little different for Lila Leeds. She parlayed her front page exposure into a low-budget quickie called *Wild Weed*, in which she played a girl who repents her wicked ways. The picture went nowhere. . . until "Mr. Pihsnamwohs," Kroger Babb bought the rights to it. Here was a man who understood the crucial link beween dope and sex. Retitling the film *She Shoulda Said No*, Babb played down the weed and played up the shapely Lila in all his advertising. His tag line: "How bad can a good girl get?"

(The answer, apparently, was "as bad as she wants." Stories from the roadshow circuit portray Lila Leeds as a party girl of prodigious stamina, who literally fornicated her way across America in support of the film.)

As the forties gave way to the fifties, and rock and roll started clamoring around in middle class consciousness (more of that demonic black influence!), America's fears of reckless youth increased, and new drug movies bombarded movie screens, both legitimate and grindhouse.

The Devil's Sleep (1949) starred Charlie Chaplin's ex-wife, Lita Grey Chaplin, as a crusading juvenile judge out to smash gangs dealing in "Bennies, Goofies, and Phenos." (The poster showed the devil leering over a pair of voluptuous women clad only in their undies.)

A young Mark Rydell was featured in *The Marijuana Story* which displayed how heroin leads to the electric chair. *Hooked* (a. k. a. *Curfew Breakers*) and *Pachuco* were dope films aimed at Latino audiences, and *Flaming Teenage* produced in Texas, featured the oldest-looking teenagers of all time.

The Devil's Sleep involved a veritable rogue's gallery of exploitation characters: It was produced by George Weiss, who operated a grungy outfit called "Screen Classics." The director was Merle Connell, whose "Quality Studios" mainly produced

Moonlighting, Hollywood Style

When Timothy Farrell wasn't portraying racketeer Umberto Scali, he was a bailiff in the Los Angeles Sheriff's Department. He got in hot water when *Paris After Midnight* (in which he appeared with Tempest Storm) was busted in a vice raid. Photos of him shooting up leggy co-star Joanne Arnold in *Girl Gang* didn't sit too well, either. It didn't stop Farrell from putting in twenty years as an L.A. deputy marshall, culminating with his appointment as County Marshall in 1971. Unfortunately, he was convicted of felony charges soon after, for the "illegal use of deputy marshals in political activities." He was hit with a six-month sentence, but received probation due to poor health. After he was fired in 1975 he opened a lumber yard in South Dakota. He died in Santa Monica in 1989.

burlesque shorts for both theatrical and arcade exhibition. The film also featured actor Timothy Farrell, who, following in the footsteps of Wheeler Oakman, orchestrated nefarious deeds in several films that constituted this new wave of vice racket pictures.

Pin Down Girl (1950), wasn't a dope film, but it did represent the first appearance of Farrell's stock character, Umberto Scali. It was a timely exposé of the treacherous world of female wrestling. Farrell played Scali again that year in *Girl Gang*, another Weiss production directed by Robert Dertano. The Scali trilogy was completed with *Dance Hall Racket* (1953), a film that survives in legend because of the involvement of comedian Lenny Bruce. Just starting his notorious career as a social critic and tester of First Amendment limitations, Bruce wrote the script and acted as Farrell's devious, hot-tempered henchman. Honey Bruce, Lenny's stripper wife, appears in the film, and his mother, Sally Marr, steals the show with some amusing monologues.

Not that the show was worth stealing. Like all Weiss productions, it was cheap, tawdry and unmarred by craft. Weiss was known for stalking his sets like Uncle Scrooge, a towel wrapped around his neck to soak up his prodigious persperation, ranting that blown takes were good enough because film cost nine cents a foot. The cameraman on most of his pictures was an old-timer named William Thompson, who'd started with crank cameras back in Edison's days. He only shot pictures when not out hunting gold mines. Thompson was fading into blindness, but was ably assisted by Art Lasky, a punchy heavyweight contender from the thirties who was blind in one eye.

The only thing missing from this outfit was an alcoholic transvestite — and that's where Ed Wood, Jr. came in.

As recounted in the 1994 Tim Burton film, Ed Wood showed up at Weiss's office one day and convinced him to bankroll his script "I Changed My Sex," inspired by the sensational story of Christine Jorgensen, the first celebrated case of a sex-change operation. Weiss didn't know at the time, of course, that the script was a by-product of Wood's own devotion to female underwear and tight angora sweaters. But, being a headline-chaser by nature, Weiss agreed to make the picture.

Farrell played a psychiatrist and voiced the typically insane Wood-penned narration. His cool ability to rescue takes when he and other actors veered off-script made him perhaps the most important member of the Screen Classics team. Wood used him again in *Jailbait* (1954), which starred Lyle Talbot and introduced future Hercules, Steve Reeves. Talbot, a legitimate B-movie actor, unwittingly drew a raid from the Screen Actor's union (which he'd help found!) when it was learned he was appearing in a non-union film. Wood finished the shoot in record time, even for him. Farrell also turned up in Wood's *The Violent Years* (1956), but escaped inclusion in *Plan 9 From Outer Space* (1959), now considered the precious nadir of American cinema.

But we've gotten ahead of ourselves. Let's step back to the dawn of the decade, when exploitation filmmakers had recovered from the WWII doldrums. Rock and roll was blaring. Peacetime money was itching to be spent. And there was a fresh young audience out there just waiting to get their first look at Adults Only movies...

A Cult Is Born

By whatever name, *I Changed My Sex, He or She?, Glen or Glenda?*, the 1953 film by Ed Wood, Jr. was an auspicious start for the man who would end up being reverently canonized as the worst movie maker o all time. The charming pathos of Tim Burton's biopic told only the first half of the Ed Wood story. We won't hold our breath for the sequel, in which the indefatigable Ed becomes a lonely drunk in a tiny apartment on Hollywood Boulevard, paying for rent and booze by cranking out pornographic paperbacks.

The 50s

Nudity is NOT Obscene

To those born after 1960, the Eisenhower years must seem like an endless episode of *I Love Lucy* or *Father Knows Best*. Repressed, stodgy, as wild as wingtips.

Nothing could be further from the truth. The 1950s was the most progressive decade in the "American Century." New consumer innovations made everyday life seem like the "World of Tomorrow" exhibit at Disneyland. The single most influential piece of domestic legislation enacted in this century, the Interstate Highway Act, built a road network that changed the way America lives. Television, for better or worse, became a fixture in households, changing the way Americans thought, learned, spoke, ate, made love, everything.

And, of course, there was another innovation — the hydrogen bomb, routinely tested to keep America's latest foreign menace — the Reds — in line. The resultant "fall out" drills made it seem as if America's garden party could end in hellfire at any minute.

In hindsight, now that the Communist menace has dissipated in public consciousness, its worth noting that the most influential person of the decade was not Joe McCarthy, or Dwight Eisenhower — it was a kind of dorky-looking guy from the Midwest named Hugh Hefner. In 1952 he took $5,000 of start-up money and created a "men's magazine" called *Playboy*.

Debate continues as to whether Hefner was a visionary or a sexist pig. There's no debate about his business acumen, or his keen timing. He parlayed his five grand into a multi-million dollar empire, all based on a simple concept: packaging sex in a way that moved it from the grindhouse to the coffee table. Well, that was the theory, anyway. Ozzie Nelson really kept *Playboy* in the desk drawer in his den, where Ricky and his buddies pawed over it surreptitiously. But once *Playboy* was in the house, the mission was accomplished for Hefner and the advertisers who provided his fortune. *What Kind of Man Reads Playboy?* Not a degenerate, but a consumer of the best newfangled gadgets, gizmos, and attitude that American ingenuity could provide. Sex was the wrapping paper: only this time around, it was being sold as healthy, worldly, and sophisticated.

Imported Euro-Skin

In the early 1950s many grindhouses became "art houses." The transformation began in the settling dust of WWII, when international geopolitics, and the arts, were being redefined in the aftermath of catastrophic warfare.

Victorious Americans were treated to lavish Hollywood spectacle. Major studios, feeling pressure from that fledgling invention, television, offered up technical wizardry—Cinemascope, 3-D, you name it — to lure customers from the insidiously accessible Philco anchored in the living room. Europe was a different story. Having bombs rain on your cities and towns puts things in a bleaker perspective. While Americans celebrated new superpower status, Europeans glumly set about picking up the pieces.

Post-war European movies reflected this world-weariness.

Most luscious female on the screen today...

SOPHIA LOREN

IS ALL WOMAN in

Woman of the River

TECHNICOLOR

with GERARD OURY
LISE BOURDIN

The Italians, particularly Roberto Rossellini and Vittorio DeSica, created a new brand of filmmaking, neo-realism, which disdained the slickness and gloss of traditional movie storytelling for a gritty, unflinching style that spoke of the struggles of common people in an unthinkably cruel world. These weren't escapist entertainments; they were art.

At first, foreign films were booked mainly into "ethnic" theaters, situated in the various immigrant enclaves in big American cities. But the anti-Hollywood approach of neo-realist directors started to capture the imagination of a younger set, particularly in university towns. There was much to discuss in these films, in terms of both style and content.

The Italian films that made it to the United States weren't admired solely for the fresh storytelling technique. The earthy sex appeal of actresses such as Anna Magnani and Silvana Mangano had much to do with their success. Arthur Mayer, who imported many of these films to the U.S., bluntly stated in his 1952 book *Merely Colossal*, that his biggest successes "...were with the pictures whose artistic and ideological merits were aided and abetted at the box office by their frank sexual content."

In *Bitter Rice* (1949), Mangano burned forever into American consciousness the image of the earthy, voluptuous peasant. Tromping through muddy fields, skirt hem tucked into her waistband, she displayed the most erotic thighs movie audiences had ever seen. Anna Magnani was already in her forties when she played in Rossellini's *L'Amore* (1948). The film is in two segments, and the second, "The Miracle," stirred up considerable controversy.

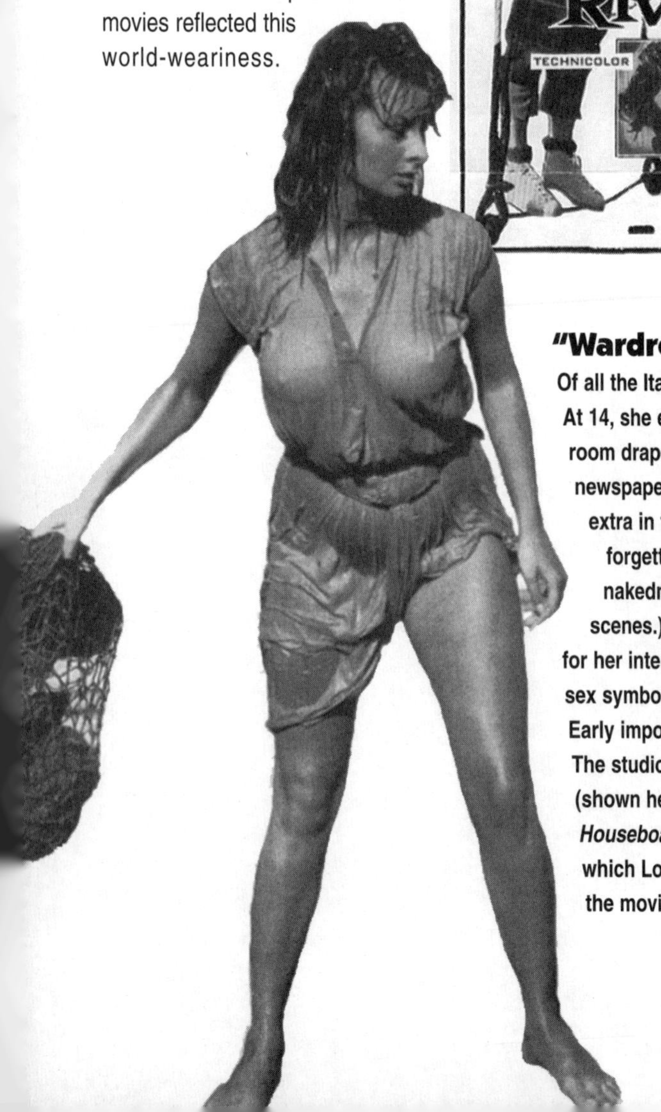

"Wardrobe! Sophia needs about five more gallons!"

Of all the Italian voluptuaries, it was Sophia Loren who gained the most lasting fame. At 14, she entered beauty pageants wearing a gown her mother made from the living room drapes. In her teens, she raised her skirts as a vampish villainess in countless newspaper fumetti (comic strips using actual models). She soon became a featured extra in films, baring her remarkable bosom in *It's Him, Yes! Yes!* an otherwise forgettable 1951 Italian comedy. ("When Sophia Loren is naked, that is a lot of nakedness," she'd later say, brilliantly explaining why she stopped doing nude scenes.) At 18 she married 40-year-old film producer Carlo Ponti, who paved the way for her international success. She waged a publicity war with rival Gina Lollabrigida for sex symbol status, much as Marilyn Monroe and Jayne Mansfield did in the U.S. Early imports such as *Woman of the River* led to a Hollywood contract in the mid-fifties. The studios promptly tried to ruin her in a series of awful pictures: *Boy on a Dolphin* (shown here), *The Pride and the Passion*, *Legend of the Lost*, *Desire Under the Elms*, *Houseboat*. The only memorable things in these pictures are the ubiquitous scenes in which Loren's clothes are drenched. "It seems to me that I spent my first five years in the movies having people throw pails of water at me," she later laughed.

Magnani portrayed a simpleton impregnated by a drifter (Federico Fellini) she thinks is St. Joseph. She gives birth to a child she believes is the "son of God."

Obviously, the Legion of Decency had to do something about these provocations. It branded *Bitter Rice* "a serious threat to Christian morality and decency." Martin Quigley, still hammering out the hard line in his *Motion Picture Herald*, called *The Miracle* an insult to traditional religious beliefs and suggested it was actually a communist plot to subvert American values. Cardinal Spellman of the New York Catholic Archdiocese attacked it as "a vicious insult to Italian womanhood." While New York film critics lauded Rossellini's film as the best of the year, a 30-month battle waged over whether the film, prohibited in New York, violated the religious freedom of Christians.

Distributors and exhibitors sensed ticket-selling potential in these challenging foreign imports, but, unsure if Americans would patronize foreign films, they relied on old grindhouse ploys to attract customers. Rossellini's *Open City* was advertised as being "Sexier Than Hollywood Ever Dared To Be." Print advertising for *Paisan*, another of Rossellini's somber studies of post-war Italy, featured a woman undressing. Even *The Bicycle Thief* — totally devoid of sexual content — was hyped with a suggestive drawing of an ample woman astride a bicycle.

"Sven, the fjord's freezing – let's swim naked."

Scandinavian skinny-dipping is what prepared America for Ingmar Bergman films. While the Italians romped al fresco amid the peasant shacks, the Swedes seemed to have a thing for naked plunges into the fjords. The trend started in 1951 with *One Summer of Happiness*, the tale of a young farm girl's idyllic summer of freedom, love, and budding sexuality — all of which is ended, Swedish-style, by a sudden motorcycle accident. Soon, Swedish filmmakers realized that it was swimming scenes that ensured an overseas sale. When *I Rok och Dans* was released, the nude bathing scene was facetiously subtitled "For Export Only." Bergman's *Summer with Monika* (1953) contained the requisite nude shots of star Harriet Andersson, guaranteeing an eventual U.S. run in both arthouses and grindhouses. Twenty years later, another round of Swedish imports would dramatically change the American film industry.

Blurring the line between grindhouse and arthouse

The Proud and the Beautiful, based on a story by Jean-Paul Sartre, told of a French woman, Nellie, whose husband falls gravely ill while on vacation in Mexico. As her husband weakens, she turns for help to a recondite, drunken doctor with a shadowy past. A sadistic bistro owner, who makes the doctor dance for his daily whiskey, tries to rape Nellie. A meningitis epidemic cuts a swath through the town. Nellie's husband dies. The doctor sobers up enough to create a serum that saves the remaining townsfolk. Nellie realizes she never loved her husband, and starts over with the redeemed doctor. Kingsley International, the major distributor of French film product, knew how to play it both ways. For urban arthouse patrons seeking the latest in existential angst, ads carried review blurbs from esteemed *New York Times* film critic Bosley Crowther and *The New Yorker*. On the grindhouse circuit, where they didn't know angst from a hole in the ground, ad copy promised a film that "Strips Bare of Prim Morality a Side of Love That Women Won't Admit — Even To Themselves!"

Louis K. Sher was a malt distributor from Columbus, Ohio who loved movies so much that in 1952 he opened an Adults Only theater in his hometown. Not to show sex films, but to prohibit squealing babies and kids rampaging in the aisles. It was so successful he expanded into Cleveland, then Akron. From there he created the Art Theater Guild, a whole chain of movie houses showing only imported fare. His success was duly noted by theater owners such as Dewey Michaels, who transformed his Buffalo, New York burlesque house into an "arthouse," exhibiting films from France, Italy, and Sweden. Soon, grindhouse owners all over the country were going continental.

Which came first, the sex or the art, was a moot issue. Some theaters catered to a sophisticated crowd: fresh-brewed coffee in the lobby, imported chocolates, the latest Dave Brubeck recording blowing cool in the auditorium. The lights would dim and the swanks would sink into their loge seats to watch...

...Exactly the same film that was playing in a smelly skid row scratch-house in some less-hip city. The marketing depended entirely on the demographics of each territory, and on what local censors would allow. The common denominator between the intelligentsia and the raincoat crowd was an eagerness to see skin. In short order, the demand for sex outpaced that for art.

It was *Ecstasy* all over again. U.S Customs started seizing foreign films, closely scrutinizing them for corrupting flashes of flesh. It was a performance worthy of the Keystone Kops, since importers routinely had the overseas vendors ship a "cool" print through Customs, and later ship the "hot" footage under separate cover.

In some cases, a foreign film picked up on the cheap would be sliced with sex stateside. William Mishkin, a New York–based distributor, routinely hired young Bergmans-in-waiting to shoot sexy inserts when the films weren't too hot.

In 1955, Kroger Babb — now calling himself "Mr. Pihsnamwohs"— bought the U.S. rights to Ingmar Bergman's *Summer with Monika* from international film agent Gaston Hakim, a Egyptian-born Frenchman whose family produced many French film successes.

(Hakim also served the Office of Strategic Services during the war, and would later produce his own sex movies.) Bergman's film starred Harriet Andersson as a restless youth shirking bourgeois conventions, living like a bohemian, and meeting a sad end. It was 95 minutes of bleak artistry. Babb was interested in the two minutes at the beach, in which Andersson doffed all for a quick swim.

He chopped the film to 62 minutes, dubbed it into "American English," and hired Les Baxter to write a peppy score to replace the dreary Swedish stuff. He retitled it *Monika, The Story of A Bad Girl*, and hyped it with an incredible exploitation campaign. The *Monika* pressbook read like Babb's showmanship primer. Its 36 pages were crammed with dozens of photos of Kroger schmoozing with priests and judges. Dave Friedman, still in the Babb camp, provided the classic tag line: "A Picture for Wide Screens and Broad Minds!" Never mind that *Monika* was in standard 1:33 aspect ratio, not the new cinemascope format.

Despite his valiant effort to create a sensation, Babb was easily outdone by a lithe Gallic coquette. It took thousands of troops storming the beach at Normandy for the United States to liberate France. Brigitte Bardot returned the favor all by herself.

The impact of *And God Created Woman* (1956) cannot be overstated. The makers, distributors, and exhibitors of Adults Only films attest that this picture was almost solely responsible for turning the "arthouse" trend into a revolution. Although Marilyn Monroe has, in death, achieved legendary status as a cultural sex icon, history will show that Brigitte Bardot was a far more influential force in changing attitudes toward cinematic sex.

Bardot was a fashion model, already

gracing the cover of *Elle*, at 15 years of age. Her parents managed her career; her mother, showing a flash of Babb-like savvy, demanded that she use the professional moniker BB for effect. BB's allure was obvious and, to many Americans, slightly perverse: she had a woman's body and girl's face, one that tempestuously shifted from playful to naughty to carnal.

She was the first of a long line of young beauties to garner the attention of film director Roger Vadim. After a protracted

"courtship" of several years (her parents tried everything, including firearms, to keep them apart), Svengali and his student were married. He immediately set to work manufacturing an international sex goddess, culminating with the release of *And God Created Woman*. In the process of creating a sensation, however, Vadim lost a wife. During filming, BB fell in love with co-star Jean-Louis Trintignant. In time, her list of lovers would outpace her film credits.

It was the BB's brazen bohemian style that so titillated American audiences. The film opens with a prolonged take of Bardot languorously sunbathing; "her round little rear

Sex Kittens for Sale

Distributors had some wild ideas for exploiting Bardot: "street bally" included guys in pith helments and butterfly nets wearing placards that read "Butterflies? No! I'm Looking For Sex Kittens — Like Brigitte Bardot." Life-sized standees of Bardot were shipped to theaters as part of a "Best Lover of Bardot" contest. "Photo fans will pose their male friends, and photograph them, presumably making love to the delectable Bardot!"

These Punch-Packed RADIO SPOTS
will tell your patrons that
BARDOT'S IN TOWN!

RADIO SPOT No. 1 *(60 seconds)*

(SOUND: IN WITH ROMANTIC FRENCH MUSIC)

ANNCR: It's BARDOT!

ANNCR II: BARDOT?

ANNCR: Yes, BARDOT!... BRIGITTE BARDOT!
More bewitching than ever!... in a role that is tailor-made for the *spirit* of BARDOT!... the *daring* of BARDOT!... the sensuous BEAUTY of BARDOT!... in ... "FEMALE AND THE FLESH"!

(SOUND: MUSIC UP — HOLD AND UNDER)

ANNCR II: BARDOT!... More woman than any man can handle!... in "FEMALE AND THE FLESH"!

ANNCR: MEN ... what would YOU do, if you were married to a woman like this...deeply in love with her...and yet, denied the *full expression* of your love?

ANNCR II: This is BARDOT ... in "FEMALE AND THE FLESH" ... DESIRED by three men!... POSSESSED by none!

(SOUND: IN WITH DRAMATIC MUSIC AND UNDER)

ANNCR: BARDOT in "FEMALE AND THE FLESH" ... a motion picture no man will forget ... with a climax every woman will remember as a new emotional experience. See BRIGITTE BARDOT in "FEMALE AND THE FLESH"!

ANNCR II: Its delicate theme is spoken in English and recommended for adults only!

glows like a peach, and the camera lingers on the subject as if waiting for it to ripen," *Time* reported. As an orphan with an unbridled libido, Bardot entices every man on the street, dances suggestively on tabletops in public, weds an older man, uses him up, seduces his son, and has her clothes ripped off several times. Make no mistake, this wasn't the sad, sexy wastrel that was Monroe's stock-in-trade. This was sexual defiance, right down to the unkempt hair and the "I don't give a damn" flash in her eyes.

Theater managers in Ohio were arrested for showing the film. Some states, like Kentucky, banned it outright. Texas censors railed that it was obscene, but it played to big crowds anyway. Police in Philadelphia confiscated prints. All over America, people were battling in court over whether the public had a right to see Brigitte Bardot's bare buttocks.

"For the first time, Americans were being shown the female nude on the screen as a work of art," Vadim said in his 1975 *Memoirs of the Devil*, "and they were told that love for the pleasure of loving is not synonymous with sin. The United States market was opened up for French films, and the Americans opened their eyes. Hollywood, sometimes licentious, but always puritanical, was not going to change overnight, but something irreversible had happened. Eight million Americans went to see my film, and although it was often mutilated by women's leagues and local censors, Americans still remember it."

And God Created Woman became the most profitable foreign movie to ever play in the United States. Bardot films, some new, some made during the early fifties, began to flood the international market. BB became a cottage sex industry. If your community refused to show Bardot films, no problem: *Playboy* and its legion of imitators all carried mail order ads selling blown-up photos of frames clipped from the films. "Each picture is an actual unretouched photograph made on the finest photographic paper," gushed a pitch from the Playboys Club of America. For two dollars you got "The 48 most exciting photographs of Brigitte Bardot from films made in Europe which were banned and forbidden to be shown throughout this country!" And, of course, they were "Rushed to you in plain wrapper."

Authorities resistant to the perceived immorality of the French imports made a couple of final efforts to fortify America's shores. In 1957, *Lady Chatterley's Lover*, a Gallic version of the infamous D. H. Lawrence novel (outlawed in the U.S. until 1960), was banned by New York state censors, a crushing blow since as much as 30 percent of a foreign film's gross rentals were expected to come from that state. The following year, Nico Jacobellis,

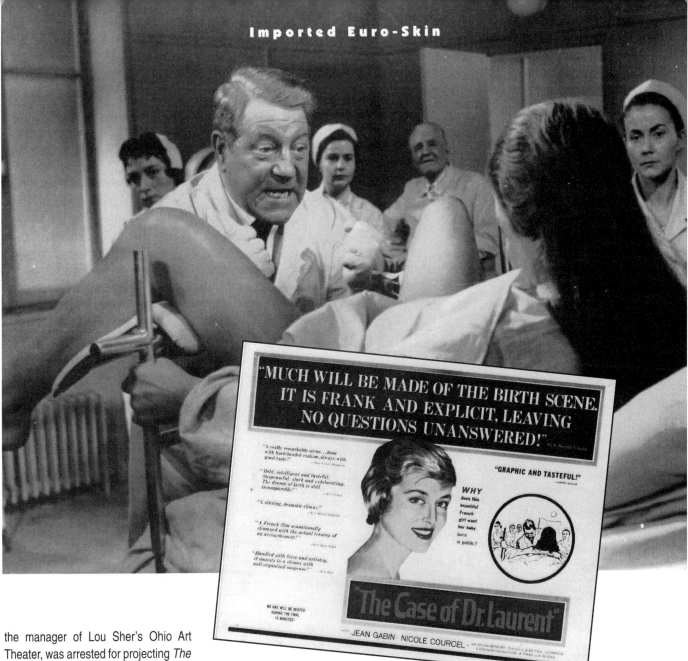

"MUCH WILL BE MADE OF THE BIRTH SCENE.
IT IS FRANK AND EXPLICIT, LEAVING
NO QUESTIONS UNANSWERED!"

"GRAPHIC AND TASTEFUL!"

WHY does this beautiful French girl want her baby born in public?

"The Case of Dr. Laurent"

JEAN GABIN · NICOLE COURCEL

the manager of Lou Sher's Ohio Art Theater, was arrested for projecting *The Lovers*, the Louis Malle film that made a star of actress Jeanne Moreau. Both films were considered dangerous because they presented stories of adultery in which the cheating lovers went unpunished.

Both cases ended up going all the way to the U.S. Supreme Court. Judge Potter Stewart struck down the ban on *Lady Chatterly*, writing a majority opinion that declared the film not obscene, and that any subject matter, no matter how controversial, was protected by the Constitution's First Amendment. In *The Lovers* case, Lou Sher, at his own cost, battled the case through a series of appellate court decisions which upheld the Jacobelli conviction, until the Supreme Court, in a decision of historical significance, overturned the earlier rulings.

Wrote Judge William Brennan: "...material that deals with sex in a manner that advocates ideas, or that has literary or scientific or artistic value or any other form of social importance, may not be branded obscenity." Asked what would constitute obscenity, Judge Stewart uttered his now-famous retort: "I know it when I see it." Right. Don't we all.

That's how the French, particularly a sex kitten nicknamed BB, crashed the gates that protected America's puritancial heart from its own libido. The course was now clear for domestic purveyors of cinematic sex. After all, how do you keep 'em down on the farm after they've seen Paris?

Maman et Papa

Sensationalism seems a little less sleazy when the French do it. Maybe it was the more subdued title, or the appearance of venerable actor Jean Gabin, that made *The Case of Dr. Laurent*, a Gallic birth-of-a-baby picture, seem classier than American films of the same genre. *Dr. Laurent* outdid *Mom and Dad* by showing the birth of triplets. The film was distributed stateside by K. Gordon Murray, who tried to replicate the *Mom and Dad* phenomenon. He misfired, however, by using a filmed lecture, not a live "sexologist." Once the scheme bottomed out, the film was retitled *Wages of Sin* and shunted onto the grinder circuit.

NUDIST MOVIES

Walter Bibo could see the writing on the wall, and it spelled a fortune. His New York–based Excelsior Pictures had churned out burlesque shorts since the end of World War II, but several court decisions in the mid-fifties, liberalizing "obscenity" laws, convinced him the world was ready for on-screen nudity. In 1954 he traveled to Lake Como, Florida, outside Tampa, and within the seclusion of a nudist camp there, shot a picture he titled *Garden of Eden.*

In the film, a vacationing mother and daughter have their car break down outside the camp, and before a reliable mechanic can be found, they've been converted to the healthy joys of nudism.

Bibo managed to screen the film in 36 U.S. cities without incident. But New York would have none of it. The Regents of the University of the State of New York, the Department of Education division entrusted with all decisions regarding decency on New York's movie screens, branded it obscene. Bibo, a conflagrationist at heart, took his case to the Court of Appeals. On July 3, 1957, Judge Charles Desmond issued a landmark ruling, stating that nudity, per se, was not indecent. He wrote that "There is nothing sexy or suggestive about it . . . nudists are shown as wholesome, happy people in family groups practicing their sincere but misguided theory that clothing, when climate does not require it, is deleterious to mental health by promoting an attitude of shame with regard to natural attributes and functions of the body."

Bibo had won, and he planned to celebrate by opening *Garden of Eden* in Times Square, with all the attendant ballyhoo he could muster.

There was only one problem: exhibitors who'd been following the case were ready with dozens of already-existing nudist movies. Overnight, New York screens were awash in happy, healthy, wholesome (if misguided) naked people.

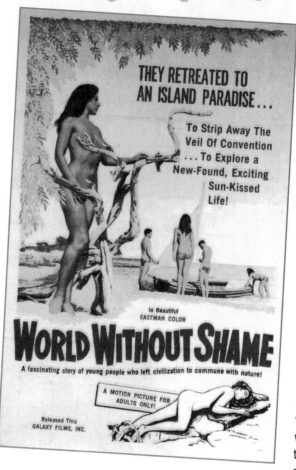

THEY RETREATED TO AN ISLAND PARADISE...

To Strip Away The Veil Of Convention . . . To Explore a New-Found, Exciting Sun-Kissed Life!

In Beautiful EASTMAN COLOR

WORLD WITHOUT SHAME

A fascinating story of young people who left civilization to commune with nature!

A MOTION PICTURE FOR ADULTS ONLY!

Released Thru GALAXY FILMS, INC.

A late entry to the nudist genre, *World Without Shame* (1962) still conformed to the rules: escaping to a Mediterranean island, three couples write, paint, swim, dance, play music — everything but have sex. As long as people were completely naked, any sexual contact was strictly forbidden by the censor boards.

Customers had to pay a little extra for the nudist experience, typically about three dollars (more than three times usual tariff). What they got for their cash was something akin to a family's summer vacation home movies, if everybody from Dad to little Janie decided to get an even, all-over tan. First some reading in the sun, then a barbecue, followed by a sack race, topped off with some vigorous volleyball. The latter was as close to physical contact as anyone came.

Judge Desmond's *Garden of Eden* ruling was also an unwitting stand for equality: now the bodies of white people could be viewed as freely as those of Africans. The great irony of nudist camp movies was that, while they revealed more skin than ever before seen in a public venue, by their very nature they repressed any sexual arousal. Nudity in the films was confined to breasts and buttocks. The only interest, truthfully, was in watching how people found endless ways to cover their genitals while pretending to be completely free of all societal constraints.

The camps where these films were shot were filled with dedicated nudists, many of whom agreed to cooperate only with assurances that the films would carry narration explaining the spiritual value of their alternative lifestyle. Since this sorely hindered any storytelling license the producers might take, they often filled up the soundtrack with droning recitation of Nudism's Code of Ethics, or other manifestos culled from the pages of *Sunshine & Health* or another nudist publication.

Nudist camp movies actually started well before the 1950s. The most famous nudist film was *Elysia* (1933), created by Bryan Foy, the producer of *High School Girl*. Its premise — a journalist visits a nudist camp to explore this fascinating phenomenon — didn't change a bit in the intervening 20 years. *Unashamed* and the German-made *This Nude World* were other nudist films of the 1930s that continued to play into the fifties. During the thirties, a young German woman named Leni Riefenstahl made nudist films of Aryan mountain girls, meant to inspire people to a healthy, natural (and no doubt superior) way of life. In the

United States, the films showed in German language booking houses, complemented by "health" pamphlets that read suspiciously like propaganda for the Reich.

In the 1950s, the puritanical opponents of nudist films asserted that they were a thinly veiled advocacy of communism. To the makers of these films, they were just the next logical step in the grindhouse "educational" genre, following in the wake of sex hygiene and childbirth movies.

The most salient aspect of these films is that they shattered the shameful, guilt-ridden mold of all preceding Adults Only fare. These films were unrelentingly sunny, not sordid. People happily interacted, did their chores, laughed a lot and enjoyed each other's company. And they never, never, looked at each other's bodies.

In a typical storyline, an overworked businessman's doctor prescribes the kind of rest and relaxation that only a good nudist camp can provide. Our nine-to-fiver enjoys a week (maybe 40 minutes, screen time) of healthy nude activity, telephoning his disbelieving and uptight girlfriend or secretary at regular intervals. He returns to society with a new outlook on life. He shares his joy with his uptight girlfriend/secretary (buttoned to the top throughout). The film's only suspense, of course, is whether or not the girlfriend, usually the most attractive cast member, is going to relent and finally experience nudism herself.

Between 1957 and 1963, dozens of nudist camp movies played across America:

The July, 1945 issue of _Sunshine & Health_, "Official Organ of the American Sunbathing Association," seems to suggest that such magazines weren't immune from smirking sex jokes. Those unclear on the gag are invited to place a thumb over the woodchopper's buttocks and reconsider what he seems to have on his mind.

Nudes at Play, Nudist Land, Nudism Today, Nudist Colony, Nudist Paradise, Nudist Life, Nudist Racket, Nudist Recruits, Nudists All, Hollywood Nudes Report, Nudes Around the World — and that's just the ones with _Nude_ in the title. (Did we mention _Career Girls on a Naked Holiday_?)

All this nakedness sounded enticing and provocative. But in the watching, it soon became clear that Rita Hayworth in _Gilda_, removing only her gloves, was sexier than all these nudist camp movies combined.

Early on, producers started to realize that the nudist genre was a rather skinny golden goose. They tried to revive it by "salting the mine." Famous burlesque stars began showing up at nudist camps, film crew in tow, to experience for themselves a revitalized return to nature. Louisiana governor Earl Long's ecdysiast paramour headlined _Blaze Starr Goes Nudist_, one of the last films of the genre.

The British, who in the early fifties had contributed sexy Diana Dors _(Man Bait)_ to the "dirty" foreign film invasion, began exporting their own colorful nudist camp movies. The Brits usually ignored the bogus "therapeutic" angle, preferring to intentionally poke fun at the obscenity laws which dictated all the silly coyness and carefully positioned tree branches. This "wink-wink, nudge-nudge" approach to on-screen sex would prove a huge influence on the next major trend in Adults Only movies — the nudie-cutie.

DORIS WISHMAN
Queen of the Nudies

Doris Wishman has a special niche in the ranks of Adults Only filmmakers. She was one of the few women to produce grindhouse fare, from her early nudist movies through rougher sexploitation films of the 1970s. Wishman also stands apart due to her singular filmmaking style. Her supporters call it "personal" and "unique." Skeptics might find "inept" more apt, if less charitable.

Like many Adults Only moviemakers, Wishman started out in distribution, gaining a working knowledge of the business of selling and showing movies. After the premature death of her husband, she immersed herself in producing films as a way of keeping busy. She quickly gravitated toward nudist movies, which were inexpensive to make and a relatively easy sell on the grindhouse circuit.

In short order, she concocted *Nudist Camp Confidential, Gentlemen Prefer Nature Girls, Behind the Nudist Curtain, Diary of a Nudist, Blaze Starr Goes Nudist*, and *Nude on the Moon*. The last is certainly one of the more imaginative spins on the genre, in which a pair of scientists discover that the lunar surface is strikingly similar to the Sunny Palms nudist lodge in Homestead, Florida.

As for plots, Wishman leaned toward international espionage. In *Behind the Nudist Curtain*, a private eye, working on orders from a mysterious client in the nation's capital, goes on a search for Mr. X, "an international spy who receives information from night club entertainers around the world." Wishman's spy films would culminate in the 1970s with *Deadly Weapons* and *Double Agent 73*, both of which starred the outlandishly proportioned Chesty Morgan. Chesty, who seems sadly comatose in both films, portrays a secret agent with a camera implanted in her breast, allowing her to photograph suspected spies after she has suffocated them with her gargantuan bosom.

Wishman's trademark is the unabashed manner in which she tried to disguise the cash limitations that prohibited synchronous sound filming. When dialogue is delivered, Wishman's camera resolutely ignores the speaker, focusing instead on the listener, the back of the speaker's head, a post, the window, a pair of shoes — anything other than the tell-tale moving lips. Those who would brand such techniques unprofessional have obviously never considered the value of being able to write a scene *after* you've shot it. And Wishman was obviously well ahead of her time, seeing how practically all television commercials in the 1990s feature jarringly unmatched sound and picture tracks.

WOMAN REPORTER POSES AS NUDIST!

DIARY OF A NUDIST

in Beautiful EASTMAN COLOR

To write this story she had to live it!

Live As A Nudist With The Most Gorgeous Campers In The World

A dramatic and personal experience in Paradise!

distributed by ATLANTIC PICTURES CORP.

AUTHENTIC! Filmed At America's Top Nudist Camps!

THE ETERNAL BEAUTY OF NATURE... So intimate... So revealing!

Witness the breathtaking story ...the secret hideout ...the mystery of woman!

Gentlemen Prefer Nature Girls

SEE WHAT WORKING GIRLS DO AFTER A HARD DAY AT THE OFFICE!

FILMED ON THE SPOT!

DEFINITELY!... ADULTS ONLY! In Intoxicating EASTMAN COLOR

A DOE-RAE-PICTURES, INC. Release

Stacey, a young reporter, is assigned by her editor, Arthur, to write an exposé of nudist camps. He joins her at the camp, to ensure that she'll reveal the ugly truth in her reports. But, as the film's pressbook relates, "Stacey refuses, saying that the members of the camp are the most honest people she has ever met." Arthur files the story instead, under the headline NUDIST EXPOSE. Enraged, Stacey reveals her true purpose to the camp director, who says that she knew all along that Stacey was a reporter, and that it didn't matter. Arthur then enters. "I have an exposé of my own to make," says Stacey, pointing to Arthur. "That's the man who wrote this article."

"I know that," says the camp director, "and he should be congratulated. The article is honest and truthful."

For the first time, Stacey reads the article aloud. To her amazement, it is for Nudism and honestly tells of its virtues. Stacey shamefully tells Arthur she is sorry. Arthur says it doesn't matter, he has suddenly realized he is in love with her.

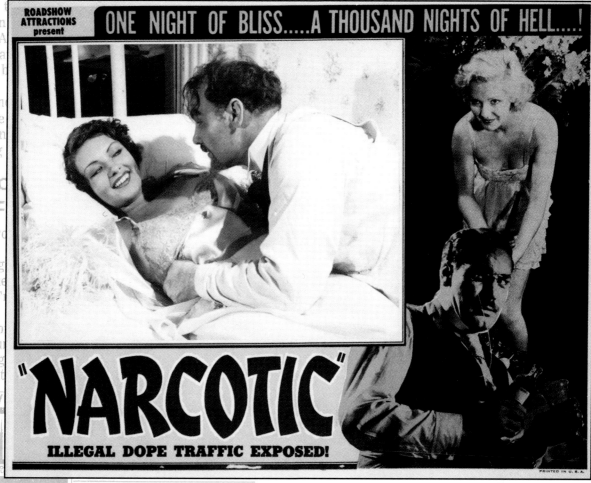

ROADSHOW ATTRACTIONS present

ONE NIGHT OF BLISS.....A THOUSAND NIGHTS OF HELL....!

"NARCOTIC"

ILLEGAL DOPE TRAFFIC EXPOSED!

HE MENACED WOMEN WITH WEIRD DESIRES!

ROADSHOW ATTRACTIONS present

"MANIAC"

A STRANGE, STARTLING LOVE!

Who Says They Don't Make 'Em Like They Used To?

Dwain Esper, the most legendary of the Forty Thieves, created several provocative Adults Only films in the early 1930s. His first film, *Narcotic* (1933), flaunted every act that had been specifically prohibited by Hollywood's Production Code Administration: Drug use, prostitution, exposed flesh — all coated in a dingy moralistic veneer. Esper's *Maniac* (1934) purported to be a study of various clinical forms of dementia, but was actually a 60-minute geek show, featuring rape, nudity, women exercising in their underwear, and a scene of a man eating a cat's eyeball.

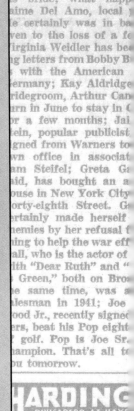

"FORBIDDEN DESIRES"

Adapted by UPTON SINCLAIR *from Famous French Play* "DAMAGED GOODS"

Clap Operas

It may look spicy, but *Forbidden Desires*, a retitled version of the 1935 film *Damaged Goods*, is actually about venereal disease. Sexual hygiene films were a grindhouse staple; exhibitors could assert that the films were "educational," not prurient. Famed author Upton Sinclair actually adapted the 1915 French stage play upon which the film was based.

Running Hot and Cold

Grindhouse features such as *Escort Girl* (1941) were always shot with a hot and cold version of the sexy scenes. Believe it or not, this is the hot one. In the censored version, the women wear robes.

Splicing in a Little Sin

Producers of Poverty Row movies — low budget films made to fill out the bottom half of double bills — sometimes got extra mileage out of a picture by shooting "hot" versions of some scenes. A more risqué dance number in a B-picture such as *Fig Leaf for Eve* (1945) would allow states rights distributors the option of pitching the film to grindhouses as an Adults Only show, as well as to regular theaters.

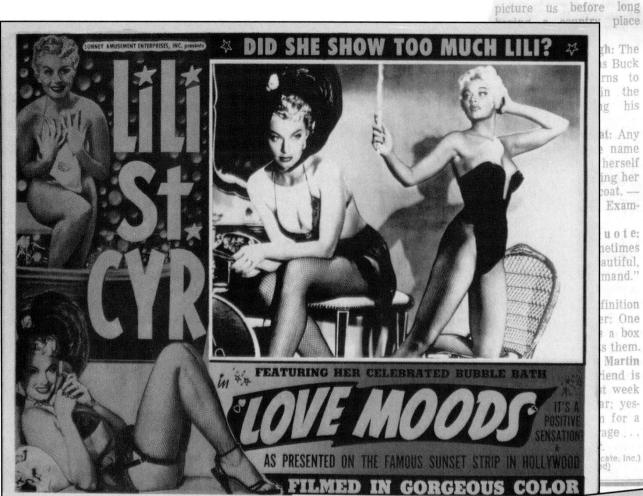

Bumping and Grinding

Burlesque had always been a popular, and particularly American, form of entertainment. After WWII there was a boom in the production of burlesque movies, as producers realized the economic advantages of filming striptease acts. Individual segments could be compiled to form a feature-length film, used as shorts on a grindhouse bill, turned into loops for arcade machines, or sold through the mail. Although feature-length burlesque films contained musical numbers and comedy sketches, there was no mistaking the main attraction. Performers such as Aleene, Lotus Wing, and Lili St. Cyr were the first bonafide "marquee stars" of Adults Only entertainment.

Imported Iniquity

Brigitte Bardot can proudly boast that during the 1950s she single-handedly saved plenty of second-run theaters in the United States from extinction. A wave of sexy French imports starring BB offered Americans their first glimpse of unabashed continental sexuality, and turned many foundering movie houses into "art houses," offering Italian roast coffee, Swiss chocolates, and French tarts.

Foreign films with sexy themes were generally an easier sell for distributors worried about the profitability of imported fare. *Street of Shame* (1956) was directed by the revered Japanese director Kenji Mizoguchi, and featured Machiko Kyo, the star of Mizoguchi's *Gate of Hell* and Akira Kurosawa's *Rashomon*.

To quote the pressbook, verbatim: "This is an unsatiable story of red light district, presented to you together with the unsolved problematical matters whether morally or politically in an agonizingly realistic surroundings and feelings, attaining the high stature of artistically appreciative picture. It is the story of women, whose lives are laden with full of miserable eking out their existence and entrusting their lives in falsely and ostensibly beautiful costumes and gaiety."

See? It's the same story, all around the world.

You Can Look, But
You'd Better Not Touch.

Nudie-cuties became the grindhouse rage in the late 1950s, once the U.S. Supreme Court ruled that nudity, per se, was not obscene. Unlike earlier Adults Only movies, which were obligated to show the shameful degradation that followed sex, nudie-cuties presented women as glorified sex goddesses, and the men who ogled them as bumbling dolts. *Tickled Pink* is a classic example of a nudie-cutie gimmick which allows an addled putz to see beautiful women nude.

In no time, the nudie craze affected popular movie stars of the 1950s such as Jayne Mansfield and Mamie Van Doren, both of whom revealed the secrets of their success in leering sex comedies of the early sixties. Mamie Van Doren was the undisputed queen of teenage drive-in movies, playing sexy tarts who led boys astray. As her young fans reached legal age, Mamie accommodated them by appearing partially nude in films such as *3 Nuts in Search of a Bolt.*

small cast (in this case,
entirely non-professional), it
left a powerful and deeply-
etched imprint.

The Pin-up and the PT Boat Skipper

Diane Webber was both a devoted spiritually based nudist (actually crowned "Queen of the Nudists" in an official convention) and one of the most photographed pin-up models of the fifties and sixties. In 1962 she starred in *The Mermaids of Tiburon* for John Lamb, a former PT boat captain and renowned underwater cinematographer. The combination of cheesecake and maritime action produced a mediocre film — and only Europeans got to see Diane swimming topless — but it's a lovely poster. Lamb would later produce the first Adults Only film to contain full frontal nudity, *The Raw Ones* (1965).

"Hold Her, Newt— She's Aheadin' fer the Barn!"

Despite the claims that there was never before a film like *Shotgun Wedding*, it is suspiciously similar to *Child Bride*, made in the late thirties by producer Lloyd Friedgan. This version, released in 1962, was written by current cult icon Ed Wood, Jr. and represents his rapid segue from daffy low-budget genre pictures into sexploitation. "Hillbilly" pictures were typically made for the southern circuit, where few customers complained about the depiction of a bunch of chicken-plucking Jethroes, mooned to the gills, pawing at backwoods jailbait — as long as they got their quota of boobs, butts, and belly laughs.

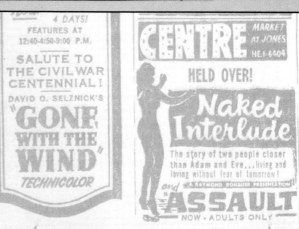

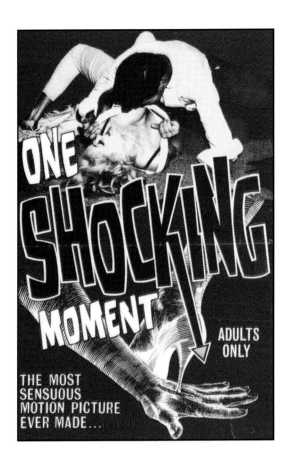

From Reverence to Rape

As the titillation of nudity wore off, filmmakers sought new ways to maintain the audience's interest (and their own). With any depiction of physical intimacy below the waist outlawed by every state censor board, violence became a substitute adrenaline rush. Films like *One Shocking Moment* (1964) spawned a whole genre known as "roughies." While it remained against the law to depict a man and woman graphically having consensual sex, there were no rules against showing a man slapping, beating, punching, or whipping a naked woman.

Same Story, New Package

The venerable plot line of most Adults Only movies never changed, from the thirties through the sixties. It was the tale of a country girl caught up in big city sin that formed the backbone of *The Playpen*, released in 1967 by American Art Films. But by this time, the movies were rougher and weirder. In this one, the country girl (played by burlesque performer Tiger Lilly) is ensnared by a lesbian stripper who forces her into prostitution. At the end of the film she is called back home to the woods by news of her mother's death. At the gravesite she is confronted by her lecherous stepfather. To quote from the pressbook: "She accused him of killing her mother and recalls to him that she knew from her mother of his killing a man in Tulsa. After a sensational chase through the woods, her stepfather kills her. AFTER DEATH, she recalls the things she will never have as her and her real father had talked of in her wishing tree as a child." If that's not enough, the film is presented in "Almost Unbelievably Beautiful Color."

Sixties Sex in One Sordid Package

The Orgy at Lil's Place (opposite page) was a film that had it all, sixties-style. Degenerate city folk invade the suburbs, and bring with them every sexy and sleazy cliché of Adults Only films. The strip dice game and the nude model in the art class were grindhouse staples since the early thirties. Films of "catfighting" women were a popular mail-order item in the fifties. Scenes of rape and torture were a nasty sixties spin on the genre. *The Orgy at Lil's Place* was one of dozens of films that depicted America's burgeoning suburban neighborhoods as virtual Sodoms and Gomorrahs, in which cocktails with the Hendersons always resulted in a naked free-for-all.

When Life Imitates Scuzzy Sex Films

No, it wasn't a double bill about Lorena and John Wayne Bobbitt. It was just a couple of low-budget Adults Only raunch-o-ramas typical of sixties fare. *The Scissors Girl* was yet another lost-innocent-in-the-big-city saga, which climaxes with the heroine gutting her abuser with the shears he'd earlier used kinkily to cut off her panties. *The Amazing Transplant* is a grisly story about a murderous loser who has the penis of his late satyric friend grafted onto him so he might overcome his vexing virginity. It was written, produced, and directed by Doris Wishman, one of the few women in the Adults Only dodge (although for this one she hid behind the name Louis Silverman).

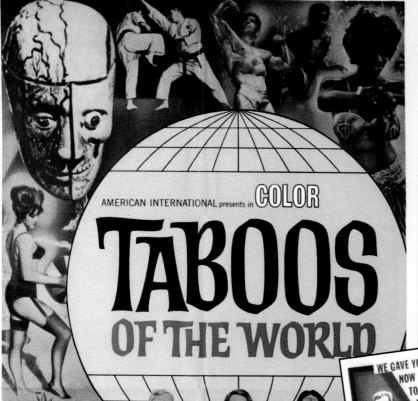

It's a Dog's World

The 1962 Italian production *Mondo Cane* spawned an entire genre of weird pseudo-documentaries, purporting to show the incredibly bizarre breadth of human behavior, running the gamut from absurd (men smashing their heads through garage doors) to the abhorrent (feeding live animals to sharks). It didn't take long for the films to veer from sardonic journalism to outright fakery, as Mondo films, in the battle to outdo each other, became suffused with all manner of staged sex rituals.

Sex Goes Uptown

In the early 1970s, more liberal laws regarding obscenity allowed sex films to move from the grindhouse to legitimate theaters. *Space Love* used every gimmick known to Adults Only producers: it exploited a topical long-running news story, in this case the Apollo moon missions; its promotional campaign coattailed on the popular *Love Story* tag line "Love Means Never Having to Say You're Sorry," and, of course, it promised something you'd never seen before: gravity-defying intercourse, lensed in Screenovision.

I Am Curious (Yellow), released in the United States in 1968, drove the X-rated industry into a frenzy. Every sex movie either co-opted the title (like the Carlos Tobalina–produced Tahitian titillater seen here) or claimed to "make *I Am Curious (Yellow)* pale by comparison." Such associations were odd, seeing as the original Swedish film was almost anti-sexual in content, and spent more time discussing the Vietnam War and Sweden's penal system than it did showing people engaged in sex.

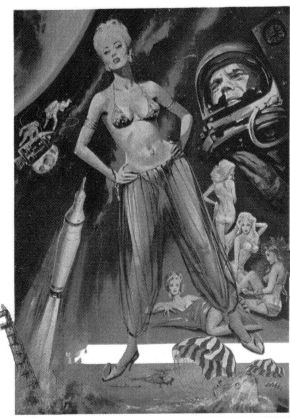

The Great Clown Prince of Dermapixville

David F. Friedman is the *Exploiteer Emeritus* of American sinema. No one had their hand in more facets of the Adults Only film business than did Friedman. He roadshowed with the legendary Kroger Babb in the late 1940s, imported foreign "art" films during the 1950s, produced some of the first nudist and nudie-cutie movies in the early 1960s, helped launched the trend in "roughies" and "ghoulies" later in the decade, and was one of the leading producers and distributors of "sexploitation" through the 1970s. Proving that he did indeed include "something for everyone" in his movies, Friedman was honored by the American Spanking Society (yes, that *is* the acronym) for "Best Spanking Scene of 1969" in *Thar She Blows*.

The posters for *The Headmistress* (1968) and *Thar She Blows* (1969) were both created by Rudolph Escalera, a young Hispanic artist who'd later be commissioned to paint the portrait of Mexican president Carlos Salinas de Gortari.

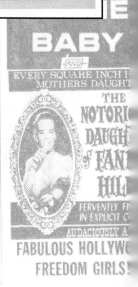

The Big Breakout

Linda Lovelace (*ne* Marchiano) made *Deep Throat* (1972) the most famous and profitable hardcore movie of all time. The film was such a cultural phenomenon it even had a Spanish language version for Mexican neighborhoods. Her skill as a fellatrix made Lovelace a household name for a while. When the spotlight dimmed, she wrote a book denouncing her involvement in sex films.

The One and Only Johnny Wadd

John Holmes was the first, and truthfully the last, male superstar of sex films. His career spanned countless couplings from the early 1960s to the 1980s. In the early seventies, he declared that he loved the work so much he'd continue it until the day he died. He succumbed to AIDS in 1985. Co-star Linda Wong died of a drug overdose. Georgina Spelvin, who began her career in sex films at the relatively late age of 38 by starring in the landmark film *The Devil in Miss Jones*, avoided such misery. She lives today in New York.

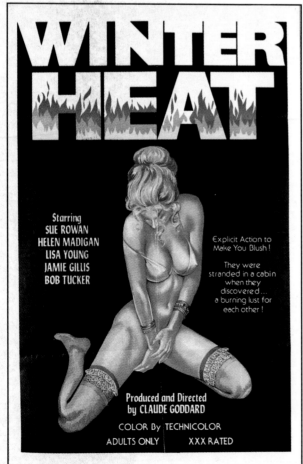

Hardcore Goes Hollywood

Makers of early hardcore films were obsessed with appearing legitimate. Posters began to emulate, and in some cases surpass, traditional Hollywood advertising. The producers of *Sweet Savage* went so far as to enlist the (clothed) services of Hollywood actor Aldo Ray to lend credibility to their carnal opus. More typical of hardcore fare was the adolescent humor of *Hot Lunch*, and the straightforward sexiness of *Winter Heat*. The trend toward theatrical "porno chic" would prove short-lived. An invention called the VCR would soon move sex films from the grindhouse right into the bedroom.

"Slap a ban on this one, Cardinal Spellman."

In 1957, producer Alberto Gout used austere sets, lavish color cinematography, and a pair of attractive actors (Christiane Martel, who played Eve, was a former Miss Universe from France) to create a faithful retelling of the Book of Genesis' third chapter: "And they were both naked, the man and his wife, and were not ashamed."

New York independent distributor Bill Horne bought the rights to the Mexican-made film, and grindhouse distributors around the country quickly snapped it up. Having regularly knocked heads with the Legion of Decency, the distributors savored the quandary this picture would present. "We showed the film to Father Masterson," recalls Dave Friedman, who distributed *Adam and Eve* through the Midwest exchanges, "and there was no way this picture could be interpreted as anything other than a verbatim depiction of the Bible."

The Legion was backed into a corner, not only by *Adam and Eve*, but by a Bette Davis film called *Storm Center*, a tale of book-burning fascism that uncomfortably paralleled the Legion's modus operandi. In response, the Legion softened its guidelines, segmenting its A (unobjectionable) rating into levels I, II and III. *Adam and Eve* carried an A-III rating, "morally unobjectionable for adults." Catholics attending the film were advised to study the Bible before and after viewing *Adam and Eve*.

"It was a picture for the pious and the prurient," Friedman says. "Something for everybody."

In Quebec, censors were sensitive to how the sight of Adam and Eve, *au naturel*, might affect the citizenry. The biblical couple's plain, off-the-shoulder frocks were provided courtesy of an artisan in the Customs department. The perforated stamp at the right of the photo signifies that the picture is now safe for public viewing. If Adam and Eve were frockless in this picture, you'd notice a glaring flaw in the film's verisimilitude — they both have navels! (You'd also notice Carlos Baena's rubber briefs, which camouflaged his vital instrument of procreation.)

IT'S ABSOLUTELY DIFFERENT

A FRENCHY COMEDY FOR UNASHAMED ADULTS

YOU'LL HATE YOURSELF IF YOU MISS IT

THE IMMORAL MR. TEAS

IT'S A RIBALD FILM CLASSIC

SEE what's on EVERY MAN'S MIND!

FILMED IN REVEALING EASTMAN COLOR

RUSS MEYER

The El Rey Theater in Oakland, California — now defunct — is a landmark in the history of Adults Only cinema. It was there that the owner, Pete DeCenzie, became pals with a photographer named Russ Meyer. A specialist in cheesecake, Meyer had provided sensational camerawork for a Tempest Storm burlesque short, *French Peep Show*, filmed in 1950 at the El Rey.

DeCenzie and Meyer struck a deal: each would pony up $12,000 to finance a full color feature filled with female flesh. Nudist camp movies were all the rage, but everyone knew that their novelty was rapidly wearing off. Nudist films weren't clever, or engrossing, or even well made.

And worst of all to Meyer, the women were ordinary. They didn't look anything like the abundantly endowed, towering Technicolor amazons that Russ Meyer craved.

DeCenzie knew Meyer was a complete professional, that he had a terrific sense of humor, that he had an unsurpassed eye for pulchritude and an unabashed skill at getting women to display it. He must have felt that his $12,000 investment wasn't much of a risk.

But he never could have imagined that *The Immoral Mr. Teas* would become the most pivotal production in Adults Only film history, returning more than one million dollars theatrically.

The finished film contained more unconstrained flesh than any movie ever made. So much flesh, in fact, that a theatrical release seemed impossible. Fortuitously, DeCenzie met a member of the Seattle censor board on a trip to the Northwest. The censor was a *paisan*, he and DeCenzie got on famously, and *Mr. Teas* was screened for him in optimum surroundings: a hotel room overflowing with pasta and chianti. It passed.

The picture drew huge crowds in Seattle. Exhibitors in Los Angeles and San Francisco braved censors and clergy, and their cash registers clanged steadily for two years. A legend, and a genre, was born.

The Immoral Mr. Teas was the first of what would become commonly known as a "nudie-cutie." It told the simple story of a regular schmoe who can't help but see gorgeous women everwhere he goes. After a trip to the dentist, he's cursed (or blessed) with an astounding ability: he sees all women naked! A series of comical vignettes ensues, culminating in an exasperated trip to a psychiatrist — female and nude, of course.

Unlike nudist movies, *Mr. Teas* didn't pretend to be educational, or espouse nudity as an alternative lifestyle. It was *about* naked women. And it was about *looking* at naked women. Promotional material for early Russ Meyer movies extolls his all-American virtues, and makes his blatant lechery sound downright patriotic. "The new film school of Bergman-type film makers had better lift up their Freud-fraught sex symbols and run for the hills. An American film maker is hot on their tails with some 'messages' of his own."

"The public was waiting for something new," Meyer is quoted as saying in the 1974 book *Sinema*, by Kenneth Turan and Stephen Zito. "I think they were becoming disenchanted with the so-called European sex films... in which there's a lot of promise but never any kind of real fulfillment... they would always cut to the curtain blowing and things of this nature. So there were a number of secondary arthouses that were floundering and they were looking for product. It was this field that we were able to jump into. Once this goddamn picture caught on, it was booked all over the country in these arthouses and the picture would just hang in there for a year and play incredibly."

Mr. Teas was, like nudist camp movies, sunny, innocent, even whimsical. It was a cheesecake calendar come to life; a voyeur's delight. But unlike nudist camp movies, it was the work of a craftsman. Other makers of Adults Only movies may have cared about their product — but Meyer was the first one with enough talent to prove it, right up on the screen. His camera work was exemplary, his colors crisp and vibrant. His staging showed thoughfulness and a genuine concern that the audience enjoy themselves. His script was as witty and sly as a four-day shooting schedule would allow. And he had a genuine feeling for his performers. His lead actually *was* Mr. William Teas, an Army buddy of Meyer's during WWII.

FILM REVIEWS — DAILY *VARIETY* DAILY

Eve And The Handyman
(COLOR)

Peep show cloaked in what is intended to be a satire. Should do good biz in houses where sex is the big attraction.

Hollywood, May 5.

Pad-Ram Enterprises release of Russ Meyer production. Stars Eve Meyer, Anthony-James Ryan. Written and directed by Meyer; camera (Eastman), Meyer. Reviewed at Paris Theatre, May 5, '61. Running time, **64 MINS.**

"Eve and the Handyman" is roughly the cinematic equivalent of one of the more sophisticated pose magazines. It is a slick slice of sex suggestion, an anatomical peepathon accompanied by that double-entendre narration that is the hallmark of caption poets from "Dude" to "Nugget" to "Playboy." More often than not, the intended satire sinks into double talk, vulgarity and low comedy, but the film is evidence that, given more reputable channels in which to direct his skill, producer-director-writer-photographer Russ Meyer (of "Mr. Teas" notoriety), who is responsible for this glorified hormone stimulant, might prove he is more than a mere flesh-in-the-pan impresario.

For its class, the picture is somewhat above average. It is superior in style and entertainment value to others of its ilk currently pulling big boxoffice at theatres that cater to the bare-babe-ogling customer, so it ought to score at least equally as well along Filmdom's "broad"way circuit.

Eve Meyer is the star attraction, undertaking a variety of roles, sole distinction among which amounts to the number and characteristic of garments in which she is frocked and/or unfrocked. Several other young ladies are intimately scrutinized, too. The degree of nudity in the film ranges from an occasional absolute zero (from an occasional aft vantage point) to form-fitting attire into which all forms fit admirably. Anthony-James Ryan is the handyman. Both he and Miss Meyer perform skillfully, considering the nature of their material.

Meyer has an affinity for extremely tight closeups. He will jam his lens right into someone's mouth for comic effect. Depending upon where he is jamming his lens, it is fairly effective. But Meyer would just as soon jam it into a ladies' toilet as he would into an eye. And some of his suggestive symbolism (notably a blast of explosives, sight gags and sound effects implying a sex act) appeals to the most arrested mentality in the way to the human animal's grosser sense of humor.   *Tube.*

THE BEST THING IN SIGHT... 48-24-36- *and we mean it!*

THE HILARIOUS NEW ESCAPADE from the producers of 'The IMMORAL MR. TEAS'!

EROTICA

Girls

Eye-Splashing COLOR

MORE ∧ THAN YOU'VE EVER SEEN BEFORE!

When it came to women, Meyer was discriminating. Not only did they have to measure up to his mammoth expectations, they had to enjoy what they were doing.

One of his calendar girls would become his wife. Eve Meyer became a partner in the business with her husband, and the star of his most successful *Mr. Teas* follow-up, *Eve and the Handyman*. In a 1986 interview with film historian Jim Morton, Russ reflected on their early days together, making nudie-cuties. "There were just the four of us: the guy who played the handyman, my assistant, and Eve, and she cooked for us and we had a really tight thing. She said 'Okay, half of this is my money, I like the idea of doing it, and let's do it,' and she broke her ass — there was never any static from her. She just said, 'Look, whatever you want to do, let's do it, okay? I'm here, I'll get up early in the morning and I'll look right,' and so on. She was special in that area and in many others as well, but with her I could do it, you know."

This kind of hardworking camaraderie, in which Meyer demanded and got the best from his people, would become his hallmark. He'd really test the grit and stamina of his actors in the coming years, when his location shoots became grueling sex and death marches, to hell and back.

If this sounds like foxhole talk, it's with good reason. Meyer was a product of WWII, and makes no bones about its formative

impact. "I was sorry to see it end," he told Jim Morton. "I liked very much that whole living by your wits, with each day being a new piece of excitement. I had mixed emotions about coming home... Everyone else wanted to go back to Alabama and start a family and all that. Not me, I just [said]: 'Gung ho, let's do it again!'"

After post-war stints making industrial films in the San Francisco Bay Area, Meyer started shooting girlie spreads for *Playboy* and other men's magazines. When he started making films, however, he rediscovered the

Double-D Day

As a combat cameraman during WWII, Russ Meyer rolled through Europe documenting the Third Army's inexorable push toward the liberation of Paris. His footage of Jacques Le Clair's Free French division proudly retaking the City of Lights was later used in the film *Patton*. In 1963, flush with the success of nudie-cuties such as *Erotica*, Meyer returned to Europe on a different mission of liberation. This time his cameras prowled the red light districts of Hamburg, Amsterdam, Berlin, Copenhagen, and Paris, allowing Meyer to revisit some sites of seminal significance from his WWII duty.

esprit de corps that he enjoyed so much in war-torn Europe.

To hear him speak of his actresses, you might have thought he was talking about the dogfaces who landed at Normandy with him: "It was like qualifying for the Olympics every day — it was the 440 and the high hurdles and everything all rolled into one. And they performed, they did it with a minimum of complaints, and rebounded at night when we had dinner and enjoyed the evening, then got a good night's sleep and got out of bed at five o'clock in the morning and they're putting on body makeup, you know..."

Well, maybe that last part wasn't like Normandy.

Nudie-cuties

The Immoral Mr. Teas had opened the floodgates. In the three years following its release, as many as 150 imitations paraded nude cuties across grindhouse screens.

A formula quickly developed that was as rigid as the guidelines of nudist camp movies. First, nudie-cuties were humorous (although in some cases, that's a generous assessment.) Comedy was of the snickering voyeur variety, of which Britain's Benny Hill would remain the world's lone practitioner. Silly schoolboy humor proved a remarkable relief for male grindhouse patrons tired of keeping a straight face during all those nude volleyball matches. In nudie-cuties, no leering wisecrack was left unspoken.

Sexual content, however, was nowhere to be found. The nudes in these films were the direct descendants of the pin-up dolls painted by Alberto Vargas, George Petty, and Gil Elvgren: lovely young girls caught unawares as they go about their daily chores. There was no touching allowed. Men and women seemed to bumble into each other only by accident: the Peeping Tom is bitten by a squirrel and falls through the clothesline, landing at the feet of his startled fantasy girl.

Women in nudie-cuties were, of course, glorified sex objects: perfectly self-contained and oblivious to the fluster they incited in the men who yearned from afar. It's the depiction of men that really distinguished the genre. They're like an endless bunch of second bananas from 1950s sit-coms. Sad sacks, dopes, young saps, and old geezers — all hopelessly idle dreamers who can only stare agog at the conga line of nubile beauties that passes them by.

Literary critic Leslie Fielder, writing in Show magazine about Mr. Teas, noted that "...There was not only no passion, but no contact, no flesh touching flesh, no consummation shown or suggested. For pornography the woman's angle of vision is necessary, but here were no women outside of Bill Teas' head; and Bill Teas was nobody's dreamed lover, only a dreamer... [he] could touch no one — not in lust or love or in the press of movement along the street... in the United

Getting an eyeful

The image at left, from Mr. Peter's Pets, sums up the entire nudie-cutie genre: a sheepish voyeur spies on a nude woman; she's an ambulatory masturbation fantasy, straight from Playboy's pages. The "party jokes" were supplied by films like Adam Lost His Apple, one of hundreds of nudie-cuties released between 1959-1963.

The Bearest movie Yet produced!
— *ADAM MAGAZINE*

The Ruined Bruin
in SUN-KISSED COLOR for UNASHAMED ADULTS!

21 beauties and a bear cavort in the GIRLESQUECAPADE of the year!

States we have long been corrupted by the pseudo arts of tease and titillation, conditioned to a version of the flesh more appropriate for peeking than love or lust or admiration or even real disgust."

The end result, Fielder wrote, "is a kind of imperturbable comedy, with overtones of real pathos."

Pathetic or not, producers cranked them out. *Not Tonight, Henry* followed in *Teas'* wake, with Frank Sinatra's Vegas cronie Hank Henry playing the dreamy loser at the center of the action. Henry, distant from his wife, is a portly putz who daydreams of romantic trysts with famous women from history. Delilah, Pocahontas, Cleopatra, and others appear, often topless, to enflame and frustrate poor Henry's libido.

Kipling's Women was another charter member of the genre, produced by Harry Smith, a veteran Hollywood soundman who grabbed his chance for independent success. The film strung together vignettes based on Rudyard Kipling's poem: "The Colonel's lady and Rosie O'Grady are sisters under the skin..." Smith united with none other than Kroger Babb to distribute the film, and Babb launched an unheard-of $100,000 promotional campaign to bring this "art film" to legitimate theaters across the country.

Babb's protégé, Dave Friedman, had formed a new partnership of his own with a young Chicagoan named Herschell Gordon Lewis, and together they produced one of the first *Mr. Teas* clones, *The Adventures of Lucky Pierre*, starring low-rent comic Billy Falbo.

Friedman proudly notes that he and Lewis shot the entire picture with 7,400 feet of "short end" film they'd bought dirt cheap.

Bears are people, too

Buddy the Bear escapes from the zoo because he longs to be human. He tries and fails to mate with a number of nubile females. The creators of *The Ruined Bruin* hit on a clever way to have the protagonist actually paw the cuties without offending the censors — dress the guy in a bear suit!

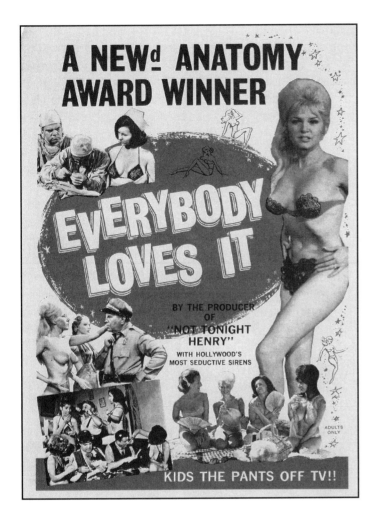

The final film ran 6,200 feet. Making a nudie-cutie was definitely a case of "No Experience Required."

In fact, nudie-cuties were directly responsible for two significant trends in the movie business.

The public acceptance of the films led to a wave of first-time producers not only taking a crack at movies, but getting their finished product distributed. Suddenly, anybody with some equipment and a few willing girlfriends was "in the business."

Secondly, nudie-cuties bailed out hundreds of movie houses around the country slated for closure due to the spread of television. Nudie-cutie advertising was packed with tag lines such as "You'll Never See This on TV!" Many of these theaters, which played art films in the 1950s, switched to sex pictures and never went back.

However, this new wave of independent producers, and crossover into semi-legitimate theaters, spelled the end of the road for that pioneering cadre of exploitation cowboys, the Forty Thieves. As the fifties waned and the sixties kicked America onto a more turbulent track, the times passed the Thieves by.

Like William Holden in *The Wild Bunch*, some of them still dreamed of a big score that would allow them to back off into retirement. But the ranks had thinned. Dwain Esper finally retired in 1962. "Steamship" Millard died in the late fifties. The prolific J. D. Kendis cashed out in 1957 at the age of 71. Willis Kent got out of the dodge when nudie-cuties hit, and passed away in 1966. "Mr. Pihsnamwohs" would never run another gaff as strong as *Mom and Dad,* and faded into obscurity in the sixties.

The old guard was gone, and the Adults Only section of the carnival would never be the same.

You've Gotta Start Someplace

Nudie-cuties represented the first step into the movie business for many aspirants. Within a few years, some would be making their fortunes selling term life insurance or running a beer distributorship. Others, like the director of *Tonight, For Sure!*, would end up creating film classics such as *The Godfather* and *Apocalypse Now*. Many cinema historians cite *You're a Big Boy Now* (1967) as Francis Coppola's first feature. Aficionados will point out that he directed *Dementia 13* for Roger Corman in 1962. But the true cineaste knows that Coppola's directorial debut was even before that, with this 68-minute nudie-cutie produced prior to his graduate studies at UCLA film school.

Let's step away for a few minutes from the blinding Los Angeles sun, beating down on a matinée crowd exiting *The Wonderful World of Girls*. Let's drift instead out past the warehouses and dry river beds, past the train tracks, into the charmless arid emptiness of El Monte, birthplace of Timothy Carey.

You remember Timothy Carey, don't you? Didn't you see *The Wild One*? He's the crazy guy who shook up the beer and squirted it in Marlon Brando's face. Did you see *East of Eden*? He was the surly bouncer at the brothel where James Dean's mother worked. Poor Tim mumbled his lines so badly that Elia Kazan had to have Albert Dekker re-dub all his dialogue. Tim thought Kazan missed the whole point. "That's the way pimps talk," he explained. How about *The Killing*, by Stanley Kubrick? He was the racist rifleman who shoots the horse at the racetrack to create a diversion for the heist. You must have seen *Paths of Glory*, another great Kubrick film— Carey is one of the three court-martialed soldiers sentenced to execution.

All his characterizations seem to inspire a common reaction: "What the hell's the matter with this guy?" Tim Carey had a uniquely twisted screen presence that many great directors tried, and often failed, to harness.

He was the only man that Kazan ever physically attacked on the set. Brando cast him in *One-Eyed Jacks,* and ended up stabbing him with a pen in exasperation. Carey didn't seem to care; he went on being Tim Carey. When new friends, like the maverick actor/director John Cassavetes, came to Carey's house for the first time, he made them wear a bulky, padded suit. He then turned his attack dog loose on them. "It's not you," Carey would howl. "He just hates that suit."

Despite his participation in several bonafide classics, the Carey film most people have seen, particularly down south, is *Poor White Trash* (1961).

Mike Ripps, the Alabama–based producer, knew a thing or two about exploitation. Print ads warned of "abnormal subject matter," and advised that uniformed police would be at every show, ensuring no children could sneak in and be turned into pillars of salt.

"You wanna see a movie, you can see a movie on television. You gotta give people a show," Ripps explained. "When they see *Poor White Trash*, they see the show before they get in the theater."

Ripps' film was actually *Bayou*, made by United Artists in 1957. Despite a *Child Bride* type storyline, it was tame enough to play a Baptist prayer meeting. Carey portrays Ulysses, a mean coon-ass who does a scary-as-hell dance to zydeco music and tries to kill star Peter Graves with an ax.

Ripps cut in new footage, using a double for nude close-ups during Lita Milan's love scene with Graves. In longer shots, the double gets her clothes ripped off in the woods by a

Timothy Carey, here pondering the future of Southern California, was a true visionary crackpot. His grand ambitions were undermined by gross indifference. When John Cassavetes claimed he had the "brilliance of Eisenstein," Carey used the quote in promos, crediting it to "John Cassaretes."

Tim Carey imitator. She sloshes around naked in the mud. Damn if *Poor White Trash* didn't make about $10 million for Ripps on the chitlin circuit.

While he could have been chasing royalties, Carey was instead creating his own Adults Only "masterpiece." He jerry-rigged it during the years 1959-1962, working as producer, director, writer, and lead actor. (He even self-distributed the movie, perhaps a decision of necessity, not control.) And being a true original, Carey steadfastly ignored any storytelling clues he might have gleaned from masters like Kubrick and Kazan.

The World's Greatest Sinner (*Frenzy* was the original, and equally apt, title) premiered at the Wiltshire Theater in Fullerton, California — the heart of conservative Orange County — and Carey got things rolling by firing a .38 over the heads of the audience. Fist fights broke out in the lobby and spilled into the streets. All before the film even started!

Once rumors of its bizarreness circulated, Carey had what was left of the tattered Legion of Decency roaring full throttle. Sight unseen (only four prints existed), it was branded sacrilegious. The American Legion denounced it as "subversive and unwholesome," a pithy and accurate assessment.

The story concerns insurance salesman Clarence Hilliard, who drops out, beatnik-style, to start his own religion (this predates Manson, remember). Clarence changes his name to God Hilliard and runs for president, proclaiming that "There's only one god, and that's man!" He gets possessed at a rock and roll show, and is soon fronting his own band as a kind of Elvis/Oral Roberts. Onstage, he does the *Bayou* dance, converting the audience, all of whom don armbands to show allegiance to the new "God." Testing the bound-

aries of his holiness, Hilliard has sex with a 92-year-old woman (then steals her money), beats up his daughter, sleeps with a 14-year-old acolyte, and forces another guy to kill himself. At the end, he stabs a eucharist he's taken from a church, and laughs that it's "nothing but a piece of bread. Mother, you're dead forever!" The black-and-white film then bursts into color, blood spurts out of everywhere, and the credits roll. The story was narrated by a snake and the score performed by a pre-Mothers of Invention Frank Zappa.

When it came to publicizing his controversial film, Carey was a one-man wrecking crew. An appearance on the Joe Pyne show (the progenitor of right-wing talk shows like Morton Downey, et al.) resulted in a fist-swinging melée in the audience. Another "premier" at the El Monte Drive-In resulted in what the theater manager called "a destruction derby," with cars smashing into each other. A 1970 midnight run in San Francisco was abruptly cancelled when an inspired patron started slashing seats apart after Carey, on-screen, announced he was God.

Although the original negative of *The World's Greatest Sinner* was lost, Carey persevered as an artist. *Tweet's Ladies of Pasadena*, an uncompleted epic, starred Carey as a gardener for an old ladies' knitting group whose goal is to clothe all naked animals. Carey's plan was to show the film one time only: it would run from the projector into a shredder and the celluloid ribbons would then be thrown into the audience as souvenirs. At the time of his death in 1993, Carey was working on *The Insect Trainer*, a film about a man incarcerated for killing a woman with his flatulence.

And to think that people make a fuss over a little old cross-dresser like Ed Wood...

Heavy Petting at the Drive-in

Rock and roll changed everything. It mixed the races, bridged the oceans, broke taboos, and rewrote the cultural agenda. And somewhere in there, it reshaped the movie business, too.

Before rock and roll, movie makers pretty much ignored teenagers. Hollywood produced product for adults and children. "Teenage" was limbo. But rock and roll aimed right at the ears and loins of the hormonally challenged. Church groups and community leaders railed about "race music," reviving again the old bugaboo about the lower-class virus that would wipe out all moral values.

Movie producers, seeing the way kids snapped up those 45s, realized there was a lot of disposable teenage cash out there.

Lawyer Sam Arkoff, reading the trend brilliantly, teamed up with theater owner James H. Nicholson to form American-International Pictures, which catered exclusively to the teen market. Monogram, the old Poverty Row studio, was revived as Allied Artists, and it began churning out "JD" pictures.

Faster than Little Richard could pound his piano, rock and roll was blasting from theater screens in an avalanche of movies made expressly for America's teenagers.

The trend also changed the way movies were shown. Patrons of "hardtops" (as regular theaters are known in the trade) wouldn't tolerate the new breed of rowdy patron. Teenagers needed their own turf. Drive-ins were the answer. Hundreds of huge screens sprouted up all over America, enabling patrons to be as rambunctious, or as romantic, as they wanted, all in the privacy of their Chevrolets.

One hundred feet tall, floating over the Midwest plains,

were *Rock Around the Clock, Don't Knock the Rock, Teenage Rebel, Juvenile Jungle, The Cool and the Crazy, Teenage Doll, Hot Rod Girl, Joy Ride, Riot in Juvenile Prison, Teenage Thunder, Live Fast Die Young, Cry Baby Killer, Reform School Girl* — a seemingly endless list. And despite the rocking soundtracks and Daddy-O dialogue, they were all throwbacks to the 1930s.

Purporting to be exposés of the dangers of juvenile delinquency, these films were sexy packages of the hottest music and the most dangerously cool actors and actresses. Ironically, what was branded Adults Only in the thirties was now being fed to 16-year-olds: tales of wayward girls, dope rackets, switchblade-wielding gangs, sold with tags such as "Hellcats on the Prowl," "The Private World of Girls Who Grow Up Too Fast," and "The Sin-Steeped Story of a Teenage Tramp."

There was no nudity, but there really didn't need to be. Suggestiveness took on new, outrageous dimensions. In *Will Success Spoil Rock Hunter?*, Jayne Mansfield took the image of the buxom blonde bimbo around the bend, posing with a pair of full milk bottles squeezed against her enormous breasts.

And then there was Mamie. If these movies were ushering America's youth down the path of iniquity, Mamie Van Doren was the usherette youth wanted.

In her movies, she rocked. Teenage boys had fistful nights after watching Mamie shimmy in a form-fitting slip while singing up a storm at a girl's prison farm in *Untamed Youth*. Billed as "The Platinum Powerhouse," she played the delectable temptress

in a series of "reckless youth" films —
all released in one rocking year, 1959:
*High School Confidential; Guns, Girls
and Gangsters; The Beat Generation
(a. k. a. This Rebel Age); Girl's Town,*
and *Vice Raid.*

In her private life, Mamie rolled. She
was sexually liberated before the two
words were ever conjoined. Mamie earned
(proudly, according to her autobiography) a
reputation as a prolific — some might say
profligate — lover. If she took all her husbands, lovers, and boyfriends (she liked
them college-age) and laid them end to end,
no one would have been surprised.

Once the fad for JD movies wore out its
welcome, producers continued to trade on
her sex appeal. In *Sex Kittens Go to College*
(1960), young Tuesday Weld eyes Mamie in
a tight sweater and moans, "Why do you
have to be so darn much of a woman?" By
the time she made *3 Nuts in Search of a Bolt*
(1963), a screwball comedy by the distinctly
unfunny Tommy Noonan, pressure from the
nudie-cuties dictated drastic action. Mamie
answered the call, performing a fiery
striptease while singing "I Used to be a
Stripper Down on Main, Now I'm the Main
Attraction on the Strip." Noonan, realizing he
was working with an unflappable star, shoe-
horned in a scene of Mamie bathing nude in
a tub of beer.

Today, Mamie Van Doren has a good-
sized cult following. In addition to her somewhat comic sex appeal, fans enjoy her
because she was able to float on the waves
of her exploitation, and not get sucked under.
Nobody exploited Mamie more than herself.
While Marilyn and Jayne, her more famous
bombshell rivals, both died tragically, Mamie
maintained her sexy little niche in the business with good humor. She garnered fans
both gay and straight, and always pops up
unexpectedly: posing nude for *Playboy* in
1984 at age 53, and again at 61, releasing a
CD in the European market in 1993, appearing regularly at AIDS fundraising parades,
and triumphantly getting her Hollywood Walk
of Fame star in 1994.

Mamie Van Doren was
unabashed about being a
sex symbol. Once, when
she appeared at an event
in a dress that barely
covered her, the
photographers asked if
she wasn't awfully cold. "I
expect your flashbulbs to
keep me warm," she
smiled.

The Girl Couldn't Help It

Jayne Mansfield caught the rock and roll wave at just the right time, bursting out of *The Girl
Can't Help It* as a top-heavy sexpot. As a youngster in Bryn Mawr, Pennsylvania, she craved
Hollywood stardom; she ended up getting more of it than she could handle. In *Promises,
Promises* (1963), Jayne became the first big-name star to appear nude. But by then, her life was
out of control. A volatile marriage to bodybuilder Mickey Hargitay, five children, several stormy
affairs, a drinking problem, serious tax trouble with the IRS, and the grind of maintaining her sex
symbol status finally took their toll. In 1964, exhausted and dispirited, she stated, "I wish it
would all end, right now, right here. What a mess I've made of my life." Three years later, after
turning down the role of Ginger on *Gilligan's Island*, she got her wish. While heading to New
Orleans with her lawyer/lover Sam Brody and three of her kids, Jayne's Buick plowed into the
back of a truck. The children, sleeping in the backseat, survived. Jayne, Brody, and driver Ronnie
Harrison all died instantly. The era of the blonde bombshell was over.

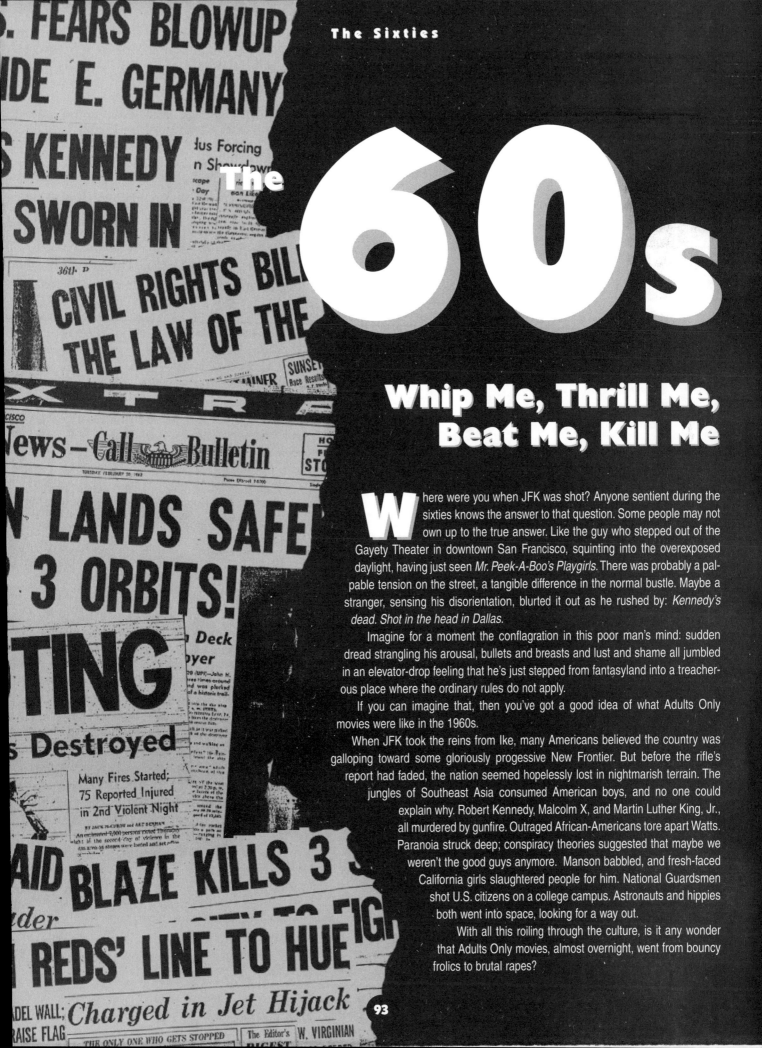

The 60s

Whip Me, Thrill Me, Beat Me, Kill Me

Where were you when JFK was shot? Anyone sentient during the sixties knows the answer to that question. Some people may not own up to the true answer. Like the guy who stepped out of the Gayety Theater in downtown San Francisco, squinting into the overexposed daylight, having just seen *Mr. Peek-A-Boo's Playgirls*. There was probably a palpable tension on the street, a tangible difference in the normal bustle. Maybe a stranger, sensing his disorientation, blurted it out as he rushed by: *Kennedy's dead. Shot in the head in Dallas.*

Imagine for a moment the conflagration in this poor man's mind: sudden dread strangling his arousal, bullets and breasts and lust and shame all jumbled in an elevator-drop feeling that he's just stepped from fantasyland into a treacherous place where the ordinary rules do not apply.

If you can imagine that, then you've got a good idea of what Adults Only movies were like in the 1960s.

When JFK took the reins from Ike, many Americans believed the country was galloping toward some gloriously progessive New Frontier. But before the rifle's report had faded, the nation seemed hopelessly lost in nightmarish terrain. The jungles of Southeast Asia consumed American boys, and no one could explain why. Robert Kennedy, Malcolm X, and Martin Luther King, Jr., all murdered by gunfire. Outraged African-Americans tore apart Watts. Paranoia struck deep; conspiracy theories suggested that maybe we weren't the good guys anymore. Manson babbled, and fresh-faced California girls slaughtered people for him. National Guardsmen shot U.S. citizens on a college campus. Astronauts and hippies both went into space, looking for a way out.

With all this roiling through the culture, is it any wonder that Adults Only movies, almost overnight, went from bouncy frolics to brutal rapes?

roughies

A SHATTERING STUDY OF THE SHAMELESS "SICK SET" FOR SHOCK-PROOF ADULTS!

Herschell Gordon Lewis and David Friedman were shooting *Bell, Bare and Beautiful* in Florida, featuring zeppelin-busted burlesque star Virginia Bell, when they realized that the nudist-movie craze was starting to peter out. They'd ridden it as hard as they could for two years, producing *The Adventures of Lucky Pierre; Daughters of the Sun; BOIN-N-G!; Nature's Playmates;* and *Goldilocks and the Three Bares.*

As a tonic to the monotony of happy nude campers, the pair produced a nasty little black and white movie called *Scum of the Earth.* In a nice display of self-mockery, the titular scum, who "dwell and thrive in a morass of depravity," were a couple of guys operating a dirty-picture racket.

Scum did fair business, but the production partners knew they had to concoct something new to leap to the fore of the exploitation pack. The next frontier, perhaps, was to show nude people actually engaged in erotic entanglements. They knew that would never pass. In 1963, the sight of a single pubic hair could bring out the riot squad. A penis penetrating a vagina? Showing that was absolutely inconceivable.

But what about a knife? Or better yet, an ax?

The duo returned to Florida with their regular stock company and *Playboy* centerfold Connie Mason. In five days they completed *Blood Feast*, a slaughterhouse of a movie. There was no sex. Instead, women were mutilated by a crazed Egyptian caterer who used their various body parts in his sacred rituals. A partially nude woman is eviscerated on a sacrifical slab; another has her brain cut out on the beach; yet another has her tongue ripped from her mouth.

For Lewis and Friedman, the production was a lark. They spent just over $24,000 and had lots of fun splashing around in new territory, wondering what kind of furor, and box office, their sanguinary quickie would drum up. When Friedman's wife described the end result as "vomitous," he promptly ordered white sickness bags imprinted "You May Need This When You See *Blood Feast*."

The old carny come-on proved infallible. The morbidly curious queued up at hardtops and drive-ins. Critics courageous enough to view the film were appalled. The *Los Angeles Times* called it a "blot on the American film industry," playing right into Friedman's hands. He was granted an injunction in Sarasota, Florida, to prevent his own film from being shown, then leaked the story to the national wire services, garnering a generous amount of free publicity.

Blood Feast was a money-maker. A pair of blood-soaked follow-ups, *Two Thousand Maniacs* and *Color Me Blood Red* oozed out in its sticky wake. These films would become known to the trade as "ghoulies," for their unsettling union of sex and death.

While Lewis continued to probe the extremes of low-budget bloodletting, Friedman, more attuned to sex than gore, moved to Los Angeles and became partners with veteran exploitation producer/distributor Dan Sonney. In his first solo outing as a producer, Friedman created *The Defilers*, a conscious attempt to emulate the smarmy thrill of an illicit stag film. It was the demon brother of the nudie-cutie, in which voyeurism was just a warm-up for the depraved protagonist: he kidnaps the unattainable beauty, locks her in a dirty basement, slaps her around, beats her with a belt, and rapes her.

A new type of adult film was spawned: the roughie. This style of sex movie would become a mainstay of grindhouses throughout the 1960s, along with its wicked siblings, the "kinky" and the "ghoulie." (More on them later.)

In a roughie, lust led to violence: women were abused, men erupted in jealous rages. The action is angry, brutal, and simpleminded. Storylines followed the old "morality play" formula — warning audiences of the dangers of depraved behavior while depicting it in detail. In *The Defilers*, for example, the kidnappers are described as "amoral hedonists" with too much time and money on their hands. And like their antecedents in vice films of the 1930s, marijuana is blamed as one of the triggers for their sadistic sex antics.

From the vantage point of the politically correct 1990s, it's tempting to brand these films as the product of a misogynistic patriarchy, punishing women for daring to assume a larger role in society. It's a tough argument to refute on face value, when you stack up the hundreds of rapes, beatings, and whippings that filled grindhouse screens between 1964 and 1970.

Roughies eventually degenerated from tales of unbridled emotion into ones of outright psychosis. Consider the synopsis of a warped picture called *Zero In and Scream*, produced in the late sixties:

> He could be the man living next door to you, pleasant, well-mannered. It was easy for him to move into the Hollywood glamour set of artists and models, but his mind did not easily accept their actions, for to him a woman was a thing of beauty, something to look at, to worship but not to touch. He found a way to get even with those who defiled the beauty of women and in his mind he became the watchman, the protector, eliminating the ugliness of mankind with one simple pull of the trigger. She became his secondary obsession and when he found her in the arms of a woman, his confused world became an unreal torment, causing him to take unspeakable actions against her.

The advertising shows various intimate sex acts, viewed through the scope of a high-powered hunting rifle.

That leaves Depraved, Deranged, Demented...

The Defilers spawned several other *De–* movies. *The Degenerates* (1967), produced and directed by Andy Milligan, has a particularly rich scenario: In the post-holocaust year 2000, a crazed man-hating lesbian Amazon named Violet rules over her sisters on a desolate farm. "Her caresses are soft and the lashes of her whip are sharp!" A trio of men from the Nuclear Attack Survival Center stumble across the farm, and soon the girls "learn how to become women from men who know all the angles." Violet, quite unprepared for the transformation, pitchforks one man to the barn and castrates him. The tasteful ad campaign for *The Debauchers* doesn't let on that it's actually a French-made bit of sleaze about a woman who answers an ad for a maid's job but ends up kidnapped and forced into stag films.

While all this seems scary and depraved, there are some behind-the-scenes aspects of the business to consider, so as not to lose perspective.

According to Dave Friedman, it's a mistake to read too much into these films. To him, they are merely an extension of the carnival experience, of the business of selling sensation. "There's no denying that the voyeur thing works," he says. "And the movie audience is the supreme voyeur."

He also points out that roughies did not exactly replace nudie-cuties, but existed side-by-side with them, at least at first. "For exhibitors that were running six weeks of nudies, a one week run of the rough stuff was a welcome change of pace."

Friedman's world view is that of the carny: you're either with the show, or you're part of the gullible audience. If you're neither, go mind your business someplace else. People who can't see behind the stage facade are rubes, i.e., *Get with it! It's all a put-on! We're not beating women and chopping their legs off — we're*

putting on a show. And the supposed "victims" are in on it. They wipe off the fake blood, have a good laugh, and collect their check. It's much more exciting than waiting tables.

The excitement generated in the early sixties by a new wave of international filmmakers was another factor in the roughie trend. Directors like Jean-Luc Godard,

Francois Truffaut, and Stanley Kubrick had made thrilling low-budget independent films, inspiring a new generation to take a stab at moviemaking. Grindhouses were a prime distribution outlet for cash-strapped producers with scant chance of cracking the Hollywood studio system.

Roughies gave young artists (we didn't say *talents*) the chance to attempt gritty dramas, filled with action and emotion. Rape, for them, was far more "cinematic" than volleyball. And hadn't Ingmar Bergman scored an international success with *The Virgin Spring*? That tale of rape and revenge would later provide the basis of one of the most notorious exploitation films of all time, *I Spit On Your Grave*.

Doris Wishman moved from nudies to roughies with *The Sex Perils of Paulette,* in which a girl from the sticks moves to New York and immediately finds herself in the midst of an orgy. Try as she might to find honest, gainful employment, she ends up becoming a prostitute, just like her cynical roomate. At the end, degraded and corrupted, she walks away from the man who loves her, saying "It is the best thing that ever happened to you, Allen." Producer/director Wishman, not wanting to hog all the glory, opted for the name Dawn Whitman as her screenwriting credit.

Bottom row (left to right): *Vice Girls, Bad Girls Go to Hell, Call Girls of Frankfurt, The Agony of Love, The Pick-up.*

In some cases these jagged little 70-minute sex films were almost direct *doppel-gangers* of more sophisticated international film fare. Consider *The Agony of Love* (1965), written and directed by William Rotsler, and distributed by Harry Novak, America's most prolific purveyor of prurient product. It depicts the secret life of a bored housewife, who, unable to get the affection she craves from her workaholic husband, sells herself as a prostitute. The film is a series of sexual vignettes, in which the protagonist (played by Pat Barrington) seeks fulfillment by becoming the fantasy object of a succes-sion of strangers. She even dreams of herself in various scenes of symbolic degradation.

Belle De Jour, produced two years later by the widely admired Spanish surrealist Luis Buñuel, is just a better-acted, more stylish version of *The Agony of Love*. (To give Rotsler his due, he probably shot his whole film in the time it took Buñuel to stage one scene.)

Despite any artistic aspirations, roughies were an extension of the essential Adults Only paradigm: maximum sensation on a minimum budget. Most of the creative inge-nuity went into simply getting a film finished. A director who could fashion passable prod-uct under these time and budget constraints was considered golden.

Lee Frost managed to do it. He directed *The Defilers* for Friedman, and despite its unnerving prurience, it's an inarguably tight, well-made film. Frost would become one of the most prolific grindhouse direc-tors of the sixties, with credits that include films as disparate as *Surftide 77* (1962), *House on Bare Mountain* (a nudie-cutie with monsters, 1962), *Love is a Four-Letter Word* (1963), *Mondo Bizarro* (1966), and *The Pick-up* (1968). His dexterity with a camera made him first choice for distribu-tors seeking someone to film well-matched sex inserts for imported movies. *Sexy Proibitissimo* (1964), *London in the Raw* (1964), *Night Women* (Claude Lelouch [!], 1966), and *Witchcraft '70* are some of the foreign items that contained new Frost footage.

After scoring a few Adults Only box offices successes toward the end of the decade, Frost attempted to make the tran-sition to Hollywood studio films. He was

Lee Frost's *The Animal* (1967) dragged the nudie film into the back alley. Picture *Rear Window* with Ted Bundy in the Jimmy Stewart role. A pervert with a high-powered telescope becomes obsessed with a wealthy socialite. "His plan — step by step — was to degrade her, to bring her down to his level of existence, and to make her an animal." As was often the case with sex films of the sixties, this plan included scenes of forced lesbianism. The pressbook notes that the film "deals with a delicate subject and was produced in Los Angeles, California with our best judgment."

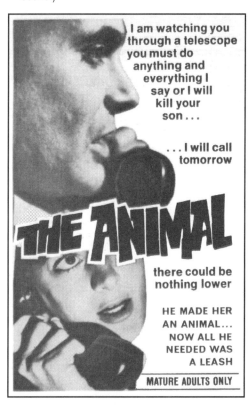

I am watching you through a telescope you must do anything and everything I say or I will kill your son...

...I will call tomorrow

THE ANIMAL

there could be nothing lower

HE MADE HER AN ANIMAL... NOW ALL HE NEEDED WAS A LEASH

MATURE ADULTS ONLY

hired to direct *Race with the Devil* (1975), an action thriller starring Peter Fonda and Warren Oates. Frost's miserly grindhouse technique betrayed him. He unnerved producers by not shooting an excessive amount of film, only what he needed. He was immediately fired.

Most of Frost's films were produced by Robert Cresse, another alumnus of the carnival midway. Cresse came to Los Angeles from Sarasota, Florida, by way of the University of Miami. He looked like a less-cuddly Jonathan Winters, and had a gift for the gabby hustle that worked just fine in Tinsel Town—after he'd paid his dues as a bike messenger at MGM. He worked himself up the production ranks, but decid-

ed to go independent when he realized there was no job security at a major studio. While Dan Sonney and Dave Friedman ran Entertainment Ventures Incorporated, the "Capitol of the Exploitation Film Industry," out of their Cordova Street complex, Cresse set up his own shop, Olympic International Films, on tonier Sunset Boulevard. Whereas MGM pompously used as its credo "Art for the Sake of Art," Olympic's banner declared "Art for the Sake of Money."

Cresse produced one of the first nudie documentaries, *Hollywood's World of Flesh*, a Shocking! All True! production in the grand exploitation tradition. All the scenes, filmed "on location as they actually hap-

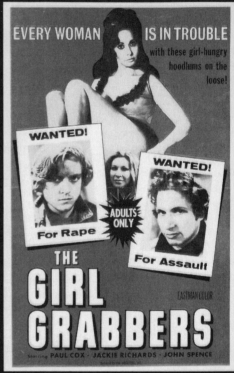

DOWN AND DIRTY

Kidnapping and rape were staples of sixties sexploitation. If you need a good head-spin, ponder this: *The Big Snatch* (1968) was produced and directed in three days on an $11,000 budget by one Danny Martin, who, according to Dave Friedman, the film's distributor, was an L.A. county deputy sheriff looking to break into the movie business. "Filmed in Color and Concupiscence" is a dead giveaway that Friedman was behind the ad campaign. He also obligingly provided newspapers with big cut-out C's to paste over the SN in the title, should community standards so dictate.

pened," were staged over one weekend, with Cresse and Frost using unpaid friends as actors. Half the footage was monochrome, half color, shot with rented equipment. The dynamic duo added a red tint to the black-and-white segments and claimed that those were hidden camera scenes filmed with a special infra-red lens. (Please refer back to earlier comments about "creative ingenuity.")

Cresse soon carved out quite a reputation. He had that me-against-the-world attitude required of an independent film producer, but his predilection for weaponry and Nazi regalia put an unnerving edge on it. He also kept two full-time bodyguards on the payroll, as a warning to people that it wasn't wise to steal from Bob Cresse. He told interviewer Mike Vraney, in the magazine *Cult Movies*, about the time

ATTENTION MR. EXHIBITOR...

NATIONAL REVIEW

HAS JUST ANNOUNCED ITS 10 BEST MOTION PICTURES, AND THERE'S ONE YOU HAVEN'T PLAYED YET

TEN FAVORITES OF 1969:
1. Midnight Cowboy
2. Ma Nuit Chez Maud
3. The Bliss of Mrs. Blossom
4. The Immortal Story
5. They Shoot Horses, Don't They?
6. Topaz
7. Devil by the Tail
8. The Wild Bunch
9. On Her Majesty's Secret Service
10. HOT SPUR IN EASTMANCOLOR

he had to collect his rental fees from a unforthcoming exhibitor by jamming a .38 into the guy's mouth and threatening to blow his head off. (Later in the interview, Cresse asserts that it was only a cap gun.)

When Friedman used Lee Frost to direct *The Defilers*, and scored a grindhouse hit, it ignited a long-running rivalry between the two outfits that veered from fraternal to ferocious.

Cresse fancied himself in the macho mold of Sam Peckinpah (although he wasn't a drinker), and toward the end of the sixties he took the roughie genre in a Western direction. He sank more money than usual into the making and promotion of a film called *Hot Spur* (1968), which he billed as "a western with the scope and quality of the largest studio...and the blatant rawness of a Saturday Night smoker film." Convinced this was his big smash, Cresse went wild on promotion, plastering 24-sheets in key cities, running radio spots, the works.

Friedman, ever the canny competitor, watched Cresse's crusade and decided to undercut him just as *Hot Spur* went into the theaters. He'd made his own quickie western, *Brand of Shame*, and convinced exhibitors to play its trailer before *Hot Spur*. Friedman's movie was a dud, but the trailer was a killer. At the bottom line *Brand of Shame* ended up out-performing *Hot Spur*, mainly because Friedman didn't spend a cent on advertising: he just coat-tailed on Cresse's ballyhoo.

Hot Spur was the archetypical Cresse production: filled with cruel, sadistic men abusing attractive women. It did prove to be Cresse's crowning achievement, at least critically, due in full measure to William F. Buckley's conservative *National Review*, which was liberal enough to include the film on its Ten Best List of 1969.

Cresse left the Adults Only business after an unfortunate encounter on Hollywood Boulevard. Heeding cries for help, he confronted two men beating a woman outside a store. Cresse ordered them to stop, and punctuated the command by brandishing the handgun he liked to tote with him. One of the men promptly shot him in the stomach, then shot Cresse's dog, then informed him that they, in fact, were the police.

Cresse had no insurance, and his seven-month hospital stay depleted most of the money he'd carefully funneled into a Swiss bank account.

THE SCAVENGERS WERE ROTTEN TO THE CORE — THOROUGHLY DISGUSTING, AND HAD A SERIOUS FREUDIAN PROBLEM... YOU'LL PROBABLY LOVE THEM

THE SCAVENGERS MAKE THE WILD BUNCH LOOK TAME AND THE DIRTY DOZEN LOOK CLEAN!
...S. THIEL

THE SCAVENGERS

EASTMAN COLOR

ADULTS

The Scavengers (1969) was Bob Cresse's lavish (by Adults Only standards) attempt to emulate Sam Peckinpah. It was released complete with ornate souvenir programs that probably cost more to produce than most grindhouse features. Apparently, the title didn't register with its intended audience, because the film was soon re-released under the title The Grabbers.

MUDHONEY

Formerly "ROPE OF FLESH"

TASTE OF EVIL!

Some sexploitation scholars assert that it was Russ Meyer who actually created the "roughie." Whether he was the first or not is irrelevant. Slinging his camera like an old-west gunfighter, Meyer swaggered into tough-ass territory and showed everybody how it was done.

Abandoning his pop-art color, bouncy scores, and buffoonish humor, Meyer created *Lorna* (1964). Here was the bible, wrapped in a *Playboy*. Set in Tobacco Road, USA, it told the brutal tale of a lonely backwoods wife who has her sexual fire ignited by an escaped convict. Her husband discovers the lovers under his own roof, and there's hell to pay. But it's Lorna who pays, accidentally killed during the men's life and death struggle. A preacher appears throughout, railing about the severity of God's impending judgment.

Many feel that Meyer's craft peaked in 1966, with the creation of *Faster, Pussycat! Kill! Kill!* In this one, Meyer took his balls-to-the-wall filmmaking style all the way around the bend, past self-parody, into a kind of surreal firmament where cultural icons are forged.

Meyer's loyal commando unit of grizzled character actors, musclebound studs and Amazonian sexbombs endured a three week bivouac in the California desert, and returned with a movie that for once could truthfully bill itself as being "Like Nothing You've Ever Seen Before!"

Faster, Pussycat! is about a trio of berserk go-go dancers who live to raise hell. Their leader, a black-clad Queen of Darkness named Varla (Tura Satana), breaks a joyriding hipster's back after a drag race and kidnaps his girlfriend. They hide out in the desert, at the home of a bitter old cripple who lives with his two sons, one a milquetoast, the other a hunky moron. When Varla discovers there's a buried fortune on the land, all manner of hell breaks loose.

GO-GO For A WILD RIDE With The ACTION GIRLS!

Faster, PUSSYCAT! KILL! KILL!

Directed by RUSS MEYER who brought you "LORNA" and "MOTORPSYCHO" Screenplay by JACK MORAN An EVE Production STARRING TURA SATANA · HAJI · Lori WILLIAMS · Susan BERNARD · Stuart LANCASTER · Paul TRINKA · Dennis BUSCH · Ray BARLOW · Mickey FOXX

The dialogue is furious, packed with trash-talk innuendo. The camerawork is sharp and the editing — Meyer's true forte — inspired. Until *Bonnie and Clyde* (1967) and *The Wild Bunch* (1969) no American filmmaker equalled Meyer's dexterity in creating exhilarating montage.

And, of course, there were the women. Could anything have been further from the 1930s image of cowering females, meekly succumbing to their lecherous patriarchs? Today, Tura Satana is an icon to bawdy feminists: a lusty leather goddess, kicking ass and not bothering to take names.

Critics who lambaste Meyer as a sexist missed a vital aspect of all his films: he esteemed women who had, as he simply put it, "guts." Headstrong women with huge appetites that matched his own. In the sexual battlefield he depicted, women didn't lie back and take it; they dished it out — but good.

Meyer perfected his hellfire-and-brimstone style in *Mudhoney* (1965). Due to his nudie-film reputation, critics were slow to acknowledge Meyer's singular style. In fact, films like *Lorna*, *Mudhoney*, *Motorpsycho*, *Good Morning and Goodbye*, and *Common Law Cabin* had less nudity than standard grindhouse fare. Meyer's films didn't engrave themselves in memory just because of huge breasts. It was the sustained turbulent tone, a boiling stew of God, the devil, lust, and dread, that put Meyer's roughies head, shoulders, and, we'll admit, breasts above the rest.

Kinkies

An idling car waits curbside at a Women's Correctional Institution. It quickly swallows up a just-released young wastrel and spirits her to a nondescript walk-up in the bowels of New York's Chinatown. Before she can experience her newfound freedom, the unlucky woman is manacled and disciplined by New York's most dreaded dominatrix: the leering, laughing Olga Petroff!

So begins *White Slaves of Chinatown* (1964), generally regarded as the first film in a genre that would become known as "kinkies." The rest of the film pretty much repeats the same scene over and over, with graphic escalations. A narrator, who sounds like a news anchorman reading one of Ed Wood's sleazy porno paperbacks, explains the shocking facts behind what we are seeing: despite the rope burns, metal bridles, flagellation, and overt lesbianism, the ersatz *raison d'être* of the film was merely an update of an old vice racket script: Olga is a Red sympathizer, working with the Syndicate to distribute narcotics from mainland China, thereby softening up America for the eventual Communist takeover.

To understand more fully the severity of this social problem, the audience is presented with numerous scenes of bound women having their clothes ripped off, being slapped, whipped, and burned with cigarettes. The worst torture of all is the deeply ennervating score, an endless loop of Chinese parade music that would make Mother Teresa confess to robbing the church coffers.

American Film Distributing, maker of *White Slaves of Chinatown*, probably was unsure how this particular brand of sex show would play on grindhouse screens; it certainly didn't spend one penny more than necessary creating it. The film is shot in dingy tenement basements, mostly without any synchronous sound recording. Like many nudist camp movies before it, budgetary limitations are "hidden" beneath the verbose, sanctimonious, and non-stop narration. Of course, the paucity of production values was irrelevant. *White Slaves of Chinatown* was the guiltiest and seamiest of pleasures for sensation-seekers in the mood for something with a bit more sting than a roughie.

Olga (played by Audrey Campbell, the wanton mother of *Sin in the Suburbs*) proved so popular with the Raunch Row crowd that producer George Weiss (no relation to the Screen Classics producer out in Los Angeles) and director Joseph A. Mawra soon cranked out *Olga's Girls,*

Producers of *The Twisted Sex* called it "a completely authentic motion picture concerning the sexual psychopaths, erotic urges, and incontrollable lusts. An incredible analysis of the sexual corruption of our age, it is a MUST for every thinking adult." Henry (enjoying himself above) "finds pleasure and pain in the form of two beautiful women: becoming the victim of their strange ecstasies."

101

Kinky antics of the fifties seemed cartoonish when confined to the pages of mail-order fetish journals. Kinkiness turned nasty when it started appearing on big grindhouse screens in the sixties.

Olga's House of Shame, and *Olga's Massage Parlor*, each one sleazier than the last. Dozens of other "kinkies" — *Violated Love, Confessions of a Psycho Cat, Slaves of Love, Take Me Naked, Spiked Heels and Black Nylons, Love My Way, The Brick Doll House, Invitation to Ruin* — followed in Olga's wake.

Kinkiness didn't begin with these films, of course. Throughout the century there had been a niche for esoteric fetish material. Underground magazines such as *Bizarre* and *Exotique*, published in New York, offered fetish fantasies primarily to mail-order customers. The intense visual stylings of artists such as John Scott Coutts (who published *Bizarre* and created the bondage serial "Sweet Gwendoline" under the pseudonym John Willie) and fetish illustrators such as Stanton, Eneg, Jim, and Gene Bilbrew had a large, loyal — and clandestine — legion of fans. Irving and Paula Klaw, a brother and sister team, produced a staggering amount of fetish and bondage photos and films for mail-order sale through men's magazines. Much of it featured charming and vivacious Bettie Page, trussed up like a Cornish game hen or dangling from elaborate block and tackle in her silk undies. Klaw's brand of kinkiness extended to short films of spankings and scantily clad women wrestling.

Most fifties mail-order kink seems tame, even innocent, by today's standards. It was intended to satisfy a particular visual craving. But by and large, those stagey antics seemed more playful than harmful. That changed in the sixties, however, when the focus shifted from fetishism to fanaticism. Women no longer paddled each others' bottoms daintily — they laid on the whip with a wicked vindictiveness.

In kinkies, the battle for sexual power that underlies much erotica came surging to the surface, generally in stories predicated on dominance and submission. Typically, women spent most of the time submitting. But just as often, it was another woman meting out the discipline. In *Obscene House* and *Invitation to Ruin*, two *Olga* clones, the dominatrix on duty is a gargantuan "mama" — Fat Mamma and Mama Lupo, respectively. *Invitation to Ruin* blurred the line between kinky and ghoulie, so repulsive was its sadism. The insertion of a hot poker into a tortured woman's vagina is no less revolting for being performed off-camera.

On a rare occasion, such as *The Daughters of Lesbos* and *Slaves of Love*, the women dominated. In the former, a secret society of angry women meets weekly to recount all the sexual indignities they've suffered at the hands of brutish males. They exact revenge by castrating the janitor who tried to rape one of them. *Slaves of Love* depicts the not-uncommon boyhood fantasy of being help captive on an island by a band of sex-starved Amazons who don't stint on the whip when their demands go unsatisfied.

Just dipping a toe into the mire of aberrant psychology, it's fairly easy to see what was going on here. Along with the nastier thrills came a heavy load of guilt. To excuse their desire to see women subjugated, men preferred to witness a woman in the role of punisher, thereby distancing themselves from the sordidness. Payback was often taken to the extreme: plenty of kinkies climaxed with castrations, as though allowing women a slice of retribution for all the humiliation.

One producer who had no such qualms about his kinky product was Bob Cresse, who apparently never cast an actress he didn't want to whip. His most notorious film, *Love Camp 7* (1968), again relied on the exploitation

rubric of "Everything you are about to see actually happened." Cresse tells the tale of a Nazi concentration camp in which Jewish women are turned into sex slaves for the Reich. Despite bookending his production with as much historical military trapping as he could muster, the film was nothing more than a series of torture scenes in which the women suffer their lashings nobly until, in the last reel, they exact bloody revenge.

arm; nipple clamps; gouged-out eyeballs; the slow hanging death of a nude woman standing on a block of ice; another boiled alive in hot oil, and Ilsa urinating on a depraved Nazi general.

The opening square-up noted that the filmmakers were obligated to show the historical truth, and that the film was "Dedicated to the hope that these atrocities never happen again."

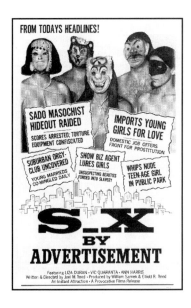

FROM TODAYS HEADLINES!

SADO MASOCHIST HIDEOUT RAIDED
SCORES ARRESTED; TORTURE EQUIPMENT CONFISCATED

IMPORTS YOUNG GIRLS FOR LOVE
DOMESTIC JOB OFFERS FRONT FOR PROSTITUTION

SUBURBAN ORGY-CLUB UNCOVERED
YOUNG MARRIEDS CO-MINGLED DAILY

SHOW BIZ AGENT LURES GIRLS
UNSUSPECTING BEAUTIES FORCED INTO SLAVERY

WHIPS NUDE TEEN-AGE GIRL IN PUBLIC PARK

S_X BY ADVERTISEMENT

Featuring LIZA DURAN • VIC QUARANTA • ANN HARRIS
Written & Directed by Joel M Reed • Produced by William Samek & Elliott R. Reed
An Instant Attraction • A Provocative Films Release

No, it's not the Red Hot Chili Peppers.

Filmmaker Joel M. Reed used the time-honored "Torn from today's headlines" come-on to promote his debauched kink-a-thon, *Sex by Advertisement*. It purported to be a documentary look at "the erotic phenomena of those who now advertise openly for their sexual outlet." Right — like the woman with the electrodes running from her nipples to a car battery. Reed departed kinky territory for the gorier realm of "ghoulies," producing what many people believe is the most tasteless film ever made, *Bloodsucking Freaks*, a. k. a. *The Incredible Torture Show.*

LOVE CAMP 7

Love Camp 7 was so successful on the grindhouse circuit that it inspired an even more grandiose knock-off. Although he disowns the film today, sexploitation maestro David Friedman — always looking to outdo his rival Cresse — accepted a deal from Canadian investors (*Love Camp 7* did incredibly well in the provinces), to produce a film called *Ilsa, She-Wolf of the SS*. The finished film didn't appear until 1974, after hardcore had been introduced, so to garner attention, Friedman pushed the kinkiness and ghoulishness to extremes.

Ilsa was shot on the sets of *Hogan's Heroes*, a popular TV sitcom about the hilarious hijinks in a Nazi prisoner of war camp. Sergeant Schulz never saw anything like this: castration within the first minute; a drunken gang rape; a victim impaled on an ominous electro-charged dildo; maggots inserted into the open wound on a prisoner's

Of course they did, in the sequels (not produced by Friedman) that soon followed — *Ilsa, Harem Keeper of the Oil Sheiks*, and *Ilsa, the Wicked Warden*. Dyanne Thorne, the Las Vegas showgirl who portrayed Ilsa, now has a devoted cult following.

Despite the fact that Ilsa is based on the very real Ilse Koch, "The Bitch of Belsen," who was executed by the International War Crimes Tribunal for "crimes against humanity," her exploits provided the basis for what's now considered a camp classic. That's attributable to several factors: Thorne dominated the proceedings with a haughty, over-the-top campiness; the production was low-rent enough to show its seams, which takes the edge off; the dialogue was intentionally hokey ("Once he has served her, it's the end of him as a man."), and, most crucially — a hip, ironic, post-everything attitude that can turn any piece of crap into a cult classic.

"You may find it incredible that two young American women would volunteer to throw themselves into the unspeakable indignities and horrifying humiliations of a Nazi Love Camp in order to serve their countries, but that is the truth of this story," declared the pressbook, adding the threatening note that "You will not live long enough to forget the things you will witness and experience inside Love Camp 7." To ensure authentic whip brandishment, producer Bob Cresse cast himself in the role of the sadistic commandant.

GHOULIES

When producer Harry Novak released *Lila* (1968), his promotion downplayed the story's sanguinary elements in favor of a straight sex sell. It bombed. The picture was re-released as *Mantis in Lace*, with ads showing star Susan Stewart in a sheer negligée wielding a meat cleaver and a dagger. It slayed 'em at the box office.

Mantis in Lace sprang from a perfect "ghoulie" recipe: take one topless dancer; combine with a series of horny men; add a dash of LSD; mix into a rough sex roux; stab the men with a screwdriver, dismember the bodies, sprinkle liberally in a vacant lot. Repeat several times, until police arrive.

As discussed at the start of this chapter, Herschell Gordon Lewis and David Friedman created the ghoulie when they cooked up *Blood Feast* and its sopping offspring. The distinction between a ghoulie and a kinky was often smeared and sticky. The trio of Box Office Spectacular bloodbaths fashioned by Friedman and Lewis, and the later gore films Lewis made on his own, were actu-ally progenitors of the "splatter" genre (*Friday the 13th* and so on) more than the sexploitation-based ghoulies.

From our subjective viewpoint, there are two distinctive aspects to ghoulies, besides the requisite sexual orientation: 1) there's an element of the macabre or supernatural, and/or 2) there's blood and death. (Kinkies deal in perversion, but typically stop short of butchery.)

Some ghoulies only used horror film trappings to spice up the sex. The Ed Wood/A. C. Stephen oddity *Orgy of the Dead* involves evil spirits who return from the grave with a compulsion to perform striptease routines. That's not a ghoulie, it's a goony. Other films use spooky dress-up to enliven the same old misogyny. *Scare Their Pants Off* tells a *Defilers*-like tale of two horny guys who get their kicks terrorizing and hypnotizing women into having sex with them. One woman is coerced into offering herself to a horribly disfigured man (actually one of the guys in a mask). In *The Last Step Down*, a group of men stage Aleister Crowley–type black masses, mesmerizing women into having lots of lesbian sex as prelude to straight phallic impalement.

Films like these offer a dark tease, but veer away from the edge of the cliff. *We're not satanists, we're just average horny degenerates.*

The serious cliff-divers were in Europe, where Spain's Jesus Franco concocted a slew of movies that splatter sex and sadism together with little regard for coherence. We'll restrict consideration of Franco to a recitation of some telltale titles: *Sadist Erotica, Kiss Me Monster, Necronomicon, Sadomania, A Virgin Among the Living Dead, Erotikill* — more than 200 body fluid festivals over the course of a 30-year career that has persisted into the 1990s. (Those seeking further edification as to the sadistic cinematic antics of the French, Germans, Italians, et al. are advised to peruse *Immoral Tales* by Pete Tombs and Cathal Tohill, which trods that territory in detail.)

Just another psycho stripper with a meat ax...

Mantis in Lace (a. k. a. Lila) was produced for $35,000 and had three different versions, with varying degrees of nudity and gore. As director William Rotsler told *Psychotronic Video,* each time star Susan Stewart chopped down with her meat cleaver "two fat guys in undershirts would toss up paper cups of fake blood." All the sex and violence was expertly lensed by esteemed cinematographer Laslo Kovacs, who'd later in the year shoot the groundbreaking *Easy Rider* for Dennis Hopper. *Mantis in Lace* is another sixties melange of sex, drugs, and gore that's become a "cult classic." Says Rotsler, "Yeah, yeah, and I haven't a clue why."

Back in the States, ghoulishness was depicted in strange items such as *Love After Death*, in which a man suffering from cataleptic fits is buried alive by his cheating wife and her lover. After breaking out of his grave, according to the plot synopsis, "he abducts a young woman and attempts to rape her in order to prove to himself that he has retained his manliness." Failing that, "he is beside himself with frustration, since his plans for revenge included the forced rape and torture of his wife when the time was ripe."

The most notorious practitioners of the ghoulie were the husband and wife team of Michael and Roberta Findlay. Under the name Anna Riva, Roberta Findlay started out performing in sex films, while Michael contributed his alarming incompetence behind the camera. One of their early bilious affronts was entitled *Satan's Bed* (1965), which featured a nearly mute Yoko Ono being variously raped and abused. The Findlay's grimy little niche in film history was achieved with the "Flesh" trilogy: *Touch of Her Flesh*, *Curse of Her Flesh*, and *Kiss of Her Flesh*, which ran the gamut of rough, kinky, and ghoulish antics. Their specialty was concocting inventive ways for nude women to be murdered: poisoned cat's claws dragged across a naked midriff, electrically charged earrings, razor-studded dildos, etc. They capped their ghoulish career with the infamous *Snuff* (1977), which earned for itself a isolated spot at the far end of the carnival midway, right down at the bottom of the huckster's barrel. Purporting to show the actual murder of a woman, the film was a fake; the Findlays concocted the whole thing out of an unreleaseable film they had shelved, after reading a story about an alleged "snuff" movie smuggled into the U.S. from South America. The media, as the Findlays planned, jumped all over the film and hyped it into a profitable scandal.

Michael Findlay's career had a bizarre denouement: heading for Europe to seek investors for a portable 3-D camera he'd devised, Findlay was decapitated by the propeller of a helicopter that crashed into the roof of the Pan Am building in Manhattan. Roberta later became one of the few sixties filmmakers to make the transition to hardcore pornography.

Ironically, it was ghoulies that had the easiest crossover path to legitimate theaters. Andy Milligan, who made a string of sex pictures quarantined to grindhouses, broke through to first-run theaters with product like *Bloodthirsty Butchers* and *Torture Dungeon*, which profitably played as R-rated features. Ivan Reitman, who'd go on to create one of the most successful movies of all time, *Ghostbusters*, christened his career with a jaunty AIP release called *Cannibal Girls*, which used the gimmick of an alarm bell to warn the squeamish of imminent bloodletting. Few censors batted an eye when American International, purveyors to American teens, began churning out films like *The House of Whipcord*, which maintained the sadism of kinkies and ghoulies, but ensured that any fleeting nudity was essential to the plot.

That violence was always more tolerable to mainstream audiences than sex once provoked Lenny Bruce to remark incredulously that Americans were more comfortable having their children see a man stab a woman's breast than kiss it.

The British are Coming, The British are Coming!

An overstatement, perhaps, but they were certainly breathing hard in 1963, when the UK was atwitter over the Profumo scandal, in which a pair of modish models-cum-prostitutes, Christine Keeler and Mandy Rice-Davies, revealed the sordid details of dalliances with political officials, including British State Secretary for War John Dennis Profumo. *The Christine Keeler Affair,* produced in tabloid Fleet Street fashion, cashed in on the story's two main features: the Cold War–inspired fear that the party girls were spilling state secrets to Communist moles, and the titillating revelation that some of Her Majesty's MP's liked to be paddled like naughty boys after a day of rigorous leadership.

The global magnitude of the scandal was such that the film was rushed into production even though its producers knew it wouldn't be approved for distribution in the UK. (England maintained rigid prohibitions against "morally questionable" films, in terms of both violence and sex.)

Two bits of cinema trivia: Profumo's stalwart wife, ValerieHobson, was a major British actress who had appeared in the horror classics *The Werewolf of London* and *Bride of Frankenstein*. The male star of *The Christine Keeler Affair,* John Drew Barrymore, was son of the legendary John Barrymore, and father of current actress/party girl Drew Barrymore.

Actress Alicia Brandet portrayed Mandy Rice-Davies in *The Christine Keeler Affair*. Mandy was for a time the most famous celebrity coquette in the world. The saga of Keeler and Rice-Davies was lurid enough to generate two films: *Scandal* (1989) was the glossier version, starring Joanne Whalley and John Hurt.

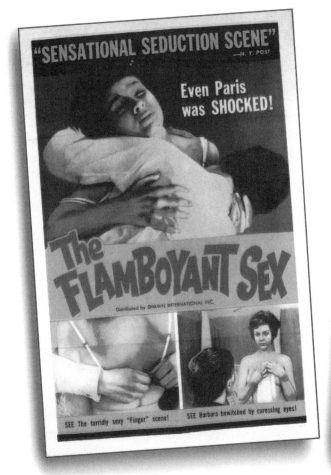

Compared with the volatile sex product in U.S. grindhouses of the mid-sixties, much of the imported European fare of the period seemed dated. Even a lurid campaign for *The Flamboyant Sex* couldn't convince potential patrons that it wasn't just another tame Continental concoction, pale in comparison with the grungier — but more immediately gratifying — American grindhouse product. *Red Lips* and *Love and the Frenchwoman* were mid-sixties imports that didn't fare particularly well trying to rekindle the market for "sophisticated sex" that French imports had pioneered a decade earlier.

Director Max Pecas even took a crack at making Elke Sommer the new Brigitte Bardot. He undraped the young German ingenue in a series of sex melodramas such as *Daniella by Night* and *Sweet Violence*. These films only became big draws on the grindhouse circuit *after* Sommer had been discovered by Hollywood. (Her biggest success being a co-starring turn opposite Peter Sellers in *A Shot in the Dark,* the second film in the *Pink Panther* series.) Following in the footsteps of Hedy Lamarr, Elke undressed less as her star status and bankability in Hollywood movies increased.

Carroll Baker, on the other hand, was a Hollywood starlet who went the reverse route...

Love is the tool that strips a jet-set widow bare of her morals and her millions!

Commonwealth United in association with Titanus Films presents

CARROLL BAKER
LOU CASTEL

PARANOIA

(X) **Persons under 18 will positively not be admitted. I D CARD REQUIRED**

Baby Doll Gets Kinky

Carroll Baker is a rare example of a performer plunging from the Hollywood firmament to the grindhouse demimonde. Combining a background as a nightclub dancer with training in the famed New York Actor's Studio, Baker emerged in the 1950s as a top shelf actress who never shelved her sex appeal. In her first major role, as Tennessee William's *Baby Doll* in the 1956 Elia Kazan production, she played a southern Lolita who slept in a crib and sucked her thumb in a most provocative manner. It inspired furious calls for censorship from the Legion of Decency. Although big name directors such as George Stevens *(Giant),* William Wyler *(The Big Country),* and John Ford *(Cheyenne Autumn)* cast Baker, they didn't really know what to do with a woman who could play smart and sexy simultaneously.

Producer Joseph E. Levine had no such problem. He tried to make Baker into the next Monroe, casting her in a pair of big budget sextravaganzas, *The Carpetbaggers* and *Harlow.*

But Baker, disillusioned by the Hollywood star-making machinery, left the studios at the height of her popularity, accepting instead lucrative offers from European producers. She also began doing nude scenes, which was at the time unthinkable for a major movie star.

Two such films made it back to the States in 1968, *The Sweet Body of Deborah* and *Paranoia (a. k. a. Orgasmo).* Baker claims that she made as many as four different films during this period that ended up being called *Paranoia.*

These were two of the very first films to carry the new Motion Picture Association of America "X" rating, under which the Hays Office's Production Code Administration was phased out in favor of multitiered warning labels assigned to each film. These pictures screened in a netherworld of second-run theaters that blurred the line between legitimate and grindhouse material.

In later years, Baker would continue to resurface in an eccentric array of roles, ranging from *Andy Warhol's Bad* (1976, in which she throws a baby out an apartment window) to Bob Fosse's *Star 80* (1983, playing Dorothy Stratten's mom) to such diverse later fare as *Ironweed* (1987) and *Kindergarten Cop* (1990).

By the late sixties, films previously relegated to the grindhouse started turning up in regular cinemas. Cambist Films, purveyors of grindhouse fodder, offered up *The Minx,* an X-rated drama "starring" Hollywood B-movie stalwart Jan Sterling. That the MPAA actually issued the X-rating, rather than totally ignoring Adults Only material, encouraged makers of sex films to attempt a crossover into legitimate theaters. All three New York dailies reviewed *The Minx,* and blurbs such as "Frankly erotic...unabashedly prurient and free of moral pretense," signaled a seismic shift in the way sex films were viewed by the media and general public. Controversy over the rating system would be further complicated as the decade ended, when *Midnight Cowboy,* slapped with an X due to its scuzzy subject matter, would win the Oscar for Best Picture.

Lessons Learned From Babb

Larry Buchanan was another filmmaker who turned away from Hollywood to pursue an independent career that frequently veered toward the grindhouse trade. Brought up from age four in a Baptist orphanage after his Texas Ranger father was killed, Buchanan ended up working as an assistant to legendary director George Cukor. When he returned to Texas to make the film *Naughty Dallas,* his course forever changed. Filming in Jack Ruby's Carousel Club must have infected him: his career would from then on be marked by an odd combination of sex and conspiracy, with a penchant for promotion gleaned from the likes of Kroger Babb.

Some ads for *Free, White and 21* (1962) were designed as subpoenas, summoning the audience: "Today Ernie Jones goes on trial. You will be the jury. Was it a criminal act or a case of consent? Since you as jurors must be adults and have mature minds, no children will be allowed. In order to render a fair and just verdict, you must see all the shocking evidence and intimate details from the beginning. The bailiff on duty will distribute ballots only to those jurors present at the beginning of each performance."

Under Age, released in 1964, encouraged exhibitors to include a lecture and a Q&A session, conducted by a community "expert on family affairs," along with the distribution of "appropriate literature." The campaign manual noted that "Without separating audiences by sexes, this is the same approach utilized in the exploitation of *Mom and Dad,* familiar to all exhibitors."

Under Age concerned a mother on trial for "raping" her 14-year-old daughter, i.e. forcing her to have sex with her boyfriend, so they would be "married in the eyes of God."

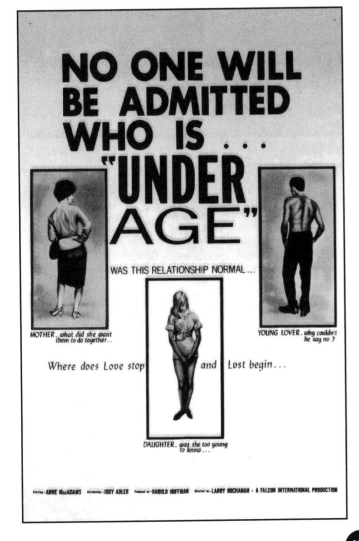

Note the same guilty, shameful pose adopted by each "victim" in these two Larry Buchanan movie posters. Do we detect a conspiracy?

Suburban Sin

Rough stuff wasn't confined to the big cities and backwoods. During the sixties, America's suburbs became a preferred location for plenty of Adults Only action.

While the vice racket films of the 1930s preyed on fears of unbridled urban development, by the sixties the trend was reversed. The middle-class exodus from the cities, and the desire for homogeneous suburban communities, inspired suspicion and dread that people "not like us," might move in down the street. Once again, the makers of Adults Only movies were poised to exploit the seamy underbelly of America's shifting demographics.

In the fifties, Hollywood had briefly considered the suburban revolution in films such as *The Man in the Gray Flannel Suit* and *Woman's World*. Adapted from bestsellers, these pictures presented a generally wholesome view of middle-class America's struggle for upward mobility. But the release of *The Chapman Report* (1962) changed all that. The potboiler detailed the bedroom shenanigans of suburbanites and changed the image of placid Maple Street from sleepy sanctuary to sizzling sleaze-pit.

In Adults Only suburbs, every barbecue culminated in drunken stripteases, bored housewives had luncheon trysts with neighbors' husbands (or each other), and organizied "swap meets" were the norm.

The depiction of sex in these movies, as in roughies, was circumspect. In a typical erotic encounter, the woman would doff her dress and slink to the sheets, clad in brassiere and half-slip, for some prolonged pawing with a panting partner. No specific acts were performed; lovemaking looked more like tentative wrestling practice. At some point in the tossing and turning, the brassiere would be removed, revealing the film's major plot points.

As for the men...it's fortunate that they often stayed clothed during sex. Perhaps these films were payback to all the dumpy chumps who could look, but never touch, the women in nudie-cuties. In sex films of the sixties, women rarely partnered with an attractive man. Rather, they had their choice of lecherous old conventioners, unkempt beatniks, paunchy businessmen, or dirty rapists. Handsome men were bound to be satanists. As raunchy as these films got, a puritanical streak still ran through them: Decent people didn't have sex. In the thirties and forties, sex stories focused on women struggling to retain their dignity by fending off sex-crazed men. In the suburbs of the sixties, however, it was women whose amatory impulses ran amok, presenting a challenge for their decent, social-climbing husbands and boyfriends.

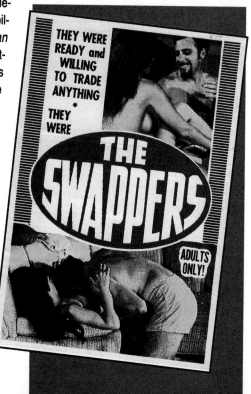

Biology professor Alfred Charles Kinsey's groundbreaking studies of human sexuality inspired numerous crass ripoffs over the years, this 1965 Albert Zugsmith production being just one of them. In addition to the "world renowned" Dr. Gladden, this film starred "two of the most beautiful girls of the teenage world," Lovey Song and Racey Tempo. Zugsmith was remarkably eclectic, producing films ranging from *Written on the Wind* to *High School Confidential* to *Touch of Evil* to *Sex Kittens Go to College*.

The standard-bearer of the genre is *Sin in the Suburbs* (1964), directed by prolific Joe Sarno. Excoriated from pulpits across America, the story depicts a daisy-chain of depravity in a cozy Northeast community. A wicked couple, pretending to be brother and sister so they can live in sin, find plenty of willing candidates for their sex cult. Plot lines converge at the cult, when an unloved teenage girl unwittingly winds up having sex with her wanton mother. Both wear Halloween masks and Druid robes during their final heart-to-heart confrontation.

Several aspects of the film put it a cut above its kin. The actors are all distinctive and entertaining, especially Woody Parker, who plays the ringleader. His seductive speeches, delivered in a gravelly, Harvey Fierstein baritone, are comedic and compelling. The women, all Jackie Kennedy wannabes, chug iced sour mash during the afternoon, and sexily peel out of their black Maidenforms. Sarno's minimalist sets are a time-capsule of early-sixties style, and the insistent jazz soundtrack, by Sam Fiedel, seems like one long riff of nasty high-hats and gutter brass, snake-charming all these sinners into debauchery.

Sarno claims the film was based on fact, and that he actually was allowed to witness the anonymous orgies that he (tastefully) depicts in the movie. Although it was a big hit on the Adults Only circuit, Sarno didn't earn much from it. The government ended up seizing the profits when it turned out that the producer, a vice president at the Manhattan–based 9th Federal Savings & Loan, had used embezzled funds to finance the picture.

A dignified city father lets his silver hair down during a lunch break with a loyal office worker in A. C. Stephen's *Motel Confidential* (1967). Born Stephen C. Apostoloff in Borgas, Bulgaria, the director fled from Communist internment in 1948, and ended up producing his own version of the tale, *Journey to Freedom*, for Republic Pictures in 1957. His career stagnated until 1965, when he crossed paths with Ed Wood, Jr. Together they created *Orgy of the Dead*, a ludicrous blend of striptease and low-rent horror. Sex films then kept both men afloat: between 1966 and 1969 Stephen produced *Suburban Confidential*, *College Girl Confidential*, *Bachelor's Dream*, *Office Love-In*, and *Lady Godiva Rides*. He and Wood united in the early 1970s for *Class Reunion*, *Snow Bunnies*, *The Cocktail Hostesses*, *Drop-Out Wife*, and *Fugitive Girls*. Wood had no qualms about eventually going hardcore, but Stephen demurred.

Sin in the Suburbs started Sarno on a long career, encompassing commercials, documentaries, children's films, and sex films both soft- and hardcore. If not all of them are memorable, some of the titles certainly are: *Warm Nights and Hot Pleasures; Come Ride the Wild Pink Horse; Scarf of Mist, Thigh of Satin; Passion in Hot Hollows,* and *My Body Hungers* are just several from a more than 20-year career.

Another notable creator of Adults Only fare from the period was Barry Mahon, who back-slid from a Hollywood career into more than 10 years of grindhouse fodder. A former RAF pilot during WWII, Mahon talked his way into superstar Errol Flynn's inner circle, and ended up as the actor's agent. A series of wild overseas deals culminated in an abomination called *Cuban Rebel Girls,* made on location with the cooperation of rebel leader Fidel Castro. It wound up being a nudie film, and marked the end of the dissipated Flynn's long Hollywood career.

It was only the start for Mahon, however, who became one of the most prolific makers of Adults Only films, churning out a seemingly endless run of movies with titles such as *Run, Swinger, Run, She Should Have Stayed in Bed, Sex Club International, Pagan Island, Prowl Girls,* and many more. Mahon made a cottage industry out of exploiting the name Fanny Hill, gleaned from a famous erotic novel. Following Albert Zugsmith's grandiose production of *Fanny Hill: Memoirs of a Woman of Pleasure,* Mahon squeezed out *Fanny Hill Meets the Red Baron; Fanny Hill Meets Lady Chatterley* (a lesbian frolic for two fictional characters), and *Fanny Hill Meets Dr.*

Erotico, in which the heroine brings Frankenstein's monster back to life and becomes his mother.

For several years, working out of a studio in Florida, Mahon produced children's films such as *The Wonderful Land of Oz, Jack and the Beanstalk,* and *Thumbelina,* while simultaneously making grindhouse product like *The Warm, Warm Bed, The Love Pirate,* and *PPS (Prostitutes' Protection Society).*

Marsha Jordan

Nobody faked it better than Marsha Jordan. Her ability to simulate sex passionately in a slew of sixties movies made her the undisputed Queen of Softcore Cinema. At a time when interchangeable actresses were paraded nude across grindhouse screens, she was the only woman to develop a devoted following.

A stewardess for Delta Airlines, she stumbled into the business when vacationing in Los Angeles in 1960. She had no qualms about doing Adults Only movies, because at the time it only meant that she had to show her body, not do anything particular with it. She looked like a corn-fed Faye Dunaway and projected a straightforward, likable personality.

Within a few years, Jordan was headlining films by all the major Adults Only producers. *The Golden Box, Lady Godiva Rides, Brand of Shame, Office Love-In, The Divorcée, Sweet Georgia, Her Odd Tastes, College Girl Confidential, The Head Mistress* — through them all Marsha performed make-believe sex with numerous men and women. She was generally paid between $100-125 per day, or $1,000 per week for her particular expertise.

Jordan often went on the road to promote her films, particularly in the Midwest and South. As she described in the book *Sinema*, "Maybe a little press conference and ads in the newspapers and TV saying I was going to be there signing or giving away 8 x 10 autographed pictures. And they would set up a little table with flowers on it in the lobby... They would say, 'Oh, you're the first real movie star I've met in my life.' And you'd want to laugh and know that you couldn't because most of them are real sincere."

It was an unexpected career for the granddaughter of a minister, who grew up in a Catholic convent, and cited John Wayne as her "ultimate hero." But she wasn't embarrassed by it, and proudly asserted, whenever asked, that she "made nude movies" for a living.

She left the business when hardcore undermined her softcore reign. "I've seen some trailers," she told interviewer Kenneth Turan, "and it's like a medical film, there's nothing left to the imagination." She guest-starred on *Gunsmoke* and an early *Star Trek,* squeezed the Charmin in a television commercial, then retired altogether.

Above and below, scenes from *The Head Mistress* (1968).

MONDO

Unusual, dare we say aberrant, behavior has always occupied a marginal place in American entertainment. Many of us grew up reading *Ripley's Believe It Or Not!:* "A man in Provo, Utah swallowed $157 in coins, then built a toothpick replica of the Eiffel Tower...actual size!" In the live version of *Ripley's,* the carnival freak show, you could marvel at the bearded lady, the two-headed fetus, and the chicken-gnashing geek. Even presentations as unsensational and high-brow as National Geographic nature specials uphold the queasy tradition: "...as they mate these ungainly storks will duel to the death, their honking cries a ghastly symphony."

What's the unifying theme? The world is weirder than you ever imagined, once you leave the comfort and safety of your home. The invention of the motion picture camera permitted everyone to realize that all around the world, animals abuse each other, humans abuse animals, and humans abuse themselves — and each other — in a non-stop frenzy of inexplicable behavior.

Happily for the curious but less adventurous among us, exploitation producers have always been willing to document the savage customs and witness the twisted rituals performed by isolated tribes, be they in the Belgian Congo or the Sunset Strip, and deliver them to the local grindhouse screen.

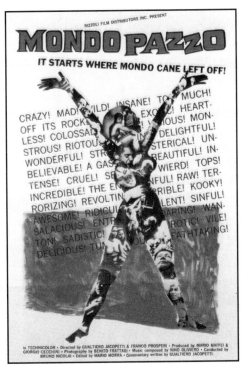

These fascinating films tend to raise more questions than they answer. The producers of *Macabro* (1966), for example, treated viewers to execution via python, Russian roulette with diesel trains, "strange jungle manhood rights," and other "secrets of the forbidden world." They then dared audiences to make the tough decisions: "Sick or bizarre? Gruesome or natural? Exotic or hideous? Bestial or interesting? Touching or disgusting?" In the shocking, strange-but-maybe-true realm of Mondo movies, there can be only one answer: "Judge for Yourself!"

Mondo movies, as they're now commonly known, are the ripe (and likely rotten) fruit that grew from the branches of the goona-goona tree. They depicted the bizarre behaviors of various species, with varying degrees of authenticity. These theoretically high-minded freak shows took their cue from a basic human need: to know what the neighbors are up to...even if those neighbors happen to be 10,000 miles away.

The prototypical example of the genre was *Mondo Cane*, an Italian documentary that became a surprise international hit in 1962, and even scored an Oscar courtesy of its melodious theme song, "More."

The film, which somehow was not retitled *Dogworld* for its American release, was written and directed by renegade foreign correspondent turned filmmaker Gualtiero Jacopetti. Even early in his career Jacopetti displayed a heat-seeking sensibility, when, in search of a story, he arranged to have himself smuggled into Vienna (off-limits then to Italians) in the locked trunk of a car.

In *Mondo Cane*'s opening narration, we are told that the curious vignettes to come are all true. "If sometimes they seem cruel," the portentous voice intones, "it is only because cruelty abounds on this planet." Gualtiero Jacopetti: journalist or carny barker? *Judge for yourself!*

Mondo Cane was a truly innovative and influential film, and not just because of its sensationalism. Jacopetti's style exhibited the core characteristics of what would become known as "gonzo" journalism; subverting objectivism in favor of an ironic, often sardonic, posture. He segues with panache from mourners at an American pet cemetery (fin-gers tracing lovingly the inscription on Rover's headstone) to preparations of canine cuisine at a Taipei restaurant (the chef deftly chopping portions of raw dogmeat).

Viewed today, Jacopetti's jump cuts, freeze frames, jaded attitude and jarring camerawork seem thoroughly contemporary. In fact, so do the tattoos, unfortunate coiffures, and body piercings.

Most of the subjects in *Mondo Cane*, in truth, are goofy. Imagine a town where all the men carry the genes (and pheromones) of legendary Latin lover Rudolph Valentino, or the tropic island where tribal tarts go light on the garments but heavy on the amatory appetites.

And so it went for all the Mondo films to come. In most cases, the response to the suggestion that you "judge for yourself" could only be "go figure."

How does one "judge" an Italian village festival in which revelers stock a garage with tons of food and drink, and then, to initiate a gastronomic orgy, men ram their heads through the doors ? (The bloody, concussed, and convulsing are carted off while the townspeople gorge themselves.) Who could know why female devotées choose to cleanse

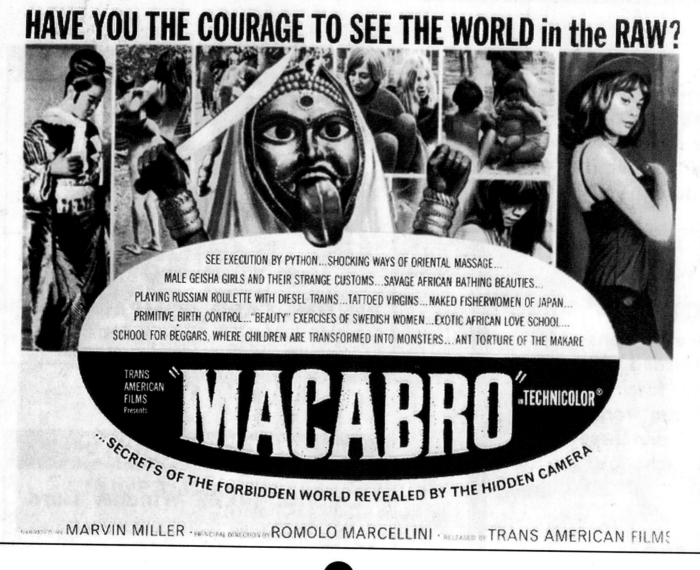

the stairway of a church with their tongues? Or what inspires a modern artist to use nude women, rather than brushes, to create a painting?

From cargo cults to cliff divers, the first Mondo films displayed an unrelenting fascination for strange human rituals and behavioral extremes.

By the mid-sixties, these "exploitation documentaries" were more commonly known in the trade as "See! See! See!" pictures, because of the midway-reminiscent pitches used to sell them. And many of them crossed over, from the grindhouse to first-run theaters and drive-ins. Joseph E. Levine, the drive-in theater magnate turned producer, was the man responsible for importing *Mondo Cane* and making it such a big hit. He followed it with another lurid goona-goona type film, *The Sky Above, The Mud Below*, which was doubly shocking to sixties audiences due to the full frontal nudity of some of the natives. (The old double standard was still firmly in place, even as a new civil rights bill was enacted throughout the land.) Levine, the man who started his producing career with *Hercules* and its countless clones, was once quoted as saying "I've never see a bad movie."

NOTHING HIDDEN IN THIS STRANGE WORLD!

WITNESS A BLACK MASS PERFORMED IN MANHATTAN BY PEURTO RICAN IMMIGRANTS

SEE THE LADY MUD WRESTLERS OF BERLIN IN A DECADENT EXHIBITION OF DEGRADATION!

LOOK AT THE POVERTY AND DISPAIR OF TIJUANA AS IT SPAWNS EVIL BEYOND DESCRIPTION IN HUMAN SLAVERY

WE DARE YOU TO SEE

THE SCENES IN THIS FILM ARE REAL- TOO REAL FOR THE IMMATURE!

ABSOLUTELY ADULTS ONLY!

mondo freudo (THE WORLD OF FREUD) IN COLOR

AN OLYMPIC INTERNATIONAL PRESENTATION

search of love," thereby putting Biff and Suzy on equal footing with the Balinese goona-goona smokers who started it all back in the early 1930s.

A vital component of Mondos was the element of the purportedly "hidden camera." All over the globe you could find crews practicing the new Mondo technique *cinema voyeur*: hanging around Spanish brothels until customers spilled out; probing around Pig Alley in Paris spying on hookers and their tricks; patiently waiting for a fight to erupt in a Hamburg bar; filming marine biologists throwing live animals into the water to attract sharks.

Mondo Freudo claimed to be "full of intimate, close-up scenes filmed without the subject's knowledge." And, indeed, how could they have known, when the pressbook asserts that some shots were taken "from as far as a mile away with the aid of a seventeen hundred millimeter telescopic lens."

In fact, plenty of this footage, particularly what was lensed stateside, was outright fakery. The bogus "hidden camera" claim was often camouflage for poorly lighted, badly shot footage of the producer's friends staging an erstaz Satanic mass in which topless women were ritualistically flogged.

Because of their penetration into legitimate venues, and the money these pictures raked in, name actors such as Vincent Price, Boris Karloff, and George Sanders were soon providing the worldly, resigned narration that was de rigeur for all Mondos. More exotic escapades and forbidden practices were showcased in *Macabro, Mondo Infame, Ecco*, and *Taboos of the World*. Other off-beat hobbies and habits were brought to light in "worlds" that were described (in the less-than-fluent Italian) as "rocky," "exotic," or "obscene."

Mondo movies soon lost all journalistic pretense, as stateside producers started cranking out their own product, issuing such deviant offspring as *Mondo Keyhole, Mundo Depravados, Mondo Teeno, Mondo Mod*, and *Mondo Topless* (Russ Meyer's personal take on the broadening trend).

Bob Cresse's Olympic International Films released the most outlandishly titled picture of the bunch, *Mondo Freudo*. This multicultural extravaganza featured not only "immigrant black masses" in Manhattan, but a "decadent exhibition of degradation" performed — as only they can — by the "lady mud wrestlers of Berlin." And proving that these productions never lost their timeliness or journalistic edge, the picture also documented "Freudian rites of American teenagers in

erstaz Satanic mass in which topless women were ritualistically flogged.

The black humor of Jacopetti's original rapidly evaporated under the crush of sensational spectale, some of it real, most of it not. Mondo films soon became single-subject documentaries such as *Prostitution and Pornography in the Orient*, or the mostly phony *Witchcraft '70*. There was even a Mondo-type film called *Manson*, claiming to be an exposé of life within the infamous cult. The Mondo ante was upped again in the 1970s, with the creation, and success, of a series of videotapes entitled *Faces of Death*, which brought gruesomeness and real-life bloodletting right into your home, courtesy of the VCR.

Of all grindhouse genres, Mondo movies have proven to be the most prescient and durable. Jacopetti's world, so exotic in 1962, is commonplace on television today — minus the irony and sarcasm. You can make your own Mondo movie by randomly running through the cable channels: *Cops*, infomercials, porno stations, wild-eyed evangelists, *America's Funniest Home Videos*, Jerry Springer, Rikki Lake, and *The Nightly News*. Provide your own Vincent Price narration.

Mondo Cane had it right, and so did *Mondo Pazzo*: the world is crazy and it's gone to the dogs.

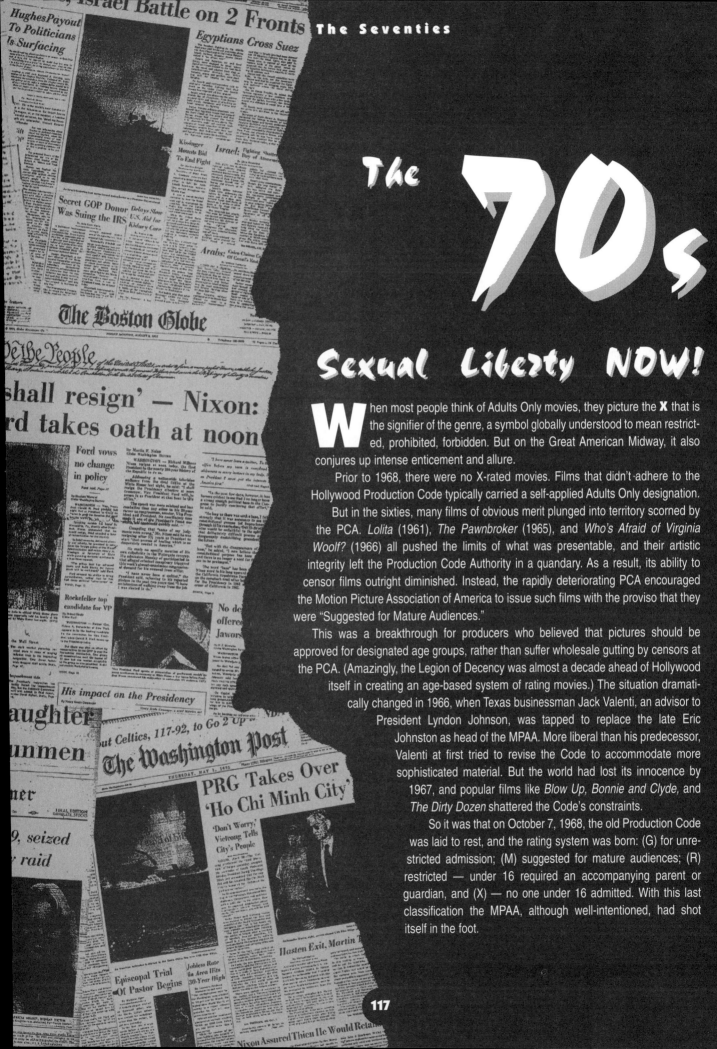

The 70s

Sexual Liberty NOW!

When most people think of Adults Only movies, they picture the **X** that is the signifier of the genre, a symbol globally understood to mean restricted, prohibited, forbidden. But on the Great American Midway, it also conjures up intense enticement and allure.

Prior to 1968, there were no X-rated movies. Films that didn't adhere to the Hollywood Production Code typically carried a self-applied Adults Only designation.

But in the sixties, many films of obvious merit plunged into territory scorned by the PCA. *Lolita* (1961), *The Pawnbroker* (1965), and *Who's Afraid of Virginia Woolf?* (1966) all pushed the limits of what was presentable, and their artistic integrity left the Production Code Authority in a quandary. As a result, its ability to censor films outright diminished. Instead, the rapidly deteriorating PCA encouraged the Motion Picture Association of America to issue such films with the proviso that they were "Suggested for Mature Audiences."

This was a breakthrough for producers who believed that pictures should be approved for designated age groups, rather than suffer wholesale gutting by censors at the PCA. (Amazingly, the Legion of Decency was almost a decade ahead of Hollywood itself in creating an age-based system of rating movies.) The situation dramatically changed in 1966, when Texas businessman Jack Valenti, an advisor to President Lyndon Johnson, was tapped to replace the late Eric Johnston as head of the MPAA. More liberal than his predecessor, Valenti at first tried to revise the Code to accommodate more sophisticated material. But the world had lost its innocence by 1967, and popular films like *Blow Up, Bonnie and Clyde,* and *The Dirty Dozen* shattered the Code's constraints.

So it was that on October 7, 1968, the old Production Code was laid to rest, and the rating system was born: (G) for unrestricted admission; (M) suggested for mature audiences; (R) restricted — under 16 required an accompanying parent or guardian, and (X) — no one under 16 admitted. With this last classification the MPAA, although well-intentioned, had shot itself in the foot.

Initially, the MPAA wasn't going to issue any rating beyond R. Valenti argued against the X brand, believing that the MPAA should clearly separate itself from independent producers who intentionally made Adults Only fare. But the National Association of Theater Owners wanted the MPAA to provide some legitimacy to Adults Only material, to protect exhibitors from arbitrary, and often costly, local prosecutions.

(They all remembered the protracted battle Louis K. Sher waged defending theater manager Nico Jacobellis in the infamous case of *The Lovers*.)

The MPAA decided to recognize the X rating, but not copyright it. That way, its review board didn't have to waste time considering films obviously designed for Adults Only: the makers could just self-administer the X rating. That was a mistake that would haunt the MPAA for years to come, as Hollywood productions ranging from *The Wild Bunch* (1969) to *Henry and June* (1990) struggled to overcome the misleading stigma of an X rating.

Nineteen sixty-eight proved to be a pivotal year in the history of cinematic permissiveness. It wasn't shaping up that way when Lyndon Johnson decided to form The President's Commission on Pornography in 1967 to conduct a study on obscenity. Twenty million tax dollars were allotted to a group of authorities so they could meet regularly, review stag movies, and determine, officially, what was "obscene." The absurdity of the endeavor was heightened when Richard Nixon assumed the presidency and appointed Charles H. Keating, Jr. to fill a vacant spot on the commission. Keating, founder of Citizens for Decent Literature, refused to attend any meetings, claiming that by its very existence, the group was promoting pornography.

The commission eventually issued a report asserting that state and local obscenity laws should be abolished, since there was no clear evidence linking the viewing of sexual material to deviant behavior. The commission stressed that enforcement should focus on preventing distribution of such material to minors, or to people who did not wish to view it. The summary, essentially, was: *Hey, it's a free country.*

Vilgot Sjöman's film is not for everyone. It may, as Vincent Canby of *The New York Times* suggested, "deeply disturb the emotionally right-wing moviegoer who has grown up in the comforting tradition of movie houses in whose ceilings little stars twinkled and clouds did everything but rain." If you are in favor of Franco's regime in Spain, some scenes of the film may irritate you. If you like your movies to come to you in a neat, tidy Hollywood package, you may not take to the film's stylistic experimentation so common to Europe's important new filmmakers. But if you are interested in what William Wolf of *Cue Magazine* calls "a landmark likely to permanently shatter many of our last remaining movie conventions." *I Am Curious (Yellow)* may be just for you. The Evergreen Film presented by Grove Press stars Lena Nyman. A Sandrews Production.

ADMISSION RESTRICTED TO ADULTS.

THEATER

That did not sit well with Commissioner Keating, who issued his own vitriolic minority opinion, asserting that the panel had created a "Magna Carta for the pornographer." Nixon, without reading the commission's full report, backed his appointee's opinion, despite the fact that polls showed more than 60 percent of the public believed Americans had the right to determine for themselves what was "obscene."

The President's Commission on Pornography, as a result of the Keating/Nixon impasse, changed nothing. Taxpayers had simply picked up the tab for the longest and most expensive "smoker" of all time.

Real changes in the laws governing obscenity would once again come through the courts, with yet another battle over an imported film.

I Am Curious (Yellow) is one of the three most famous Adults Only movies ever made, along with *The Immoral Mr. Teas* and *Deep Throat*. Yet it has so little in common with those two films that it seems absurd to group them.

I Am Curious concerns the efforts of a young woman, Lena Nyman, to forge her identity amidst the confounding political, social, and sexual turmoil of the late sixties. The film is strident, didactic, talky, unpleasant, bitter — and almost resolutely unerotic. It did, however, dare to treat sex unflinchingly. Intercourse, fellatio, and cunnilingus were suggested or simulated with what, for America in 1968, was alarming frankness. (In Sweden, where it was made, the film was restricted to patrons over the age of 15.)

Grove Press, a publishing house with a penchant for First Amendment battles, bought U.S. distribution rights to *I Am Curious*, with the full knowledge that it would be opening a Pandora's Box. From a business standpoint, it was almost essential that the film generate controversy, for there was no way that the average American would otherwise ever have sat still for a film so deeply concerned with the Swedish penal system. So when the Customs Service seized the first print of *I Am Curious (Yellow)* to enter the country, the big brouhaha was underway.

One could argue that the film was targeted because of its socially progressive attitudes, particularly its empathy with radical feminism. Ms. Nyman, who played herself, was a free-thinking challenger of the status quo, and her approach to sex was unlike anything that had ever been presented in an American-made film. She liked it; she wanted it; she had it. Sometimes it was good, sometimes not. How she felt about her partners seemed to have a bearing on her reactions.

Consider this testimony, given by film critic John Simon to attorney Edward DeGrazia during the film's obscenity trial at the U.S. District Court, Southern District of New York, in May, 1968:

Q: Are there other films that you know about and have seen exhibited in the United States which in their sexual aspects go as far as the sexual scenes of this film?

A: Well, in the explicit sense they don't go as far, but I think a film that implies a great deal might in some senses be said to go farther and farther in the direction of confusion, nasty insinuation, encouraging the viewer to fantasize and possibly supply indeed quite illicit things, where spelling out something might almost be said to my mind to be going less far, if by "going far" we mean overstepping some kind of sensible, healthy...kind of boundary. If by "going far" we mean going far in the direction of honesty and attempts to understand, then this one goes quite a bit farther...

Such interpretations were simply mind games to the prosecution. Sex was sex, and tender or terrible, it didn't belong on the movie screen. Here's Lawrence Schilling, assistant U.S. attorney, cross-examining Dr. Charles Winick, a professor of sociology at City College of New York and censorship consultant to NBC:

Q: Can you think of any other films which have the equivalent amount of emphasis on male and female nudity?

A: Well, I think it is necessary to take the overall intent and theme of the film. It is not really meaningful to take the amount of time devoted to nudity or sexuality and make judgments from that.

Q: Whether it is meaningful or not, I would appreciate an answer to the question.

YOU HAVE NEVER SEEN ANYTHING LIKE IT BEFORE!

This is the first film to enter the U.S. from Denmark since its liberalization of permissiveness!

REPRINTED FROM THE "HOLLYWOOD REPORTER"

'Without Stitch' Cleared by Trial; Ruled Not Obscene

Year's most clothesless film, the Danish import, "Without a Stitch," has been cleared for viewing by American audiences as a result of a finding by a seven man—five woman jury in U.S. Federal Court here that the picture, impounded by customs authorities, is not obscene as charged.

Verdict, following a five-day trial before presiding Judge A. Andrew Hauk, has been hailed as one of the few affirmations of constitutional freedom of expression guarantees without resort to appeal in higher courts.

"The pattern in obscenity cases has been that for the most part we have had to win on appeal," commented attorney Stanley Fleishman, who defended the movie. "There has been a large number of favorable decisions handed down in the Supreme Court and Appellate Court. This is one of the few instances where a jury found the material to be protected."

Victory for Jack H. Harris, president of VIP Distributors, which will release the film domestically, was rendered when the jury found against U.S. Customs attempts to have the picture "forfeited as obscene material."

without A stitch

introducing ANNE GRETE
(pronounced "GREAT!")
directed by ANNELISE MEINECHE
based on the novel by JENS BJØRNEBOE
Admission Restricted to Adults

Color by De Luxe

RATED (X)
Persons under 18 not admitted.

Danes Do It Too

Within months of all the *Curious* furor, distributor Jack Harris imported *Without A Stitch* from Denmark, capitalizing on that country's liberalized laws regarding sexual material. Based on a book by respected Norwegian novelist Jens Bjørneboe (which, ironically, was banned in Norway), the film was a lighthearted satire of current sexual trends. Star Anne Grete's name never appeared in print without a reminder that it was *"pronounced GREAT!"*

LEE HESSEL presents

RELATIONS
THE LOVE STORY FROM DENMARK

Starring GERTIE JUNG · Bjorn Puggard Muller · Paul Glargard · Produced by Sam Lomberg · Written and Directed by Hans Abramson

ADULTS ONLY   A Cambist Films Release InCOLOR

"NOW I'VE SEEN EVERYTHING."

"It combines all the qualities of 'Sister George,' 'Candy,' 'I, A Woman,' 'Belle De Jour,' and the rest of the sensual lot in one complete package.

Had me so thoroughly turned on it would be impossible for me to recall just what did happen."
—Beverly Hills Courier

From Sweden
A Cannon Production

"YES!"
(COUNT THE POSSIBILITIES)

GUNILLA IVANSSON
GUN FALCK
LARS LIND

Distributed By Cannon Releasing Corporation

THIS PICTURE RESTRICTED TO ADULTS ONLY

THEATRE

A: Certainly. Several of the Andy Warhol films, such as *Chelsea Girls* and a film like *I, A Woman* and *Love Affair* have perhaps as much, I would say, proportionately, nudity and non-marital sex and sex of a kind that is not traditional.

Q: You say perhaps as much, and you mentioned things other than nudity. Again, I would appreciate an answer to the question.

A: Well, addressing myself to nudity and sexuality, I would say that *I, A Woman* and *Love Affair* have approximately as much sexuality and nudity.

Schilling: Your Honor, I ask that that answer be stricken as unresponsive. My question dealt with the emphasis on male and female nudity and on the male and female genitals.

Judge Thomas F. Murphy: I think he answered the question.

The defense paraded psychiatrists, sociologists, ministers, writers (including Norman Mailer), and director Vilgot Sjöman himself before the jury, all arguing that the sex and nudity were in the service of ideas. The prosecution called only one witness, the Rev. Dr. Dan M. Potter, a Protestant cleric and censorship advocate. The jury deliberated two hours and upheld the Customs ban, branding the film obscene.

I Am Curious (Yellow) was thus instantly notorious, and had taken its first step toward profitability.

Months later, in 1969, a Court of Appeals overturned the earlier decision. Judge Paul Hays issued a written opinion stating that:

...although sexual conduct is undeniably an important aspect of the picture and may be thought of as constituting one of its principal themes, it cannot be said that "the dominant theme of the material taken as a whole appeals to a prurient interest in sex." Whatever the dominant theme may be said to be it is certainly not sex....*I Am Curious* does present ideas and does strive to present these ideas artistically. It falls within the ambit of intellectual effort that the First Amendment was designed to protect.

With that precedent established, *I Am Curious (Yellow)* was virtually immune from obscenity prosecutions. And at every turn, the bluenoses who railed against the film kept it alive. Without the tumult, it probably would have sunk like a stone, so far removed was it from what the American general public wanted in its movies. But the furor over illicit acts resulted in huge initial grosses wherever it played. The picture didn't have "legs," however, once word got around that it was boring and unsexy. Its second installment, *I Am Curious (Blue)* generated little interest.

But its legacy was evident early on. *I Am Curious* broadened the limits of what was permissible on-screen. Penises could be shown, although erections prodded the boundaries of tolerance. The awkward groping and wrestling of the sixties would be replaced by more defined and explicit (if still simulated) sex acts. The reality of intromission and ejaculation were the only taboos left.

The success of *I Am Curious (Yellow)* was, in truth, based entirely upon its name. Although Sjöman had meant the title to reflect his protagonist's incessant questioning of the status quo, it surpassed any enticing title Adults Only producers had conceived. It was mysterious and titillating, a perfect example of a carnival come-on. Once the grindhouses got hold of this trend, all things Scandinavian suddenly seemed salacious. Swedish pancakes and Swedish massage and Swedish-designed furniture all assumed a prurient patina.

So it was that the 1970s were ushered in with a tidal wave of sex films, some imported, some homegrown, but all equating themselves in some way with the notorious Swedish import.

America Answers

The Curious Female was only one of a slew of films that cashed in on the public's obsession with *I Am Curious (Yellow)* and Swedish sexuality. There was also *Love, Swedish Style, Sexual Customs in Scandinavia,* and *Sweden, Heaven and Hell,* an Italian production released stateside by Avco Embassy Pictures. From the pressbook: "The publicity attendant to Sweden's *I Am Curious (Yellow)* will doubtless boost the appeal of this import among those craving voyeurism, Swedish style. This is not to say that *Sweden, Heaven and Hell* is as explicit as *Curious,* but it's definitely 'dirtier' in tone and intent, and boasts even more provocative angles."

The first films to show sexually explicit material — the real thing, not simulated — were facetiously known in the trade as "white coaters." Taking a cue from the Scandinavians, producers showed sex as a normal and healthy aspect of life, validated by a doctor who presided over the graphic lovemaking, wearing a white lab coat and brandishing a clipboard.

A classic example of this type of film is *Man and Wife*, produced in 1970 by the "Institute for Adult Education." (You know the one, on Hollywood Boulevard.) The head of the Institute, Matt Cimber, had impeccable credentials: he was the former husband of Jayne Mansfield. In *Man and Wife*, two couples, sharing the goal of improving modern marriages, display about 40 different positions in which they have intercourse. Cimber followed this up with the daring *He and She*, which did not pretend that the coupling duo were husband and wife. Special mention must be made of the purple prose with which Cimber attempted to sanctify his "dirty" movie:

He and She is about one young man — who is all young men; one young woman — who is all women. The people of the streets whom they move amongst is the world of today. Your world, their world. They are like islands unto themselves, their mutual love a verdant, emerald green freshness rising from the sea of humanity... Love has its own special language. The language of silence. His eyes have glimpsed paradise, his love, worthy of the name.

Cimber had his own special language, as well.

With his next release, *Africanus Sexualis (Black Is Beautiful)*, Cimber co-opted 30 years of goona-goona films in which blacks were embarrassingly presented as being akin to jungle animals. In this picture, the same associations were made, but with a new, positive, seventies spin: black males were more "in touch" with their natural selves. Lusty sexual urges, the film asserted, made "the modern black man the happiest, best-adjusted of all humans." African-Americans responded to Cimber's obvious sincerity, helping him turn a strong profit.

A "white coater" of special note is *Sexual Communication*, which featured an actual doctor, Sheila Rossi, Ph. D., as a counselor who puts her money where her mouth is, so to speak, by actually performing, in unsimulated close-ups, various demonstrations of masturbation, fellatio, and intercourse with a pair of sexually dysfunctional couples seeking therapy.

Another similar film is *Together* (1971), which encouraged hip and happening people to experience healthier sex lives through sensitivity training. Although it was a modest hit, its creator, Sean Cunningham, soon learned that the real money was in spilled blood, not semen. His series of *Friday the 13th* splatter films would later earn him a fortune.

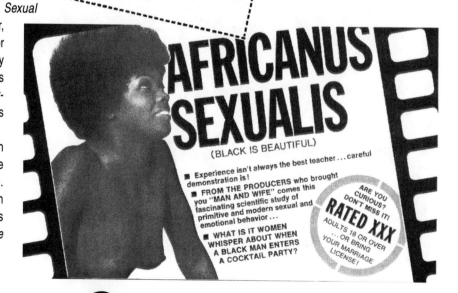

The amusing bit of promotion at left is from the 1970 release *Sexual Freedom in Denmark*, made by American John Lamb, whose 1965 film *The Raw Ones* was the first to show full frontal nudity (minus any sexual contact).

Swingtown, USA

The liberal attitudes of the Scandinavians invaded the cinematic suburbs of the seventies much like the "reports" of Kinsey and Chapman had in the early sixties. Only this time around, there was significantly less "sin" in these suburbs. Guilt and shame were out, man. Pleasure was in. *Can you dig it?*

Exhibitors had a field day. Not only were they virtually immune from local prosecutions thanks to the MPAA's new X rating, but they didn't have the Catholic Church to worry about anymore. The Legion of Decency hadn't survived the sixties. Its downfall was brought about by *The Pawnbroker*. The Legion had chosen to condemn that film for its brief flashes of nudity, and in so doing, seemed to trivialize a picture that was almost unanimously praised as one of the most ambitious, thoughtful dramas Hollywood had ever attempted. Even Episcopal bishop James Pike praised the film *and* its tasteful handling of the nudity.

Sensing that the Legion was an anachronism, the Church reformed the organization, mixing professional laypeople and students in with the members of the International Federation of Catholic Alumnae who acted as reviewers. In 1965 the Legion of Decency became the National Catholic Office of Motion Pictures (NCOMP). That organization, and its unfortunate acronym, would be dissolved once the MPAA adopted its ratings system.

By the early 1970s outcry against sexually explicit movies had little effect. The new permissiveness on America's movie screens was the result of an odd synergy between a rapidly maturing generation emerging from the rebelliousness of the sixties, and an older generation of exploitation producers looking to cash in on this younger crowd's liberal attitudes. Although the new crop of Adults Only movies was about young, fresh-faced swingers, it was grizzled old exploiteers who still ran the business.

The Very Friendly Neighbors, directed by old warhorse Albert Zugsmith, was a perfect example of this new twist on the suburban genre. Advertisements blared:

"THEY try extra-marital affairs.
THEY try wife-swapping.
THEY try many partners.
THEY try communal marriages.

THEY are a new generation of young adults who are dedicated to pleasure-seeking. Is theirs a NEW MORALITY? Or is it as immoral and decadent as the critics and censors say? NOW the Supreme Court has ruled in your favor. NOW YOU can see for yourself. NOW YOU can be the JUDGE!"

According to the garbled pressbook, "Our present day society has fostered upon the middle income groups the necessity for extra-sexual expression in line with their income."

David Friedman's Entertainment Ventures Inc. jumped on the bandwagon and drove it to a "swapping center" in *Love Thy Neighbor...And His Wife,* which, in his inimitable style, he described in ad copy as "A Blow By Blow Description of the D-Generation!"

Friedman's synopsis of the film all but sums up the typical bill of fare in a swingin' seventies sex romp:

"Cadillacs, speedboats, dune buggies, split-level homes, vacation hideaways, and beautiful and passionate wives mark the "D" generation. Boredom and a ready willing-

The enticing all-American look of this Swinging Wife was just a promotional ruse to bait U.S. audiences. She never appeared in the film, which was made entirely in Germany. A bogus sex documentary crossed with a nudie-cutie, it asked the question: "How thin is the line that separates a nymphomaniac from a housewife?"

Swinging Wives

IN VIVID COLOR

ADULTS ONLY

ness to try anything characterize these 'beautiful people.' A prominent attorney, his client and their wives weekend at a lakeside cottage. Inhibitions vanish as the liquor gushes and stag movies are shown. Lovers are exchanged. No holds are barred. The wives experiment between themselves. Across the lake, a trio of college co-eds, accompanied by a comic but lecherous professor, have rented a cabin. Two raunchy nomads have invaded the vacation paradise. Lured by the sweet smell of burning grass, the co-eds soon acquaint themselves with the roughies. Much action follows. The two groups meet at a cozy tavern. Initial hostilities soon disappear and the inevitable orgy ensues. *Love Thy Neighbor...And His Wife* is a study of friendship and sharing."

Producer Matt Cimber shelved the white lab coats and clipboards long enough to take his stab at the swinger genre, with *Love Me, Love My Wife,* which asked the age-old question "Why do some women want to watch their husbands make love to another woman?" One-time Hollywood ingenue Pier Angeli "sheds her innocence with a vengeance," as the "innocent pawn" in this tawdry X-rated offering that "graphically portrays three beautiful people in a sensual love pact."

Orgy, American Style combined suburban swingers with a parody of the popular television comedy anthology *Love, American Style.* The film starred Sharon Kelly (billed as "The New Marilyn Monroe"), a striking redhead who'd have a long career in X-rated films under her real name, Colleen Brennan. The most notable aspect of this Carlos Tobalina production is the mangled grammar of its advertising: "What is the maximum task for masculinity?" the promos ask. "Why do women swing and how many ways are there to enjoy the social pleasures? The whole shocking reality presented with detailed clarity."

Then there were the "Wife" films: *Suburban Wives* ("There's a lot you can do in an eight-hour day...and they did it!"), *Lonely Wives* ("Just Because You Ignore Your Wife...Doesn't Mean Somebody Else Does!") *Swinging Wives* ("I Do...Is Just the Beginning!"), *The Executive's Wives* ("Your promotion is simple...The boss makes it, or you don't...And you pay your dues with YOUR WIFE!"), to cite just a handful.

The genre spilled over into R-rated fare, from the popular Paul Mazursky film *Bob and Carol and Ted and Alice,* to less successful gems like *Group Marriage.* Trans American Films, producers of *The Swappers* (1970), issued bogus news stories with their press kits, which referred to (uncredited) surveys indicating that the flourishing new fad of mate-swapping was "not made up from homosexuals, perverts, or free-love advocates, but normal married couples, accepted in all social levels operating through secret and highly organized clubs." Its catch line was a howler: *Remember when all the guy next door wanted to borrow was your lawnmower?*

Hollywood Swinging

Swinger movies were not merely figments of producers' imaginations. Publications like *Swinger World* became common in the early 1970s, complete with region by region listings of people seeking casual sex. Examining the cover of this issue, two things become perfectly obvious: 1) it must have been intense embarrassment over their clothes that drove people into nude encounters, and 2) lesbianism as a lifestyle choice can be traced directly to this guy.

"Love Thy Neighbor" became the most overused catchphrase in the swingers' genre. But take a closer look at the ad to the right. It's not for a movie at all. It's an ad for a singles apartment complex that actually ran in the *Denver Post* in 1973. Ah, those were the days: every unit came with hanging macramé plant holders, a fondue pot, orange shag carpeting, and a lecherous leisure-suited Lothario in the next apartment.

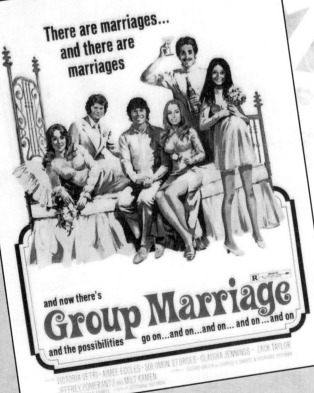

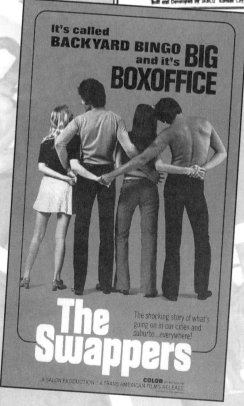

Reefer Madness Redux

One of the most popular films on the midnight movie circuit of the 1970s was *Reefer Madness.* But in re-release the moldy oldie was hooted at by college students sharing a doobie in the darkened theater. Some enterprising young exhibitors, cracking into the theater business with garage-sized revival houses or college campus cinemas, had learned that the copyright on the old anti-weed movie had expired and not been renewed. *Reefer Madness,* the campiest of many titles used over the years for the original *Tell Your Children,* became more popular as a comedy than it had ever been as the cautionary melodrama it was meant to be.

Dwain Esper, outraged at being ripped off, paid kids five dollars for every new poster they'd bring him advertising a screening of "his" movie, and he'd comb the trade sheets for news about upcoming screenings. Esper, who had stolen from everybody in his heyday, was amassing evidence for the lawsuit he imagined bringing against this new generation of thieves. It never happened, and the whole episode proved to be a pathetic coda to Esper's notorious career.

Reefer Madness was just the ironic apex of the big comeback of drug use in Adults Only movies during the early 1970s. Now, however, the "square up" had disappeared. The daffy demises of dope-smokers that climaxed vice racket and JD films in earlier decades were missing from the third act. Not that marijuana didn't serve the same function in 1972 that it did in 1936 — getting the girls out of their clothes, and making them lose all inhibitions. But the youth of the seventies didn't want to trash apartments and auditoriums; they wanted to tune in, turn on, and drop their drawers for a love-in.

Although the free love- and LSD-infused Haight-Ashbury might seem a world apart from the suburbs, they were two sides of the same coin to the makers of Adults Only movies. Hippies and social-climbing professionals shared the same goals in the world of the grindhouse: get naked and go at it. And grindhouses offered a bizarre bridge across the generation gap: it's where Dad, the

Poster art for *The Wild Scene* (left) had it all working. "From Berkeley to Woodstock... Today's Explosive Revolution Exposed in Uncensored Action and Dialogue!"

guy most repulsed by the rebellious antics of America's hippie culture, paid several dollars to see just how free all that love really was.

The irony was pervasive and a bit unsettling. In interviews, many sex film actresses assert that they got into the business, not for money, but as a reaction to being unloved, particularly by their fathers. Grindhouses of the early seventies were filled with fathers viewing their worst nightmare: their "daughters" having sex with unemployed, draft-dodging, scraggly-haired hippies.

Some exhibitors learned to exploit both age groups. San Francisco–based Harold Greenland, who operated a chain of grindhouses, bought product from young art school filmmakers, provided they'd insert the requisite amount of sex. His advertising pulled both the raincoat crowd and hipsters looking for "cutting edge" experimental cinema. He titled one film *Underground* (attracting the arty types) and in ads used a drawing of a man and woman crawling out of a sewer (a none-too-subtle tipoff as to the potential for depravity).

Love-In '72, distributed by New York sex movie maven William Mishkin, brought together all the pressing issues of the day. "Steve Hilton has just arrived at the Community, a Canadian hideout of American hippies, runaways, and draft dodgers," explains the pressbook. "Being one of the latter, he is shocked at the aura of promiscuity and the lack of political fervor he finds. He is befriended by Sunny, one of the most voluptuous members of the Community..." Mandala-print wall hangings, yarrow stalks, love beads, "The spirit of total liberation is especially evident during the Community's Love-In (Orgy) where not only does 'anything go' but it goes on completely in the open." The action, ads promised, was "more explicit than anything from Denmark!"

While films from the West Coast typically displayed a loopy acid-

"Come Along With a Blonde On a Trip You'll Never Forget!"

"Blonde on a Bum Trip"

ADULTS ONLY

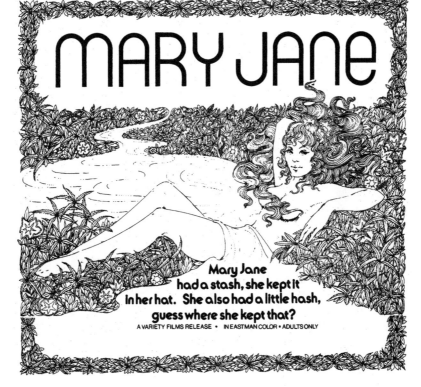

Mary Jane had a stash, she kept it In her hat. She also had a little hash, guess where she kept that?

A VARIETY FILMS RELEASE · IN EASTMAN COLOR · ADULTS ONLY

fueled faith in the healing powers of sexual liberation, New York–based films, such as *Blonde on a Bum Trip,* hewed closer to the old *Reefer Madness* formula: "It didn't start out as a sex exploit film," exclaimed the ad copy, "it just ended up that way! Director Ralph Mauro, guiding his camera and crew among the hippie 'pot-holes' of New York, discovers the psychedelic sadism, lust, & mutilation!" Validating the film's authenticity, viewers learned that LSD stood for "Lovely, Sexy, and Dangerous." *Alice in Acidland, Wanda the Sadistic Hypnotist,* and *Depraved* were other films that used LSD as the pretext for wild sex displays. There were also plenty of Mondo-style drug epics, such as *Wild Hippy Orgy* and *The Evil Pleasure.*

Plenty of R-rated product explored the drug culture, as well. Jack Nicholson was an acid-head in *The Trip* and *Psych-Out* before he got famous pretending to smoke dope for the first time in *Easy Rider.* A rock and roller rides the youth revolt to the presidency and gets Congress stoned in *Wild in the Streets,* and Groucho Marx and Jackie Gleason trip in Otto Preminger's utterly bizarre *Skidoo.*

But the "revolution" in sex, drugs, and rock and roll provided the biggest boon to X-rated producers. Whereas in the bustling days of 1960s sexploitation, performers were often fledgling professional actors, the early 1970s saw an influx of free-spirited "talent" more interested in the sex than the acting. Appearing nude on-camera was another form of rebellion against uptight society. Haight-Ashbury's cultural influence on San Francisco was directly responsible for that city emerging as a hotbed of hardcore filmmaking in the early 1970s: there seemed to be an endless supply of groovy hippie chicks wearing nothing but the flowers in their hair, who'd have sex on-camera in exchange for some really good dope.

"Get a good grip on your popcorn!

He'd created the nudie-cutie and he'd mastered the roughie, so in 1968, seeking his next milestone, Russ Meyer decided to produce the most erotic picture of all time. No peek-a-boo teasing, no frenetic comic book–style melodrama, just the real goods: straight-on, hard as a rock, bang the bedpost sex.

Of course, in a Russ Meyer film, straight-on sex revolves around hijackers,

RUSS MEYER'S **VIXEN** IS A "**SMASH HIT**" Newsweek *Sex and the Arts*

RUSS MEYER'S **VIXEN** COULD VERY WELL BE THE MOST EXPLICIT FILM EVER MADE. ROGER EBERT *Chicago Sun Times*

RUSS MEYER'S **VIXEN.** X RATING

INTRODUCING **ERICA GAVIN** AS VIXEN RESTRICTED TO ADULT AUDIENCES IN **EASTMANCOLOR** PRODUCED AND DIRECTED BY **RUSS MEYER** AN **EVE** PRODUCTION

draft-dodgers, raging rednecks, ideological battles between democracy and communism, miscegenation, incest — all of which, in the end, wither under the onslaught of nature's most powerful force: rampant female sexuality.

Vixen, starring Erica Gavin as the sex-obsessed wife of a Canadian bush pilot, was the first American-made Adults Only film (it carried one of the first X ratings) that could be called a gender crossover hit. In addition to the usual clientele, *Vixen* proved

surprisingly popular with women. Meyer's simple explanation for this is that his film was the first sex picture in which a woman "called all the shots." Like *Faster, Pussycat! Kill! Kill!* it struck an off-kilter blow for women's liberation. Erica Gavin's character may have been an affront to normalcy (she does, after all, have sex in the shower with her brother) but it's clear that Meyer loved his Vixen; she was his kind of woman.

She was not, however, Charles Keating's kind of woman. Citizens for Decent Literature, a Keating-founded organization, attacked the film as the foremost example of the morally debilitating filth that was corrupting American society. Keating's group solicited donations from the pious to keep such smut off movie screens. Meyer ended up spending $250,000 in legal fees defending, not only *Vixen*, but the public's right to view whatever it wanted.

While such unexpected costs would have eaten all the profit of some Adults Only movies, for Meyer they were only an unfortunate nuisance. That's because the public, despite Charles Keating's strident assault on its First Amendment rights, lined up behind Russ Meyer at the box office. *Vixen* became, on a profit to cost ratio, one of the most successful motion pictures ever made: Meyer had spent $72,000 getting his vision of erotica on the screen. People paid more than $7.5 million to see it, grossing for Meyer more than $104 for each dollar invested.

(In the blue corner, Russ Meyer: produces films that show well-developed people engaged in simulated sex acts and charges free-thinking people several dollars each for the viewing pleasure. In the red corner, Charles Keating: curries favor with influential politicians to deregulate banking laws, with the result that he is eventually convicted of bilking elderly people out of their life savings through fraudulent investment schemes. Which man is morally corrupt? *Judge For Yourself!*)

Darryl Zanuck, then chairman of 20th Century–Fox, believed that Meyer's smooth handling of erotic material would translate to Hollywood product. He and Meyer entered into a multi-picture deal, and the renegade filmmaker soon found himself in charge of a whole battalion of unionized grips, gaffers, and gofers, producing *Beyond the Valley of the Dolls* (1970).

The film, based on a screenplay by critic Roger Ebert, would be the quintessential Russ Meyer movie were it not for the aberration of a large budget ($2 million), grand sets, and sprawling cast.

Although the original story borrowed characters from Jacqueline Susann's tawdry bestseller, the author's threat of a lawsuit forced changes to the script that made the film uniquely Meyeresque (Meyerian?). The tale of a female rock-and-roll band groping its way through the sex- and drug-saturated Hollywood scene provided Meyer with a sturdy premise from which he could launch all sorts of satiric sorties and rambunctious sexual tomfoolery.

"It's a blending of violence, melodrama, hoke, parody, satire, [and] really unbridled sex, the kind of sex people fantasize about," is how Meyer described his style to Kenneth Turan in the latter's book, *Sinema*.

At the time, critics were uncharitable; they'd lambasted the film version of *Valley of the Dolls*, a turgid and lugubrious bitch-fest, so there was no way they'd approve of a "rip-off" by a nudie director. But Meyer and Ebert had the last laugh, for *Beyond* holds up as a mad and macabre comedy more than 25 years later. It's as though Meyer possessed a quirky prescience when making the film, mocking things that most people hadn't yet grasped in 1970 as ripe targets for social slapstick. It's the secret of Meyer's success: he makes films that are already parodies of themselves, so the joke just gets funnier with age.

Unfortunately, his second film for 20th Century–Fox, an adaptation of Irving Wallace's *The Seven Minutes*, was a disaster. Meyer tried to relate the anti-censorship theme of the book, but without a sufficient amount of sex and violence to splash around, the film seemed to drain Meyer of his essential bodily fluids. When Richard Zanuck, Darryl's son, was booted out at Twentieth, Meyer, too, was cut loose.

Returning to independent filmmaking, Meyer was faced with a dramatically altered marketplace. Hardcore had started to take hold in the grindhouses, and in legit theaters Marlon Brando was having buttery anal sex in *Last Tango in Paris* (1974). The originator suddenly was the odd man out. Meyer refused to go the hardcore route because he found it too lazy; there was little imagination, no wildness, just the jarringly unarousing spectacle of genitalia, up close and sadly impersonal.

Meyer took a run at crashing the growing market for blaxploitation films with *Blacksnake* (1972), but the film got lost in limbo between white and black audiences. So, rather than try to calculate the market, Meyer returned to his own unique formula. *Supervixens* (1975), *Up!* (1976), and *Beneath the Valley of the Ultravixens* (1979) were Chuck Jones Roadrunner cartoons for adult boys, filled with crazy crackers, Dudley Do-Rights, and nefarious Nazis spinning like dervishes around an ever-broadening bevy of balloon-breasted beauties.

By the 1980s the formula had run out of gas, and Meyer stopped making pictures. He became the Orson Welles of sex films, grandly talking of plans for his ultimate epic, but only shooting in fits and starts. The man once blamed for corrupting American morals could no longer pull an audience. His vision of sex was too tame, too straight, and too light-hearted at its core. Today, he can relish his legendary status, although it means that the times have passed him by.

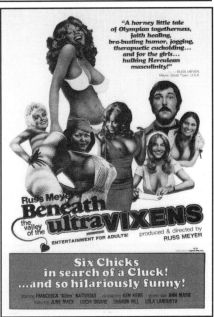

Mr. Novak's Sex Factory

Harry H. Novak was, not to put too fine a point on it, the Louis B. Mayer of sexploitation films. Quantity, not quality, was the name of the game. If you thought one of his films was a low-brow, slapdash exercise in crudity, spiced with T & A — you only had to wait a couple of weeks for another one just like it.

Novak understood the market and never spent one nickel more than necessary to get a film produced and into the theaters. From the Los Angeles–based headquarters of Boxoffice International Productions, Novak kept a keen eye on the industry, reading trends. If *The Godfather* looked like a sure hit, he'd be ready with *The Godson.* When *The French Connection* took off, Novak answered with *A Scream in the Street,* about "The Brave Men Who Put Their Lives on the Line to Break...The Connection!" The latter film is about a rapist, however, not drug dealers.

Novak's specialty was selling and distributing movies, not making them.

He began his career with RKO in the 1950s, designing advertsing campaigns. When the studio went belly up in 1957, Novak landed at National Film Service, where he learned the ropes of distribution. In the early sixties he took his first steps toward independence, acquiring a pair of nudie-cuties, *Mr. Peter's Pets* and *Knockers Up!* for distribution.

A diligent penny-pincher, Novak started out shooting on "short ends," without direct sound recording. His first big success came with the goofy, low-budget monster-nudie *Kiss Me Quick!* (1964), directed by Pete Perry and photographed by the young Laszlo Kovacs. The film's combination of sophomoric humor (an alien named Sterilox comes to earth to abduct women — strippers, of course — for his home planet of Droopiter, but he ends up at the castle of Dr. Breedlove, who mesmerizes women into sex slaves) and "soft" nudity would become a Boxoffice International staple.

Over the next 10 years, Novak mastered the business of churning out sex-saturated imitations of Hollywood movies on minuscule budgets, and squeezing the maximum profit out of them with lurid, tantalizing ad campaigns. Crime thrillers, roughies, Swedish sex education knock-offs, ghoulies,

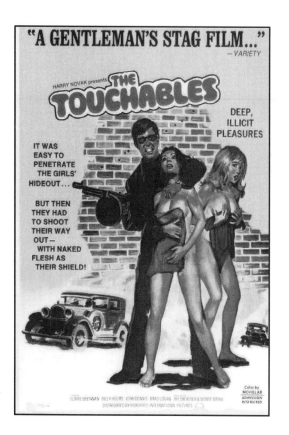

Fans of Harry Novak like to say he had the "Midas touch," because he could make money in any genre — as long as there was sex. *Four Kinds of Love* (1968) was sincere erotica Swedish style; *The Touchables* (made in 1961 but rereleased by Novak in '66) was a gangster send-up, and *The Takers* (1971) was a rape-filled roughie.

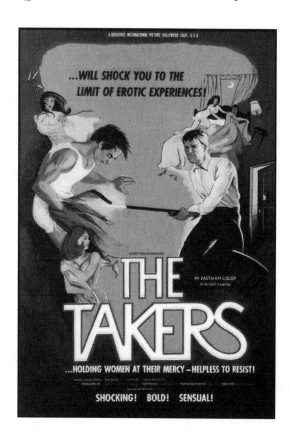

suburban sin fests, low-rent science fiction, period costume comedies — Novak never saw a genre that couldn't pay off with the addition of some softcore sex. In all, he either produced or distributed more than 200 exploitation movies, most of them restricted to Adults Only.

William Rotsler, who'd later become a prolific writer and illustrator, directed two of the better Novak-produced films, *Agony of Love* and *Mantis in Lace*. He recalled his experiences with Boxoffice International in a 1994 interview in *Psychotronic Video:* "Harry knew nothing about how films were made, but pretended he did, but we all knew. The budgets were about $15,000 for black and white. I kept fighting the front office who simply didn't understand why my paperwork wasn't up to the minute every second — on five-day shoots! Eventually it was all front offices that drove me out of the directing business and to my typewriter."

At the height of his success, Novak operated a full pro-

"Did ya hear the one about the farmer's daughter?"

For a guy living high on the hog in Hollywood, Harry Novak had an affinity for the rural south. Between 1969-1971 he released more than a dozen "hillbilly" movies. These were mostly drive-in fodder for folks who liked young girls splashing naked in barnyard slop. Look for the trademark pig in every poster. In addition to the films pictured here, there was *Sassy Sue, Indian Raid, Indian Made, The Pigkeeper's Daughter, Country Hooker, Sweet Georgia,* and *Teenage Bride* (yet another *Child Bride* re-do).

duction studio at Boxoffice International, complete with kitchen, baths, cocktail bar, and screening rooms. When he expanded into the international market, selling his patented brand of American sex product overseas, film buyers could be squired straight to the studio, tidied up, feted, contracted, and shipped back to the airport in most expeditious fashion.

Mr. Novak's sex factory was a long way from the days of the Forty Thieves.

By the late 1970s there was no longer a market for Novak's softcore product, and Boxoffice International was transformed into Valiant International Pictures, purveying hardcore titles such as *Sissy's Hot Summer, Sweet Surrender,* and *Moments of Love.*

Considering the incredible amount of product Novak released, it's remarkable that there's not a memorable film in the bunch.

The rediscovered popularity of many of his softcore films on video has more to do with an eager suspension of taste and discrimination than with any quality latent in the product.

But, as Harry Novak himself remarked in an interview with *Cult Movies* magazine, "When I was a kid, my Daddy told me, 'There's a buyer for everything.' And I lived to find out that he was right."

So was P. T. Barnum.

Carlos Tobalina

Harry Novak's attempts to dress up his drek (with releases like those on the previous page) paled in comparison to the grandiose offerings of Carlos Tobalina, supreme egotist of erotic cinema. If Novak was an ersatz Mayer, Tobalina was an off-brand Orson Welles. Credits for *Affaire in Rio de Janeiro* list Tobalina not only as lead actor, but producer, writer, director, director of photography, editor, and composer of the theme music.

In his mid-thirties, Tobalina fashioned a lusty lifestyle for himself, jetting to exotic locations to shoot low-budget sex dramas, many starring himself as the worldly Latin lover quenching the amatory urges of beautiful women. While his movies weren't memorable, his tax returns (if filed) must have been legendary.

Obsession with "critical acclaim" was a Tobalina trademark. *The Last Tango in Acapulco* was, according to his promo blurbs, the first-prize winner at international film festivals in Cannes, Berlin, Tokyo, and Rio de Janeiro. Unmentioned, no doubt due to space

restrictions, was that these prizes were bestowed by a small group of sex film aficionados with no connection to the official festivals. Tobalina was also fond of plastering on his posters a big number 1, surrounded by laurel branches, which declared his films to be "Considered by world critics as one of the 10 best pictures." How did we miss *Infrasexum* (1970) between *The Bicycle Thief* and *Rules of the Game?*

Another charming Tobalina trait was his gratitude. He'd lavish appreciation on any entity that afforded him an air of respectability — Bank of America, Eastern Airlines, Lloyd's of London, San Juan Investment Company, Fuji Film Manufacturing, et al. — and helped pad his acknowledgments to impressive width and international breadth.

Unfathomable credits were another hallmark: "This story is fiction; created and copyrighted by Carlos Tobalina. The behavioral patterns and psycho dynamics revised by Dr. Gabino Tobalina, MD. Psychiatrist. Locales were chosen for pictorial value only, there is no implication of similar conduct of real people." Of equal significance were Tobalina's pioneering technical achievements, such as the introduction of TobaScope Hi-Brilliance Wide Screen Cinematography, and TobaPhonic Multi-Channel Stereo Sound.

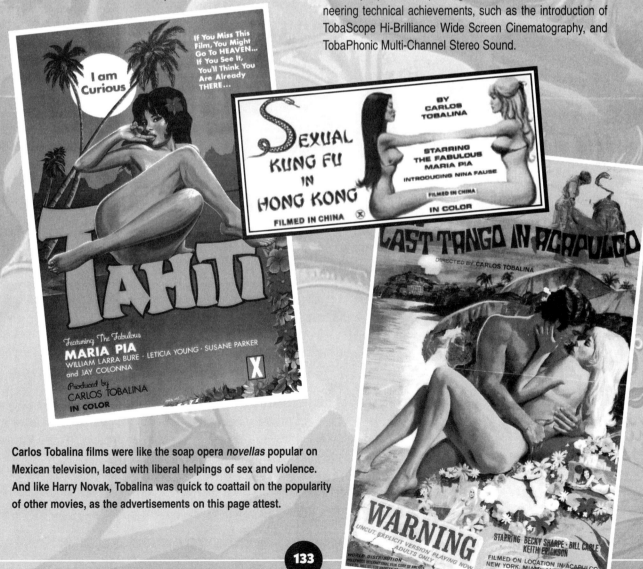

Carlos Tobalina films were like the soap opera *novellas* popular on Mexican television, laced with liberal helpings of sex and violence. And like Harry Novak, Tobalina was quick to coattail on the popularity of other movies, as the advertisements on this page attest.

DAVID FRIEDMAN
The Sensational Seller Of Sinful Sexploitation

"I have to admit I've made a pretty good living exploiting the lust, greed, and ignorance of the American public."

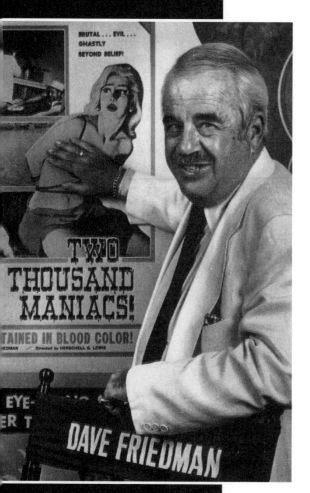

Dave Friedman has always been a gambler. He relishes the thrill of the card and dice tables in Las Vegas, betting on his ability to draw to the inside straight or toss six the hard way. On the fairgrounds and midways of the carnival circuit, he gambles on the good weather and flush crowds that spell the difference between an engagement being a "red one" (a big payday) or a "larry" (a stinker). Friedman's biggest gamble may have been in 1949 when he left the glamor and security of Paramount's publicity department to sign on with exploitation impresario Kroger Babb. Few people would fold a hand that contained a solid, steady paycheck and a chance to climb the ladder of one of Hollywood's premier studios.

To Friedman, however, the life of the itinerant roadshowman seemed to be what carnies call a flat joint — a game rigged to take big money from the rubes. Censor boards, church groups, restricted viewing laws might all threaten to overturn the table at any given time, but Friedman was primed for the game: He knew early on that he had what it takes to sell a little sin to the skeptics, to "turn the tip," in carny slang.

The essence of Friedman's career — and perhaps the Adults Only film business as a whole — is this: no matter how volatile, competitive, or offensive the business may get, it's all just a big con game. And few people ran the scam better, or had more fun doing it, than David Friedman.

Born in Birmingham, Alabama, Friedman grew up living in hotels with his father after his parents divorced when he was eight years old. The elder Friedman was an editor of the conservative *News* in Birmingham, and much of Friedman's youth was spent with his uncle, traveling with motorized carnivals and circuses throughout the south. From the start, Friedman was "with the show," separating him from the "rubes" and "suckers" off of whom carnies made their living. His earliest ambition was to be a carnival press agent.

He showed discipline enough to get an electrical engineering degree at Cornell, but went into the service during WWII and promptly forgot everything he'd learned. He was, however, assigned to communications duties, and picked up the rudiments of motion picture production. Discharged, he worked as a craps croupier in notorious Phenix City, Alabama, a virtual Sin City that catered to the military. Phenix City wasn't policed, it was quarantined. This is no doubt where Friedman gleaned much of the guts and guile that sustained him through his career.

Selling a pair of Army surplus searchlights to Kroger Babb in 1946 changed everything. Babb brought carny hustle to the independent film business, and Friedman would eventually leave a cushy job as a Paramount press agent to live the roadshowing life with Babb's phenomenal *Mom and Dad*.

During the 1950s, Friedman absorbed the nuts and bolts of making, distributing, and exhibiting movies. But he never lost the carny attitude: nothing was better than pulling a fast one on the rubes, scoring a big payday, then savoring your fortune over a fine meal, "cutting up jackpots" until all hours with a bottle of good Scotch. This was the way of the roadshow man, and it was as far from corporate Hollywood and its Wall Street underpinnings as you could get. No stock portfolio compared with a roll of hundreds hanging large in your pocket.

After his apprenticeship with Babb, Friedman developed another partnership, with Herschell Gordon Lewis. Their co-productions, *Blood Feast, Two Thousand Maniacs,* and *Color Me Blood Red* ushered in the notion of gore as entertainment. (Today, Lewis runs a hugely successful direct mail marketing company, with clients such as the Franklin Mint. He also writes a regular column for *SELL!NG* magazine on proper business correspondence.)

Splitting from Lewis in 1964, Friedman left his Chicago home base and headed to Hollywood. There he bought into Sonney Amusement Enterprises, sharing the driver's seat with Dan Sonney, son of the man, Louis Sonney, who started the whole roadshow exploitation market back in the 1920s.

With Sonney, he produced a string of films that defined the softcore sexploitation genre of the sixties: *The Defilers, The Notorious Daughter of Fanny Hill, A Smell of Honey, A Swallow of Brine*, and dozens more. The duo soon changed the name of their company to Entertainment Ventures Inc., and became the nation's leading producers and distributors of Adults Only product. Friedman came into his own in the late 1960s, turning out films that reflected his irreverent sense of humor: *Thar She Blows, Starlet, Trader Hornee, The Lustful Turk, The Long Swift Sword of Siegfried, The Erotic Adventures of Zorro*.

There was a standard formula to the sex: female masturbation scene, hetero sex scene, lesbian scene, sadomasochism scene — Friedman calls it the "something for everyone" approach.

Making sure they had all the bases covered, Sonney and Friedman bought theaters as well, starting with a ramshackle place on Fifth and Hill in L.A. that became the flagship of a chain of sleaze emporiums known as the Pussycat Theaters. (Friedman eventually sold his interest, and the theaters were run by Vince Miranda.)

"On opening day of a new film you could almost call roll," Friedman recalls of The Guild, a Pussycat theater he ran in North Hollywood. "The same guys were there, week after week." Matinées were always stronger than nights, thanks to the businessmen. "We had a pay phone in the lobby,

and you could always hear them: "Hello, Grace, this is Joe. I can't keep my appointment because I'm going over to 3M and won't be back in time.' Then they'd go in and watch the movies for an hour or so.

"Once in a while you'd get a woman, or a stray couple," Friedman relates, but it was primarily a male — and nervous — clientele. "Guys would stand out front reading the one-sheets so long you'd think they were studying the Gutenberg Bible." Once inside, the unwritten law "was that there was no sitting next to, in front of, or behind, anybody else. Eventually, Sonney just took every other seat out to solve the complaints."

During the 1960s, the Adults Only market exploded, even though only about 20 producers and distributors comprised what Friedman calls "the factory." There were about 14 on the West Coast, six on the East Coast. "In 1960 there were maybe 20 theaters around the country — former burlesque houses or art theaters — that showed adult pictures exclusively. By 1970 there were 750. The Pussycat chain actually built 25 theaters, from the ground up, to show X-rated movies. There were 47 Pussycat theaters in California alone."

(There's no delicate way to describe the purpose of these theaters. Robert Downey, father of the popular young film actor, described in the book *Sinema* making a sex film in the sixties for producer Bernard Sackett and being told by Sackett that such films were either one-, two-, or three-hatters, referring to the number of chapeaus older men brought with them, into which they would ejaculate. A good picture was a three-hatter. Downey was upbraided by Sackett for creating *The Sweet Smell of Sex,* deemed a "no-hatter" by Sackett.)

During his career David Freidman became a crusader for First Amendment rights, and a leading foe of the righteous censorship forces. He relished dealing with ignorant local censors. "I was hyping a picture with the tag line *Nubile Virgins Sucked Into a Vortex of Passion!* and this guy told me that I couldn't use the word 'nubile' because he knew that it meant 'naked.' He didn't care about the *Virgins* or the *Sucked*, but he wasn't going to stand for any of that *Nubile* stuff."

More intriguing condradictions in Friedman's

She Freak (1967) was Friedman's paean to the carnival life, a sexed-up remake of Tod Browning's *Freaks* (1928). It was directed by Byron Mabe, (a. k. a. B. Ron Elliot), who'd played the psycho lead in *The Defilers* (1965). Friedman's association with Mabe ended with *Space Thing* (1968) when the director's wife, hired as a costumer, bristled when Friedman vetoed her expensive designs. "Don't you think we should respect the director's vision?" she asked. "The only thing we respect around here," Friedman responded, "is the producer's wallet."

personality: he's a staunchly conservative boot-strap Republican (who voted *six times* for Nixon, he notes) who has fought more than any civil libertarian against other conservatives who want to dictate what people can watch. He bristles at the memory of earlier days when the Knights of Columbus could burn a movie screen and the police wouldn't do a thing. "This is a free country, and if they don't like something, they don't have to watch it," he declares, dropping his typically bemused demeanor for a burst of genuine rancor. "But, damn it, they don't have any right to dictate what you or I or anybody else wants to do."

His articulate First Amendment arguments made him the natural first choice as president of the Adult Film Association of America, a lobbying group of sex film producers (pornographers to their critics) formed in 1969 to combat censorship of the burgeoning sex film industry. Ironically, it was hardcore that eventually dulled Friedman's enthusiasm for the business. "The old con was working just fine," he's

"I've got a high school education in making movies," Friedman says. "But a Ph.D. in selling them." He excelled at hyperbolic, pun-filled promotional copywriting.

fond of saying, "until a few assholes decided to go hardcore and show the last act right up front." To Friedman, it violated every principle of good showmanship.

He maintained a sort of Emperor Emeritus status, often acting as an official spokesman for an industry he no longer really enjoyed. He produced several hard-core films — *Seven Into Snowy, The Budding of Brie,* and *Matinée Idol* among them — but left the business in the mid-1980s, returning not only to Alabama, but to the carnival circuit as well. At 72, he still brandishes, but doesn't light, the big Havana cigars, and still likes nothing more than cutting up jackpots over a few drinks, laughing like hell about the exploits of the Forty Thieves and their progeny.

The only time he turns serious is when he considers the kernel of pathos lurking at the center of his grandiose grindhouse con game. "I've exploited the basest human emotions," he admits. "But the one I exploited most was loneliness. That's who was paying my way, a lot of very lonely men."

BOY MEETS BOY & GIRL MEETS GIRL

It's called a "girl / girl" in the industry argot, and during the sixties and seventies it was a staple of every Adults Only movie. It might be suggestive (the budding teenager seduced, off-camera, by the worldly neighbor in *Sin in the Suburbs*) or explicit (a tangle of lascivious lesbians in *Daughters of Anomaly*), but it was always there.

While the primary audience for Adults Only fare — white males, age thirty to sixty, college-educated, middle-class, gainfully employed — was no doubt confounded by the idea of male homoerotica, it had no problem watching women engaged in sex play with each other. Explanations for this paradox run the gamut: some feminists claim that it's a way for men to assert dominance, by forcing women into unnatural acts; others read it as a hidden indicatator of male self-loathing. Makers of sex films contend that the trend started because women could "simulate" arousal better than men, and still avoid the censor's shears. In a full body tussle between two women, for example, the director didn't have to worry about hiding the erection of one of the performers (at best an amusing, if disingenuous, explanation).

Even though girl / girl scenes were common to mainstream sex films — and remain so to this day — there have always been less-closeted "gay" movies for male, rather than female, homosexuals. Women might pretend to be lesbians in front of the camera, but it was virtually impossible to find real lesbians behind the camera, making films about their lives or fantasies.

In the 1960s, however, films about gay men started surfacing in "specialty" cinemas (sex between men was anathema in mainstream grindhouses). Gay films generally came in two varieties: the underground "art" film (such as Kenneth Anger's *Scorpio Rising* or Andy Warhol's *I, a Man)* and down and dirty loops and short features, known as "meat racks," and featuring titles such as *Stud Farm* and *Heavy Loads*. The former typically played cinematheques and film festivals; the latter, tiny urban "screening rooms."

There were exceptions. Los Angeles–based Pat Rocco made a series of romantic shorts that were like gay Hallmark cards, celebrating (in non-graphic style) "the beauty of male love." One of his films, *Discovery,* was a 25-minute encapsulation of a gay date at Disneyland, which ends up with a bout of nude kissing on Tom Sawyer's Island! Rocco had his own 500-member Southern California fan club, called SPREE (Society of Pat Rocco Enlightened Enthusiasts).

The Picture All Women are Whispering About

HOLLYWOOD THEATRE
506 St. Charles St.   St. Louis, Mo.
Beg. FRIDAY MAY 3

"CHILDREN of LONELINESS"

More Dramatic Than The Sensational Book "WELL of LONELINESS"

MYSTERIOUS FASCINATION

A Thrilling Motion Picture of UNNATURAL LOVE THAT IS FORBIDDEN

ADULTS ONLY

Lesbian love was the subject of the Adults Only film *Children of Loneliness* (1934).

Wakefield Poole is regarded as the director who moved gay films out of the dingy screening rooms and into better venues, with *Boys in the Sand* (1971), a little $8,000 male bonding anthology that grossed more than $400,000 in the few metropolitan theaters that played gay movies. Its star, Casey Donovan, became the first "marquée" gay performer, under the pseudonym Cal Culver.

Jaguar Productions, formed by Gorton Hall in 1971, was the first company to produce films regularly for the 22 U.S. theaters that catered exclusively to gay audiences. Jaguar earned a reputation for titles with polished production and thoughtfully crafted storylines. Barry Knight, who directed many of Hall's features, was a veteran maker of television commercials.

One notable but rarely seen gay film was *Vapors* (1965), directed by Andy Milligan. Although he'd later become notorious for artistically deprived gore-fests such as *The Ghastly Ones* (1968), *Torture Dungeon* (1969), and *Bloodthirsty Butchers* (1970), Milligan's short featurette is a gritty imitation of *cinema verité*. A young homosexual, taking his first steps out of the closet, visits the St. Mark's Baths in Greenwich Village. He meets an older man, haunted by the death of his son and sadly distant from his wife, who is drawn to the baths by the promise of intimacy. They talk of their lives while a gaggle of queens dish the neophytes. After a chaste kiss, the married man flees, leaving his waiting partner with only a paper flower. Crushed, the young man decides to replace lost intimacy with blunt sex. A new stranger approaches, eagerly stroking his penis, and the film goes black.

Vapors is effective in large measure because of Hope Stansbury's script, which balances a compassionate view of the desire for a same-sex liaison with a snide take on flamboyant gays who trade in their real selves for cartoon versions. Milligan, himself a homosexual, showed a feeling for his characters not evident in his other, more sanguinary, work. After a long career churning out absurd low-budget splatter films, Milligan succumbed to AIDS in 1992 at the age of 62.

Hardcore changed gay films as dramatically as it did straight sex fare. The dreamy fantasies of Rocco and surreal imagery of Poole were replaced by films that advertised sex like boxing matches: "Be Sure to see Wrangler vs. Cassidy in the rock 'em, sock 'em load-fest of the year!"

A pair of *Vicious Blondes* take time out for a "lesbian" love scene typical of sex films in the '60s and '70s.

RADLEY METZGER's

Elegant Erotica

Although cinematic sex flourished in the early seventies, and critics such as Vincent Canby, Judith Crist, William Wolf, Norma McLain Stoop, and the ubiquitous Bob Salmaggi paid obeisance to the trend, it was the rare film that inspired both pundits and public to simultaneously invoke the words *erotic* and *art* when discussing these films.

New York filmmaker Radley Metzger was able to provoke that response regularly. Starting in 1965, Metzger produced and directed a series of exceptional Adults Only films. In place of the leering, adolescent titillation common to most American sex pictures, Metzger offered a high-toned, sophisticated approach to sex. Where most producers stinted on production values, certain that viewers cared only about unveiled bodies, Metzger displayed lavish attention to his filmed environments, suggesting that erotica had more to do with ambience and attitude than with nudity. While the cameras of most sex film-makers stalked and probed, Metzger's glided about like a tuxedoed gentleman observing an orgy, interested but respectful.

Beyond the physical edge...

"BODY TO BODY IS THE NAME OF THE GAME."
—WCBS-Radio

Radley Metzger's

"The Lickerish Quartet"

AN EROTIC DUET FOR FOUR PLAYERS

WITH SILVANA VENTURELLI, FRANK WOLFF, ERIKA REMBERG, PAOLO TURCO. IN EASTMAN COLOR.

Distributed by Audubon Films   Persons under 18 not admitted

T H E A T R E

sound to editing to devising ad campaigns. At Janus he met Ava Leighton; together they formed Audubon Films in 1960, and began importing "blue" movies from overseas. Audubon's specialty in the early 1960s was reworking European films for American audiences. They added new footage to *The Twilight Girls* (1957), forged *The Nude Set (The Fast Set* wherever the word "nude" was banned) from *Mademoiselle Striptease* (the Agnes Laurent version, not the Bardot one), performed reconstructive surgery on the filmed version of Boris Vian's cult novel *I Spit on Your Grave,* and added 40 new minutes to *Soft Skin on Black Silk* (1959). In all, Audubon released more than 50 adult-themed pictures from all over the globe.

Audubon's first production was *The Dirty Girls* (1963), about three women from varying social strata who use sex to pay their way in the world. Metzger shot it in Europe, and began cultivating an Old World style and attitude. The influence proved so strong Metzger would end up shooting almost all his subsequent films on the Continent.

Audubon's financial breakthrough came in 1965, with the stateside

If Max Ophuls had made sex films, they'd probably look like Radley Metzger movies. Such continental flair and craftsmanship earned Metzger a reputation as "The Aristocrat of Erotica."

It was quite an achievement for a kid from the Bronx who, in a bit of glorious irony, got his start in the movie business in 1950, trimming "nasty bits" from imported films for the New York censor board. He also, serendipitously, performed the synchronization editing for the dubbed version of *And God Created Woman* that would take America by storm. Radley Metzger was, it seems, destined for a career in erotica.

After serving in the Korean war, Metzger started making low budget movies in New York. His first, *Dark Odyssey*, could only get play-dates at Greek theaters, so he re-dubbed it in Greek to accommodate the exhibitors. At Janus Films, a major importer of foreign fare, he edited trailers and shot inserts. He worked in all areas of film craft, from

release of *I, A Woman*, one of the first of a new wave of imported sex films that took a more mature approach to the subject. The story concerned a young woman (the uniquely beautiful Essy Persson) learning the boundaries of her erotic urges. Metzger tightened the film up for domestic audiences, but maintained the thoughtfully stylized eroticism. *I, A Woman* afforded its female protagonist character and dignity, and was never lurid or demeaning. It's also a much sexier film than the more famous *I Am Curious (Yellow)*.

Thérèse and Isabelle, produced in 1968, was an impressively realized adaptation of Violette Leduc's memoir *La Bâtarde,* about the relationship of two young women at a French boarding school. Essy Persson plays Thérèse, who returns to the desolate school years later and relives the pleasure and pain of a romantic idyll she shared with her classmate Isabelle (Anna Gael). Through graceful camerawork, dextrous editing, and evocative performances by both actresses, Metzger fashioned a mesmerizing movie about memory and regret. There is a sense of erotic anticipation that, in its subtlety and intensity, surpassed anything previously achieved by any American director.

Metzger has remarked that his only regret about the film was the decision to shoot a "safe" ending, in which the middle-aged Thérèse walks away on the arm of her fiancé, as though her memory of Isabelle was being shelved as she finally began her "real" life. Metzger spent years rounding up and destroying these prints, made to appease the all-important drive-in crowd.

Camille 2000, filmed the following year, exploded the cloistered black-and-white world of *Thérèse and Isabelle;* it was a vision of jet-set partiers in Rome shot in spectacular three-strip Technicolor, a photographic process which had been all but abandoned by that time. This film and

"THE BEST PORN FILM OF THE YEAR"
HUSTLER MAGAZINE

"Some of the most luscious dishes this side of a blue movie camera provide a mouth watering treat."
Reggie Danzig, HIGH SOCIETY

A film in four courses

"BARBARA BROADCAST"

STARRING
Annette Haven, C.J.Laing, Constance Money, Suzanne McBaine, Jamie Gillis

DIRECTED BY Henry Paris   Ⓧ

A Sexual Smorgasboard

Annette Haven played a notorious prostitute being interviewed by a curious reporter in a New York restaurant-cum-bordello in Metzger's 1977 film *Barbara Broadcast.* The film was shot in the bankrupt Manhattan Hotel at 44th and 8th, with the lobby serving as the grand restaurant set. Scenes were filmed from 8 P. M. til 6 A. M. Metzger had to work fast — an auction house was selling off the furnishings as the film was being shot.

its follow-up, *The Lickerish Quartet,* solidified Metzger's image as an arty bohemian who made movies about beautiful people in beautiful places engaged in beautiful-filmed sexual escapades.

Lickerish, Metzger's first film to receive an X rating, was shot in an Italian castle and told the tale of a female circus daredevil (Silvana Venturelli) who seduces, one by one, the family living there. Its unique quality prompted Vincent Canby to lose all self-control: "A fruitily beautiful movie," is how he described it. When the film was finally released in Italy, it was called *Erotica, Exotica, Psychotica, Fab!* — exactly the words Bob Salmaggi used to describe the film in U.S. promo blurbs.

It wasn't long before Metzger, feeling the pressure in the marketplace from the introduction of hardcore films, moved into explicit, non-simulated sex. Four films in particular, *The Private Afternoons of Pamela Mann* (1975), *The Opening of Misty Beethoven* (1976), *Barbara Broadcast* (1977), and *Maraschino Cherry* (1978) are still considered to be the best theatrically released hardcore movies ever made.

"What we did was take the eroticism that we had done previously and simply extend it to hardcore," Metzger told interviewer Jay Kent Lorenz in 1994. "As far as the choreography, the stuff was

usually planned around some central idea, and it became an extension of the character... The other ingredient that might make a difference is the magic element of time. We spent more time making the films because we controlled the distribution, the production, the writing, everything. We had that flexibility."

Metzger used a pseudonym, Henry Paris, for his hardcore products. His reason was twofold: he wanted to distinguish the softcore and hardcore clearly, and more importantly, he was afraid of prosecution. A Supreme Court ruling in 1973 returned "obscenity" prosecutions to local authorities, creating an uncertain marketplace for distributors of X-rated product. "The big fear that everyone had were the federal regulations about crossing state lines," Metzger said. "So the legal aspect of it forced me to change my name."

Since 1978, Metzger's film projects have been few and far between, and he has moved away from eroticism. He directed *The Princess and the Call Girl* for Playboy's cable channel in 1984, but has since elected to rest on his laurels, collect art, and divide his time between Manhattan and Morocco.

Radley Metzger has accomplished a singular feat: making films that are included in every well-stocked porno video emporium — and in the permanent collection of the New York Museum of Modern Art.

PORNO CHIC

America went hardcore in 1972. That was the year in which "dirty movies" were suddenly fodder for the *CBS Evening News,* and husbands took their wives to a local grindhouse to see an X-rated spectacle. Sometimes they actually had to wait in line. The film they queued up for was *Deep Throat,* inarguably the most famous X-rated picture of all time.

Not that it was the first hardcore feature to combine a narrative storyline with explicit, non-simulated sexual activity. That distinction belonged to the 1970 release, *Mona: The Virgin Nymph,* a 16mm production that squeezed a full range of dirty dalliances into its 60 minutes. It was produced by Bill Osco, who began creating sex loops while still a teenager. Hardcore movies made him a millionaire before he was 25. But Osco never attained the combustible mix of title and timing that made *Deep Throat* an unexpected addition to the American vocabulary.

The success of *Deep Throat* is, in hindsight, a truly amazing phenomenon. Just several years earlier theater owners in many states could be jailed for showing even simulated sex on-screen. But in 1972, Linda Lovelace became a bonafide celebrity, a fixture on talk shows, a mainstay of Johnny Carson monologues — a certified household name — due entirely to a seemingly gluttonous appetite for fellatio. The film's cultural cachet was secured by its linkage to the Watergate scandal, "Deep Throat" being the code name of reporters Woodward and Bernstein's secret White House source.

The phenomenon started when an opportunistic photographer-cum-hustler-cum-pimp named Chuck Traynor introduced his girlfriend Linda to hairdresser-turned-filmmaker Gerard Damiano at a Manhattan party. Traynor showed off his woman like a trick pony, bragging that he'd trained her to provide depthless oral service by using special breathing techniques he'd seen demonstrated in Bangkok. Suitably impressed, Damiano wrote a script around her unique talent, and convinced two New York associates, Phil Parisi and Lou Perry, to invest $24,000 in what he assured them would be the wittiest, most well-crafted hardcore movie yet made.

Wit is in the mind of the beholder, of course. But plenty of people thought the tale of a frustrated young woman who can only reach orgasm by providing oral sex (her clitoris somehow being biologically misplaced in her throat) was a hoot. Al Goldstein, who'd carved his own niche in the smut business with the scurrilous and silly *Screw* magazine, provided an orgiastic review of the film — headlined "Gulp!" — after an advance screening. This no doubt helped the film post eye-opening grosses when it premiered at the New World Theater, a grindhouse in Manhattan.

Further fueling its success was an NYPD bust of the film. But unlike the old days, the film continued to play as theater owner Bob Sumner awaited trial on charges of exhibiting allegedly obscene material.

In the ensuing months, as the wheels of "justice" slowly ground, theater turnstiles spun. The media came down with fellatio fever. Critics as revered as the *Village Voice*'s Andrew Sarris were reviewing Damiano's circus show, and stories about it appeared in everything from the *Los Angeles Times* to *Women's Wear Daily. New York Times*

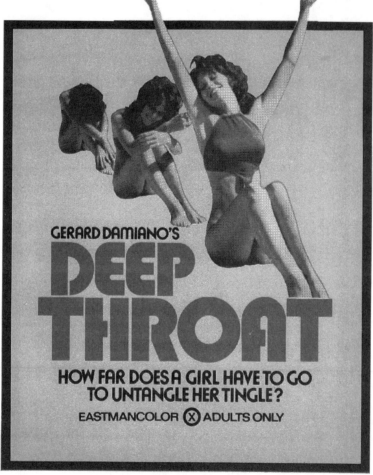

GERARD DAMIANO'S
DEEP THROAT
HOW FAR DOES A GIRL HAVE TO GO TO UNTANGLE HER TINGLE?
EASTMANCOLOR ⊗ ADULTS ONLY

No Credit Where It's Due

Despite his above the title billing on this poster, it wasn't Gerard Damiano's craftsmanship that made *Deep Throat* a sensation. The film's peculiar renown was due entirely to the unique ability of fellatrix Linda Lovelace, here unaccountably uncredited.

critic Vincent Canby is generally credited with coining the term "porno chic" to describe the trend that lifted hardcore sex from the grindhouse to the penthouse. Middle-aged women leaving screenings were interviewed by the evening news for their opinion of Linda Lovelace's contribution to American culture. Of course, it didn't matter whether they liked it or detested it. All that mattered was that *Deep Throat* was on everyone's lips, so to speak.

Sumner's trial ended with a conviction, a stunning fine of $3 million, and the judge railing that it was "a feast of carrion and squalor...Sodom and Gomorrah gone wild before the fire...a nadir of decadence..." in short, promotional copywriting that Damiano was far too modest to have penned for himself. (Sumner had the good humor to post on his marquée: JUDGE CUTS THROAT, WORLD MOURNS.)

With that kind of reputation, *Deep Throat* quickly became the bellwether of blue movies, reaping profits that put it among the top ten grossing films of 1973. Linda Lovelace appeared everywhere, touting her depthless sexual stamina and fun-loving attitude. There was even talk — this is not a fabrication — of a Vegas-style show being created for her, as Sammy Davis, Jr.'s opening act. Linda Lovelace quickly became the poster girl for sexual liberation, American males' first hardcore fantasy figure: she did it all, she liked it all, she always had a smile on her face. Publishers rushed out several volumes of her "intimate diaries," in which she extolled the pleasures of a life dedicated to sexual abandonment.

While controversy swirled around *Deep Throat*, Gerard Damiano forged ahead, determined to produce a film that would unite traditional filmmaking and hardcore sex. *The Devil in Miss Jones* (1973) was hailed — even by mainstream critics — as the first "artistic" hardcore success. It was an inverted *It's a Wonderful Life*, telling the tale of a lonely spinster who commits suicide, only to have the Devil offer her a chance to live her life again. On the second go-round, she engages in all

The immense popularity of *Deep Throat* infuriated many women in the growing feminist movement, who had adopted a vociferous anti-pornography stance (*Deep Throat* was the first time many women were exposed to sex films, and plenty of them found it a demeaning debacle). Feminist writers such as Gloria Steinem, Nora Ephron, and Ellen Willis lashed back at those who claimed the film set a new standard for good, clean adult fun. (Willis called the film "about as erotic as a tonsillectomy.")

Linda Lovelace was in the fourteenth minute of her allotted fame when she was arrested in Las Vegas on drug possession charges. What happened next still inspires furious debate between pro-porn and anti-porn crusaders. Suddenly, Linda Lovelace did an about-face. All the feckless fellatio and hundreds of interviews in which she chirped happily about her insatiable sex drive, were, she declared, a fraud. Instead, she asserted that she was held prisoner by Chuck Traynor and forced to perform sexually, under punishment of death. Suddenly, the woman who had called herself a "comedienne," in the mold of Marilyn Monroe, was telling sordid tales of gang rapes in hotel rooms, participating in cocaine and amyl nitrate-infused orgies, and engaging in coitus with a canine for a Traynor-produced stag loop.

Lovelace was the new *cause célèbre* of the feminists, who used her as living "proof" that pornogrpahy was, for all intents and purposes, the same as rape.

Lovelace's fans turned on her, asserting

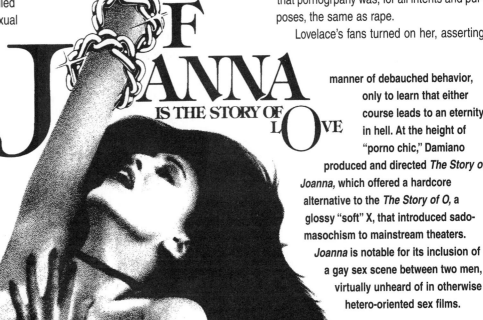

manner of debauched behavior, only to learn that either course leads to an eternity in hell. At the height of "porno chic," Damiano produced and directed *The Story of Joanna,* which offered a hardcore alternative to the *The Story of O,* a glossy "soft" X, that introduced sado-masochism to mainstream theaters. *Joanna* is notable for its inclusion of a gay sex scene between two men, virtually unheard of in otherwise hetero-oriented sex films.

that her claim of victimization was an opportunistic new way for her to sell books, and try to rekindle her dimming public flame.

Chuck Traynor never denied any of the disgusting allegations Lovelace leveled in her two post-Traynor books, *Ordeal* and *Out of Bondage*. He merely asserted that Lovelace was a willing accomplice, and her change of tune was prompted by jealousy (he dropped her for another budding porn superstar, Marilyn Chambers) and the spell cast by yet another controlling male. (Traynor has also told interviewers that he sees no distinction between women and horses.)

The Linda Lovelace saga set an ugly and virulent precedent, as the semantics of the argument directly equated cinematic sex with actual rape. *Look at her on-screen,* the pro-porns argued, *Linda loves it! No one could fake that!* On the other side of the fence, Andrea Dworkin, the most strident anti-porn crusader, asserted that a man merely viewing *Deep Throat* was committing an act of violence against women.

Back when on-screen sex was simulated, there were never debates like this, because regardless of how demeaning a film might be, it could always be excused away as make-believe. Linda Lovelace, however, did not fake what she did — so the issue became clouded by subjectivity. *Was she, or was she not, a "consenting" adult?*

The politicization of hardcore was, as a result, one of the legacies of *Deep Throat,* and its (reluctant?) star.

The film's male lead, Harry Reems, achieved his own notoriety. A crusading U.S. attorney in Memphis named Larry Parrish, determined to strike a God-fearing blow against the evils of pornography, decided to prosecute the creators of *Deep Throat,* not for obscenity, but for criminal conspiracy. Reems, who'd worked on the picture for one day and been paid $100, found himself rounded up and arrested by the FBI. Parrish was basing his case on a broad interpretation of the Supreme Court's 1973 *Miller* decision, which shifted the legal focus of the obscenity debate from national to community stan-

dards. In conservative areas, unsolicited distribution of objectionable material could be considered racketeering, and prosecuted as such.

(Exposing the shallow roots of this proposition was the attempted prosecution, in Albany, Georgia, of *Carnal Knowledge,* a high-profile Hollywood product.)

Summertime will be a love-in there...

Even since the days of the Barbary Coast, when seafarers could find any form of relaxation or stimulation in its International Settlement, San Francisco has had an unsurpassed tradition of tolerance. In the early seventies, that reputation was bolstered by hardcore filmmaking and exhibition. As many as 25 theaters showed hardcore films, and directors Lowell Pickett, Bob Chinn, Alex deRenzy, and Jim and Artie Mitchell — among many others — cranked out hundreds of sex movies. Mary Rexroth, daughter of legendary local poet Kenneth Rexroth, was one of the first in a long line of hardcore actresses from San Francisco. "We knew we might have to take a bust," Lowell Pickett said in the 1993 book *Bottom Feeders,* "but we also knew we'd never have to go to jail in San Francisco... We'd have been hung in Alabama, but in San Francisco, people generally felt that adults should be free to decide whether they wanted to see a pornographic film. The courts shouldn't make that decision for them."

Between 1973 and 1976, when the *Deep Throat* case finally went to trial, Harry Reems became a celebrity, attracting immense support from free speech advocates who felt the case signaled a return to McCarthyism. In the trial, the judge instructed the jury to ignore First Amendment issues and consider *Deep Throat* only as the average Tennesseean would. Everyone was convicted. Predictably, the judge's unconstitutional admonition backfired, as most of the convictions were later overturned on appeal. The prosecution's tab, picked up by U.S. taxpayers, totalled $5 million.

During the course of Parrish's quixotic crusade, hardcore movies flourished. Despite early trepidation on the part of filmmakers that the *Miller* decision might destroy their industry, nothing could have been further from the truth. By the mid-1970s, X-rated cinema had become ingrained in the culture. Conservatives factions still railed, echoing the words of Supreme Court Chief Justice Warren Burger, who, in handing down the *Miller* decision, commented that "One of the hallmarks of a decent society...resides in the prerogative of government to prevent consenting adults from engaging in degrading conduct."

Good luck, your honor. Perhaps the Constitution might make good summer reading.

The makers of *The Final Blow, Sometime Sweet Susan, Desires Within Young Girls, Lips, Candy Stripers, Pleasure Masters, Sensations, Honey Pie, Mash'd, Eruption, Sex Family Robinson* — and literally hundreds more — certainly had no trouble finding consenting adults to both perform in, and view, their cinematic offerings.

By the mid-1970s, the X-rated industry had become a Bizarro universe version of Hollywood, complete with its own hierarchy of stars, *auteur* directors, and product ranging from grungy "loop carriers" to grandiose spectacle. A new generation of Forty Thieves was taking over Adults Only entertainment from the old guard. They may have preferred lines of coke to fifths of gin, but the basics were still the same: promise 'em something they've never seen before. But once you really deliver — *what next?*

Sex Education, Seventies-style

Some hardcore films followed the lead of popular books of the time, like *The Sensuous Woman* and *The Joy of Sex*, which offered hip variations on the *Kama Sutra*. John and Sharon were a far cry from *The Story of Bob and Sally.*

OUT OF THE LUSTY WEST— came the wooly wild-cats who brought every man to his knees ... the only way they knew how!

BAD, BOLD, BEAUTIFUL...

Truly outstanding —an early contender for the best this year!
Al Goldstein
—Screw Mag.

TEENAGE COWGIRLS

Starring the unbelievable
LONG JOHNNY WADD
in COLOR

The top male sex superstar was John C. Holmes, a. k. a. "Johnny Wadd," whose claim to fame needs no explanation. Holmes began his career in the 1960s, in loops and stag films, but the seventies hardcore boom made him a featured grindhouse attraction. Adding to his celebrity were the endless rumors, the most popular being that Holmes was actually Ken Osmond, who played Eddie Haskell on *Leave It to Beaver.* (Although there's a physical similarity, Osmond became an L.A. cop, not a porno star.) For almost 20 years Holmes swaggered through a life of sexual excess, paid to copulate with thousands of women, augmenting screen work with freelance service as a rent-a-stud for rich swingers who wanted to give their wives something different on their anniversary. Although he told interviewer Kenneth Turan in 1974 that he'd continue making hardcore films forever because he didn't smoke, drink, or do drugs, Holmes hit the downward spiral in the early 1980s, getting tangled in an L.A. drug-and-murder conspiracy. When he died from AIDS in 1985, the rumors swirled again: Holmes was either gay, or that he was injected with the virus as payback for ratting out his associates.

MARILYN & the X MITCHELL BROS.

San Francisco's reign as the capital of Adults Only movies was due in large measure to Jim and Artie Mitchell, brothers from the blue collar Bay Area suburb of Antioch, who in their teens moved to San Francisco with the ambition of having lots of fun and making lots of money. Jim Mitchell particularly saw the city's "free love" movement with the eyes of an entrepreneur.

Ten bucks and a joint could get any number of groovy hippie chicks to pose topless. Jim would sell the photos to bookstores and smoke shops on Market Street, where businessmen could privately buy nude pictures of the Haight-Ashbury hippies they publicly scorned. Jim graduated to shooting "loops" for local grindhouses, and soon enlisted brother Artie in the business.

From the start, Jim was the savvy businessman; Artie was the wild free spirit. Jim had the sense to reinvest profits into a theater, so the Mitchell Brothers could control every dollar, from production through exhibition. They added more theaters to their growing pornographic mini-empire. Before long the boys from the Sacramento delta had scored the Dark American Dream: they could buy anything on a whim, had the best booze and drugs, a loyal coterie of colorful intellectual friends, and gorgeous women willing to perform any sexual feat.

So far, it was a typical story of cash-for-sex-cinema. But the brothers weren't common sleaze peddlers. More than anything else, they wanted to be perceived as buccaneers on a new Barbary Coast. Their father, whom they idolized, had been a swaggering, gambling rapscallion, and both boys were eager to follow in his footsteps. They lived to flip the bird at authority, and reveled in confrontations with City Hall over the "obscene" nature of their enterprise. Every time a bluenose politico like city supervisor Dianne Feinstein (later mayor and senator) complained about the Mitchell Brothers, she may as well have been shoveling coal into their promotional boilers.

Even though their ambition far exceeded their talents as filmmakers, the brothers decided it was their calling to produce the first great hardcore movie.

If it hadn't been for Marilyn Briggs, the Mitchell Brothers would probably have remained small-time pornographers. Ms. Briggs was a Connecticut-born "girl next door" type who'd come to San Francisco at age 19 hoping to further her own modeling and acting ambitions — but especially to irritate the straight-laced parents whom she felt had never loved her.

She answered a newspaper ad offering roles in a "major motion picture," but bailed out of the casting call upon realizing that she misunderstood the part about "bowling or non-bowling" parts. The guy on the phone was saying *balling,* not *bowling.*

But Jim and Artie, who thought Marilyn looked like fashion model Cybill Shepherd, talked her into taking the lead in their "big budget" production of *Behind the Green Door.* Marilyn proved to be exceptionally adventurous as an actress. She had declined to read the script, figuring that her performance — as a woman kidnapped and forced to perform sexually before an audience at a mysterious sex club — would be more genuine if she had no idea what she was getting into.

Cinematically, the Mitchell Brothers really didn't uphold their end of the bargain: the production looked only marginally better than the sleaziest stag film. But Ms. Briggs — renamed Marilyn Chambers by her producers — was a startling revelation. No actress had before (or since) so compellingly conveyed carnal abandon. Despite poor camerawork, lousy sound, and erratic editing, Marilyn Chambers burned up the screen and ushered in a whole new standard for sex in the movies.

Just as the film was about to be released Marilyn found herself in an unexpected bind. Two years earlier she'd modeled for Procter & Gamble. Now they were using a sweet shot of her, cradling a baby, as the new image on the Ivory Snow detergent box. This twist of fate, milked for all it was worth by the media-savvy Mitchell Brothers, made *Behind the Green Door* a colossal moneymaker. People everywhere headed to a local grindhouse to watch the Ivory Snow Girl be ravaged by insatiable lesbians and perform fellatio, with stunning stamina, on men in trapezes. The notorious international reputation of the Mitchell Brothers was secured.

Some people might say that Marilyn Chambers owed everything to the Mitchells. In truth, the opposite was more accurate. She made a

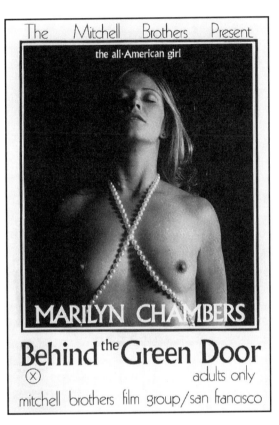

The Mitchell Brothers Present
the all·American girl

MARILYN CHAMBERS

Behind the Green Door
Ⓧ adults only
mitchell brothers film group/san francisco

couple more successful porno films with them before heading off on her own treacherous course — as the leading lady of sleaze Svengali Chuck Traynor, who held her in a drug-induced thrall within months of dropping Linda Lovelace.

But whenever the O'Farrell Theatre — the Mitchell Brothers' flagship — needed a burst of nasty publicity, Marilyn came back to bail them out. She performed live shows in the club that outstripped anything the brothers dreamed up in *Green Door.* Some nights, Marilyn would end up locked in a pillowed room with more than a dozen men, living out sexual scenarios that few people once would have imagined, let alone dare film.

By the early eighties, the Mitchells had become a large thread in San Francisco's social fabric. They headed up the so-called Irish Cultural Mafia, a ragged band of Celtic intellectual hipsters who found political significance in bad-boy hijinks. For a time, Hunter S. Thompson was the night manager of the O'Farrell, drinking, carousing, and belching out a weekly column for the *San Francisco Examiner.* Although they liked to depict themselves as loving family men (they both had large broods), the brothers' saga had become a wild montage of sex, drugs, court battles, political tomfoolery, and intellectual posturing. Jim wanted to venture into new, more legitimate enterprises with his cronies. "Party Artie" couldn't stand to see the wild days winding down.

Those who knew them understood that Jim had always been his brother's keeper, and by the 1990s Jim watched in frustration and exasperation as his brother spiraled so far into drug and alcohol abuse that it seemed certain he was either going to kill himself or someone else. It all came to a biblical end on February 27, 1991 when Jim Mitchell shot his brother to death with a hunting rifle. Everyone was shocked, but no one really seemed surprised.

Jim argued that his brother was deranged, and that he shot him in self-defense. He was convicted of manslaughter and drew a relatively light six-year sentence. He maintains his interest in the O'Farrell (often morbidly refered to as the Mitchell Brother Theater), but of late it has been surpassed by raunchier sex emporiums in the area.

Today, Marilyn Chambers is a happily married mother of a young daughter. She has never renounced her career as a sex performer, although she was lucky to survive a wild ride through drug addiction and an abusive marriage to Traynor (who now owns a survivalist's gun range in Las Vegas). Her stint in legitimate movies, such as David Cronenberg's *Rabid,* fizzled out, but she's clean and sober and alive.

Like any product in a mercantile culture, X-rated movies were soon customized for the widest possible range of customers. For those who couldn't cross the imaginary moat of iniquity at the grindhouse threshold, the "soft" X was created. In these, audiences were denied (or spared, depending on your tastes) the sight of actual intromission. In place of explicitness, producers lavished attention on sets and costumes and Hallmark card imagery — all calculated to replace the stench of the scratch house with the aroma of romance — and attract more women customers.

Last Tango in Paris (1972) was certainly a challenging change from typical X-rated fare. But Bernardo Bertolucci's existential sex drama was truly more of an aberration than a trailblazer. It's the only film the revered Italian director ever made that was sold as a "sex" film, and although its prurient subject matter gained the film incredible notoriety, Bertolucci's artistic aloofness clearly separated him from the garden variety sex peddler.

Emmanuelle (1974), released in the U.S. by Columbia Pictures, was the film that really blazed the trail from grindhouse to multiplex. Based on the 1957 novel by Emmanuelle Arsan (a pseudonym), the French production was an attempt to replicate the phenomenon of And God Created Woman. This time Sylvia Kristel portrayed the nubile gamine willing to try anything, and Just Jaeckin was the director dedicated to sophisticated erotica à la Vadim. Emmanuelle advertising clearly reached for a new market, with tag lines such as X was never like this and Lets you feel good without feeling bad. "The intelligence of the story, and the elegance with which it is handled result in a film that doesn't make you fidget in the explicit scenes, or slink down into your seat. And after the film is over you don't find yourself making a hasty departure while scrupulously avoiding eye contact," ads instructed.

Jaeckin followed Emmanuelle with The Story of O, another anonymously penned classic of erotica that used glossy photography, opulent sets, and Continental sophistication (more often pretension) to make its saga of sadomasochism palatable to the broadest possible audience. Even emerging star Richard Dreyfuss headlined an interesting X-rated offering called Inserts (1976), about a prodigal Hollywood director of the 1920s reduced to shooting seamy stag films.

What was the world coming to? Smut films and sado-masochism socially acceptable? Had everyone forgotten that Adults Only movies were supposed to exist in shadowy, marginal alleyways at the intersection of Shock and Shame?

John Waters certainly hadn't forgotten. In the early seventies he presented a series of outlandish cinematic fever dreams that, for all their grostesque contemporary excess, were throwbacks to the days when Adults Only movies were meant to stun, disturb, and insidiously shake the hell out of the status quo.

While most makers of X-rated films seemed bent on gaining acceptance and respectability for their films, Waters delved gleefully into perversity. Pink Flamingos (1972), his most infamous film, was about a competition between a group of outrageous sickos to capture the crown of "the filthiest person alive." Waters' friend Glenn Milstead, a 300-pound transvestite better known as Divine, copped the grand prize by eating freshly excreted dog feces. That was the cherry atop a putrid cinematic sundae of rape, bestiality, incest, homosexuality, and cannibalism. Savvy to the advantages of a catchy nickname, Waters began billing himself as "The Prince of Puke."

The link between John Waters and exploitation pioneers like the Forty Thieves is evident in Multiple Maniacs (1970), his precursor to Pink Flamingos. It wallows in the dirty doings of a troupe known as the Carnival of Perversion, and pays homage to the heady mix of sin and sensation that was the stock-in-trade of early Adults Only movies. Female Trouble (1974) puts a twisted spin on old vice racket and JD films. Its "case study" of criminal Dawn Davenport (Divine again), plays like a berserk version of Confessions of a Vice Baron.

Divine (Glenn Milstead), who once symbolized the furthest edge of perversity, ended up playing a romantic lead opposite Tab Hunter in John Waters' Polyester (1981), and crossed over into non-drag roles in mainstream films such as Alan Rudolph's Trouble In Mind (1985).

In his early days, Waters seemed like a descendant of vintage roadshowmen; he'd play his films anywhere he could find an audience, and was far more interested in the theatrics of staging a carny-style screening than he was in producing well-crafted films. His popularity swelled through midnight screenings that recaptured the nasty allure of "forbidden" offerings of the early thirties.

Waters' own carefully cultivated character, however, was something new (or at least freed from the closet) on the mainstream cultural scene: the fey, catty queen dripping with irony and attitude, so far above it all that everything, no matter how grisly, was giggle-fodder. It's a pose that's practically institutionalized in today's hipper-than-you media.

Beneath Waters' flippant, cynical veneer is the distinct possibility that he is actually disturbed by the pervasiveness of poor taste and inhuman behavior rampant in the culture. His own excesses seemed like an attempt to plant his flag at the perimeter of bad taste, and in so doing establish a secure sense of order: at least someone with obvious wit and intelligence was standing guard over the boundaries of the cultural compost pile.

John Waters, however, proved to be far from the last word in poor taste. Today, there's something almost quaint about his brand of outrageousness. His shockers from the early seventies now seem like backyard carnivals staged by a squirrely, attention-craving brat. The ferment of daily television has, in sheer volume, surpassed the most egregious of Waters' excesses, and John Waters now produces polished Hollywood products — *Hairspray, Cry-Baby, Serial Mom* — that are notable for the taste and restraint exhibited by the once-notorious "Prince of Puke."

End of the Roadshow

In 1975 the world was introduced to the video cassette recorder, a device that accomplished what God-fearing prosecutors and Bible-thumping censors never could — it closed down hundreds of Adults Only theaters all across America.

No longer did the curious and horny have to drive to a dicey part of town, buy a ticket from a greasy-haired Richard Speck look-alike, and slink into a dark auditorium reverberating with moans of passion, the screen emblazoned with gigantic brightly lit close-ups of acts usually confined between facing bedsheets.

Starting in 1975, a person could find all manner of illicit sex right in their neighborhood, behind the canvas curtain.

Fast Forward

Let's make a conservative estimate: the videotapes on these pages each contain at least a dozen scenes of hardcore sex; There's eight tapes to a shelf, eight shelves to a rack; fourteen racks in the Adults Only section of this particular video store. That's approximately 10,752 individual hardcore sex acts contained in this one retail establishment.

A suburban community may have six video stores, a large city more than 100. We'll split the difference at 50. That gives us an average of 537,600 sex scenes available on tape in the average city. For California, we'll conservatively multiply that figure by 100 major communities, which gives the public 53,760,000 hardcore sex acts available on videotape. Extend that over the 50 states and we're looking at — *hit the fast forward button!* — 2,688,000,000 specific acts of intimate interaction that, 30 years ago, would have gotten exhibitors jailed if projected in a theater.

The VCR has made the sex business bigger than ever.

The battle over acceptable community standards for film exhibition has been rendered moot; people are free to view whatever they wish in the privacy of their own homes. Unlike film exhibition, videotape rentals are an individual, not community, concern. To assert otherwise is to violate the sanctity of a person's home, where privacy is a constitutionally protected right.

Today, the sex film business bears little relation to the days of the Forty Thieves. (One similarity, however, is the importance of the come-on. As much time and money is spent on the production of an enticing video box, as is spent on the actual production of the encased video.)

In tonier porno products, superstar actresses command thousands of dollars a day for their performances, and employ retinues of stylists, attorneys, and accountants. Women may not control distribution of the product, but smart female performers who rise to the top know they have the business by the balls, as it were. They use hardcore to capture an audience, then really rake in the money with live, non-explicit performances in the plethora of "men's clubs" that have replaced grindhouses in many cities.

At the other end of the hardcore spectrum, enterprising sex peddlers coax horny Americans into providing homemade erotic tapes. For little or no remuneration, thousands of people capture very different "magic moments" on their camcorders, and offer the tapes to distributors for inclusion in "amateur anthologies." Sort of like *America's Dirtiest Home Videos*. The "performers" apparently get a vicarious thrill. The distributor makes a fortune.

Somewhere, P. T. Barnum and H. L. Mencken are sharing a hearty laugh.

Afterword

A remarkable thing about our world, particularly the outlandish open-air bazaar of the capitalist marketplace, is that it turns itself forever inside out, like a Möbius escalator serving the Great American Midway, conveying people to the outer reaches, then returning them to safety, again and again.

The market never rests, tirelessly stretching the boundaries — of price, utility, and good taste — so as not to miss any chance to close a sale. And it's always waiting patiently to reassure those shaken and chastened souls seeking to reclaim their roots. Smart money says there will be a box office, a checkout counter, and a cashier waiting to collect.

In the realm of sex-as-entertainment, even the video explosion, once representing the furthest edge, today seems quaint. Cybersex is the new frontier, and the Internet the virtual terrain where prudes and permissives presently wage war over what constitutes "obscenity," and how much censorship should be imposed.

That debate, in essence, hasn't changed, even though delivery has shifted from theater to television to terminal. The next step, no doubt, will be "jacking in," to mainline wet-wired neurological transfusions of second-hand imagery and sensation.

As a consequence, many of the venues that once exhibited Adults Only movies have returned to their carnival roots, offering live shows. Step inside, our girls are waiting breathlessly — *just for you!* Once all taboos have been demystified on film, there's nowhere left to turn but back to reality.

A prescient little sex picture called *Café Flesh,* released before the scourge of AIDS, depicted a future in which the remaining "sex positives" perform in murky nightclubs for the delectation of high-paying customers who have been rendered "sex negatives" by a mysterious plague. The film, made in the mid-1970s, appears to have been unsettlingly ahead of its time.

Meanwhile, out at the fairgrounds, it's business as usual. When we last checked in with David Friedman, he was back on the carnival circuit, running old gaffs for a new generation of rubes. This time around, however, he was joined by a new colleague — Radley Metzger, the Aristocrat of Erotica, late of Sutton Place, upping-and-downing an inflatable pitch game on the same "Sucker Belt" once plied by the Forty Thieves.

Metzger no doubt is recapturing the guilty pleasure of the come-on, that tingling sale of temptation that has always been the true hard core of the forbidden world of Adults Only cinema.

Our grindhouse ride has come full circle. We know you got your money's worth. Please exit through the curtain to your left.

Bibliography

Books

Friedman, David F.: *A Youth in Babylon: Confessions of a Trash Film King,* Prometheus Books, 1990.

Hubner, John: *Bottom Feeders: From Free Love to Hard Core—The Rise and Fall of Counterculture Heroes Jim and Artie Mitchell,* Doubleday, 1992.

Lovelace (Marchiano), Linda: *Out of Bondage,* Lyle Stuart, Inc., 1986.

McCarty, John: *The Sleaze Merchants: Adventures in Exploitation Filmmaking,* St. Martin's Griffin, 1995.

Miller, Frank: *Censored Hollywood: Sex, Sin & Violence on Screen,* Turner Publishing, Inc., 1994.

Milner, Michael: *Sex on Celluloid,* Macfadden-Bartell Corp., 1964.

Morrocchi, Riccardo; Piselli, Stefano & Singer, James Elliot: *Bizarre Sinema! Wildest Sexiest Weirdest Sleaziest Films; Sexploitation Filmmakers, Masters of the Nudie-Cutie, Ghoulie, Roughie and Kinkie,* Glittering Images *edizioni d'essai,* 1995.

Schaefer, Eric Paul, Ph.D.: *Bold! Daring! Shocking! True!: A History of Exploitation Films, 1919-1959,* UMI Dissertation Services, 1995.

Silver, Gary: *The Dope Chronicles, 1850-1950,* Harper & Row, Publishers, 1979.

Sjöman, Vilgot: *I Am Curious (Yellow),* Grove Press, 1968.

Sullivan, Steve: *VaVaVoom! Bombshells, Pin-ups, Sexpots and Glamour Girls,* General Publishing Group, Inc., 1995.

Thomson, David: *A Biographical Dictionary of Film (Third Edition),* Alfred A. Knopf, 1994.

Turan, Kenneth & Zito, Stephen F.: *Sinema: American Pornographic Films and the People Who Make Them,* Praeger Publishers, Inc., 1974.

Vadim, Roger: *Memoirs of the Devil,* (American edition) Harcourt Brace Jovanovich, 1977.

Vale, V & Juno, Andrea: *Incredibly Strange Films,* RE/Search Publications, 1986.

Wortley, Richard: *Erotic Movies,* Roxby Press Ltd., 1975. U.S. edition issued by Crown Publishers, Inc.

Magazines

Cult Movies, published by Buddy Barnett, Hollywood, California.
"Harry Novak: The Producer with the Midas Touch," issue #8, uncredited interview.
"Bob Cresse," issue #9, interview by Mike Vraney.
"Mondo Mahon," issue #11, interview by Frank Henenlotter.
"Dan Sonney: Last of the 40 Thieves," issue #12, interview by Mike Vraney.

Psychotronic Video, published by Michael Weldon, Narrowsburg, New York.
"Timothy Carey," issue #6, Summer, 1990, interview by Mike Murphy and Johnny Legend.
"Stephen C. Apostoloff, Bulgarian Nudie Director," issue #8, Winter, 1990, interview by Frank Henenlotter, Johnny Legend, Peter Clark, Bal Croce, and Mark Isted.
"Go-Go Tura!!! Satana!!!" issue #12, Spring, 1992, interview by Mark Isted.
"Umberto Scali Lives: The Timothy Farrell Interview," issue #14, Winter, 1992-93, interview by Rudolph Grey.
"The Erotic World of Radley Metzger," issue #17, Winter, 1994, interview by Jay Kent Lorenz.
"William Rotsler's Women," issue #18, Summer, 1994, interview by Bill Warren.

The Movies

Boldface denotes illustrations

The Players

Italic denotes major themes

"Your Honor, despite the preceding 158 pages of evidence to the contrary, my clients — Eddie Muller (left) and Daniel Faris — do not spend all their time watching Adults Only movies.

We can call at least two witnesses who have seen both these men making constructive contributions to society. Mr. Faris, for example, is considered something of a pioneer in the business of motion picture memorabilia, having opened The Cinema Shop in San Francisco in 1967. *The Worst of Hollywood*, which Faris produced for television in the seventies, was considered a vital breakthrough in the treatment of insomnia. Mr. Muller has been a journalist for fifteen years, as well as a graphic designer and museum curator. He founded the San Francisco Historical Boxing Museum in 1987. In 1993 he edited and designed *Who Shot JFK? A Guide to All the Major Conspiracy Theories*, for Simon & Schuster's Fireside imprint. Mr. Muller has selflessly funneled all proceeds from this work back into his local community, particularly in so-called 'bad areas.' In closing, we beg the court's mercy — please don't tell their mothers about this book."